UNHINGING THE NATIONAL FRAMEWORK

sidestonepress

UNHINGING THE NATIONAL FRAMEWORK

PERSPECTIVES ON TRANSNATIONAL LIFE WRITING

editors

Babs Boter, Marleen Rensen
& Giles Scott-Smith

Published by Sidestone Press, Leiden
www.sidestone.com

Imprint: Sidestone Press Academics

Lay-out & cover design: Sidestone Press
Photograph cover: © Vintage world map. Colorful paint, watercolor on grunge paper | Photocreo Bednarek | Stock.adbobe.com

ISBN 978-90-8890-974-0 (softcover)
ISBN 978-90-8890-975-7 (hardcover)
ISBN 978-90-8890-976-4 (PDF e-book)

CLUE+
RESEARCH INSTITUTE FOR
CULTURE, COGNITION, HISTORY AND HERITAGE

VU VRIJE UNIVERSITEIT AMSTERDAM

Contents

Introduction

Babs Boter and Marleen Rensen

Living in an increasingly transnational world we are no longer surprised to learn that many of our colleagues in academia focus their research on subjects, texts and ideas that transgress national boundaries.[1] They examine the effects of social media on diasporic communities,[2] or study the lives of those involved in internationally operating criminal, terrorist or social activist networks.[3] They carry out surveys on UN fighters working abroad, analyse transnational movements of fascism and feminism, or investigate a European-based resistance movement during the second world war.[4] They

---

1 We are grateful to Susan Legêne for sharing her comments on a first draft.

2 Koen Leurs, *Digital Passages: Migrant Youth 2.0. Diaspora, Gender & Youth Cultural Intersection* (Amsterdam: Amsterdam University Press, 2015); Bart Cammaerts, "ICT-Usage Among Transnational Social Movements in the Networked Society: To Organise, to Mobilise and to Debate," in *Media, Technology, and Everyday Life in Europe: From Information to Communication*, ed. Roger Silverstone (Aldershot, UK: Ashgate, 2005), 53-72.

3 Francis J. Pakes, *Comparative Criminal Justice* (New York: Routledge, 2014); Efstathios D. Mainas, "The Analysis of Criminal and Terrorist Organisations as Social Network Structures: A Quasi-Experimental Study," *International Journal of Police Science & Management* 14, no. 3 (September 2012): 264-282; Tatah Mentan, *Dillemmas of Weak States: Africa and Transnational Terrorism in the Twenty-First Century* (Aldershot: Ashgate, 2004); William A. Gamson and Micah L. Sifry, "The #Occupy Movement: An Introduction," *The Sociological Quarterly* 54, no. 2 (March 2013): 159-228.

4 David Samuel Malet, *Foreign Fighters: Transnational Identity in Civil Conflicts* (Oxford: Oxford University Press, 2013); Samuel Huston Goodfellow, "Fascism as a Transnational Movement: The Case of Inter-War Alsace," *Contemporary European History* 22, no. 1 (February 2013): 87-106; Arnd Bauerkämper and Grzegorz Rossoliński-Liebe, eds., *Fascism without Borders: Transnational Connections and Cooperation between Movements and Regimes in Europe from 1918 to 1945* (Oxford, New York: Berghahn Books, 2017); Gay W. Seidman, "Gendered Politics in Transition: South Africa's Democratic Transitions in the Context of Global Feminism," in *Globalizing Institutions: Case Studies in Regulation and Innovation*, eds., Jane Jenson and Boaventura de Sousa Santos (New York: Routledge, 2018): 121-144; Ranjoo Seodu Herr, "Can Transnational Feminist Solidarity Accommodate Nationalism? Reflections from the Case Study of Korean 'Comfort Women,'" *Hypatia: A Journal of Feminist Philosophy* 31, no. 1 (Winter 2016): 41-57; Ranjoo Seodu Herr, "Reclaiming Third World Feminism: Or Why Transnational Feminism Needs Third World Feminism," *Meridians: Feminism, Race, Transnationalism* 12, no. 1 (March 2014): 1-30; Ismee Tames, "Transnational Approach to Resistance: Turntable the Netherlands," Working Paper (Amsterdam: Institute for War, Holocaust and Genocide Studies, 2016).

explore a transnational framework for understanding the experiences of 1930s Jewish refugees, or the 20th century globally enmeshed lives of Australians.[5] Still others write the lives of transnational colonial individuals and families.[6]

This cutting-edge research asks how individuals and groups experience a globalised world, and what kinds of transnational consciousness and identity arise from living in a world where national borders can more easily be transgressed yet seem so significant at the same time. It questions which tools, instruments, and frameworks we should employ when studying the lives and textual expressions of subjects who are increasingly mobile and moving.

A first book-length collection bringing together a great variety of research projects approaching lives from a perspective of global mobility was *Transnational Lives: Biographies of Global Modernity, 1700-present.*[7] Its case studies focused on the ways in which, since the 18th century, national identity has been destabilised for a whole range of subjects, from "the elite to the subaltern." Our current volume moves on from there. It offers a wider scope in the sense that it focuses on subjects beyond the English-speaking world; places its case studies in a more specific framework of Life Writing studies, and focuses on the late 19th and 20th century lives of men and women. Working from an interdisciplinary angle it explores how these narrated lives add innovative transnational perspectives to the entangled histories of the two world wars, decolonisation, the Cold War and post-colonialism.

Life writing and identity

Life Writing is an umbrella term for a wide range of writings about personal life experiences, such as biography, autobiography, travel writing, memoir, letter, diary, oral history and auto-fiction. It challenges the traditional genres of biography and autobiography that privileged the history of great (white) men, military leaders, men of state, intellectuals and artists. Building on the democratic ideal that all lives and modes of life documentation are of interest and deserve recognition, Life Writing studies aims to be more inclusive across subjects and genres. In the last few decades it has grown into an active field of research where much work has been done to write and study the lives of 'ordinary citizens,' 'women' or 'postcolonial subjects' as relevant historical actors in their own right.[8]

5 Debórah Dwork, "Flight and Exile," in *A Companion to Nazi-Germany*, eds., Shelley Baranowski, Armin Nolzen, Claus-Christian W. Szejnmann (Hoboken, NJ: Wiley Blackwell, 2018): 449-463; Desley Deacon, Penny Russell, Angela Woollacott, eds., *Transnational Ties: Australian Lives in the World* (Canberra: Anu Press, 2010).

6 Robert Bickers, *Empire Made Me: An Englishman Adrift in Shanghai* (New York: Columbia University Press, 2003); Elizabeth Buettner, *Empire Families: Britons and Late Imperial India* (Oxford: Oxford University Press, 2004); Patricia Ann Schechter, *Exploring the Decolonial Imaginary: Four Transnational Lives* (London: Palgrave Macmillan, 2011); Caroline Drieënhuizen, "Social Careers Across Imperial Spaces: An Empire Family in the Dutch-British World, 1811-1933," *The Journal of Imperial and Commonwealth History*, 44, no. 3 (2016): 397-422.

7 Desley Deacon, Penny Russell, and Angela Woollacott, eds., *Transnational Lives: Biographies of Global Modernity, 1700-present* (London: Palgrave Macmillan, 2010).

8 Barbara Caine, *Biography and History* (Basingstoke: Palgrave Macmillan, 2010); Margaretta Jolly, ed., *Encyclopedia of Life Writing: Autobiographical and Biographical Forms.* 2 vols. (London: Routledge,

Both in the academic and non-academic world the interest in Life Writing has been given a boost. Within the Humanities the recently signaled so-called Biographical Turn and Autobiographical Turn offer evidence that scholars such as biographers and historians increasingly take into account the role of individual actors.[9] Occasionally moving away from investigating large social and political structures, they have come to focus more on personal experiences. Outside of academia we also recognise a renewed attention for individual subjects. Life stories are immensely popular and figure on top of many bestseller lists. This is significant, as it has now been widely established that life stories have particular societal relevance, as they emotionalize history and appeal to the readers' faculties of empathy and identification. Consequently, they are increasingly employed to claim citizenship or protect human rights through an 'ethics of recognition' across nations.[10] In addition, life stories are particularly valuable sources that offer intimate access to the complex layers of identity. They help gain insight into the multiple ways in which individuals negotiate their attachments to local, regional, national and transnational communities. While the national framework is still dominant in the Life Writing field, new transnational approaches are being developed to give a more adequate representation of the lives of individuals who literally crossed national borders, or who implicitly or explicitly renounced a framing of themselves as national citizens.

Transnational lives

In the 19th and 20th centuries, scores of well-known artists, intellectuals, and politicians, but also ordinary citizens such as labor migrants, exiles, refugees, expatriates or frequent travelers, each with their own unique set of expectations, exchanges and evaluations, operated outside their own nation's boundaries, or negotiated with them. Many left traces that we can use to construct their lives – lives that questioned and transgressed the national boundaries that existed or emerged since the 19th century. The chapters presented here trace the casual border-crossing encounters of everyday life, the building of familial, socio-cultural and professional networks outside of the national sphere, and the travel and translations of life stories as they have been recorded in different media. Jointly they make a strong case for reclaiming personal narratives that have been passed over by more orthodox, often nation-state-focused approaches in which the biographies of great political leaders were incorporated into imaginaries of the nation. In conjunction they also offer an analytical lens that enables researchers to go beyond the taken-for-granted mono-national framework. In order to unhinge our national framework(s), Life Writing scholars need to rethink our concepts,

---

2001); Sidonie Smith and Julia Watson, *Life Writing in the Long Run* (Michigan: Michigan Publishing Services, 2016); Sidonie Smith and Julia Watson, *Reading Autobiography: A Guide for Interpreting Life Narratives* (Minneapolis/London: University of Minnesota Press, 2010).

9 See, for instance, Hans Renders, Binne de Haan, and Jonne Harmsma, eds., *The Biographical Turn: Lives in History* (London/New York: Routledge, 2016).

10 Kay Schaffer and Sidonie Smith, *Human Rights and Narrated Lives: The Ethics of Recognition* (New York: Palgrave Macmillan, 2004); Gillian Whitlock, *Soft Weapons: Autobiography in Transit* (Chicago: University of Chicago Press, 2006).

methodology and standard narratives.[11] That way they will be able to loosen up the restrictive context as it has been selected and constructed by (literary) historians, and study the transnational subjects, their agency, social networks and discursive contexts in a new light.

By drawing on personal records and other primary sources, the chapters in this book release many layers of subjectivity otherwise lost, enabling a richer understanding of how individuals move through, interact with and are affected by the major events of their time. They follow the trajectories of individuals where the transnational dimension lies at the surface because they migrated, went into exile or experienced the fluidity of borders in the turbulent history of the 19th and 20th centuries. They also investigate the cross-border connections in the lives of people who were firmly rooted in their homeland but travelled, worked or studied abroad, had international friends and acquaintances or used 'foreign' media. In addition the chapters situate transnational explorations in a configuration that includes categories such as class, gender, religion and race, arguing that these categories are not bound by the nation-state frame. The case studies at hand thus contribute to an 'unhinging' of the national context of (literary) history-writing.

The unhinging theme is a central theme of the book. It involves a challenging or even destabilizing of the national frame. The transnational quality of these subjects' lives does *not* mean that in their lives national identity and the nation-state have become unimportant, let alone that the subjects lead post-national lives that freely float in a universe of denationalised and deracialised discourses. Whereas they do negotiate, expand and transgress national and cultural boundaries, the subjects studied are not outside of a national paradigm or framework, even if their life histories are considered to be non-national or anti-national. Indeed, they may be firmly rooted in particular localities and local, regional or national networks, and may even at the same time reinforce national boundaries. National and transnational allegiances can add up, overlap and conflict.

Case studies

The various case studies in this volume take up transnational Life Writing in four different ways, which correspond with the four sections of the book.

Section One, "Archival Traces," includes three studies of women who, through the diverse and fragmentary records that they have left behind, enable us to taste the social norms, prejudices, and cultural violence of their colonial environments. Their personal accounts bring to life the meaning of crossing boundaries related to nation, citizenship, and race, and how they both negotiated and challenged the social and cultural dividing lines of everyday life, taking life-changing decisions to do so. The fact that the 'archive' of their beliefs and actions is incomplete only adds to the sense of fragility of human experience, and emphasizes the task of the researcher to piece together the traces to recreate each subject. Ernestine Hoegen's chapter focuses on the Dutch figure Mieke Bouman-van den Berg who lived through the transformations of decolonisation in Indonesia in the 1950s. After her husband's departure from Indonesia she took up counsel for

11 Ulrich Beck, *Power in the Global Age: A New Global Political Economy* (Cambridge, UK: Polity Press, 2005).

the defence of two Dutch businessmen who had been arrested in Indonesia in 1958 for having allegedly attempted to undermine the Indonesian state. The international campaign she started to gain support for the case brought her all the way to America. Evidence shows that her desire to be recognised and taken seriously as a woman drove her border-crossings in a fundamental way. Her letters show that she was both entitled to, and developed, the individual skills and abilities, networks, resources and opportunities to transgress the gender, socio-legal and national conventions and boundaries of her time. Eveline Buchheim studied fragmentary archival sources and private documents about the wartime relationship of the Dutch-Belgian Marie-Thérèse Brandenburg van Oltsende-Geyssens, a member of the colonial elite in Indonesia, and the Japanese officer Sakata Minoru. Buchheim subtly pieces together the contested evidence of a wartime marriage that van Oltsende-Geyssens, under suspicion of collaboration after the war, vehemently denied. Buchheim concludes that the position in which the two protagonists found themselves was much more complicated than could have been expected based on historical writings. The time of war challenged the strict borders between enemies and turned colonial networks into quite unique transnational ones. Barbara Henkes examines the practices of 'doing race' in the daily life of a white Dutch migrant woman in 1950s South-Africa. Analysing the woman's perspective on the racial divide and policies of apartheid in the letters she weekly sent to family in the Netherlands, Henkes demonstrates how the protagonist gradually familiarised herself, and identified, with the dominant politics and culture of racial inequality. Henkes further explores how the letter-writer negotiates the ambiguities that the racial order of apartheid society implied, looking closely at what she tells and what she ignores.

The second section, "Networking," includes research that deals with a type of transnationality that is more collectively constructed, in the respective networks of a writer, a social activist and an intellectual. Diederik Oostdijk shows that for the Jewish American poet Adrienne Rich travelling abroad, frequenting international circles and establishing friendships with foreign artists such as the Dutch poet Judith Herzberg intersected with issues of language. Translations of her own or other writers' poetry helped broaden her horizon as much as travelling, and helped Rich to become more emphatic and reach out to disenfranchised women and men around the globe. Rich took themes and motifs from the poems she translated and made them her own. The act of translating foreign literature thus profoundly shaped her poetic imagination, her expression of self in poetry, and her transnational life. Lonneke Geerlings researched the visit that African American leader W.E.B. Du Bois and his wife, Shirley Graham, undertook to the Netherlands in September 1958. Geerlings takes up a multi-biographical approach to connect the Du Boises, the Suriname-Dutch communist activists Otto and Hermie Huiswoud, the Dutch translator Rosey Pool, and the Dutch antiquarian Paul Breman. In combination with an analysis of the visit this approach allows Geerlings to consider the Netherlands as a contact zone of Black Atlantic networks. Thomas D'haeninck introduces digital humanities techniques such as Nodegoat to explore the international correspondence networks of Belgian intellectual Emile De Laveleye across space and time from the 1850s to the 1890s. De Laveleye expanded his fields of expertise as well as his agency and reach by travelling abroad and exchanging letters. He actively participated in debates related to social and political reform, and was simultaneously involved in Catholic and socialist debates, cross-fertilising both as a consequence. D'haeninck's open-source network analysis and visualisation software package provide the means to link sources in new ways, and to establish De Laveleye, the intellectual-cosmopolitan, as a mediator between several ideologies, disciplines and nation-states.

Section Three, "Circulation," presents a set of chapters that examine how, instead of lives, texts, archival narratives and/or bodies circulated beyond the borders of the nation-state. Marijke Huisman rhetorically asks whether transnational Life Writing needs a human subject. Objects are used, exchanged, traded, and re-used. They are central to the transnational flows of trade that typify global capitalism, and affect all subjects, including those who themselves are not mobile. Employing the theoretical notion of 'banal cosmopolitanism' Huisman explores African American educator and writer Booker T. Washington's 1901 biography *Up from Slavery*, which travelled around the world, and discusses the ways in which the text impacted the transcultural connections between the United States and the Netherlands, including its colonies. Ciraj Rassool discusses various areas of biographic dispute, one of which involves the proclamation of personhood and the composition of life narratives for South Africa's Khoisan subjects whose bodies and bones were unlawfully unearthed, commodified, and integrated into the collections of natural history and anthropology museums as objects of race. Rassool's biographic work tells the story of Klaas and Trooi Pienaar whose bodies had been disinterred from their graves in South Africa's Northern Cape in 1908. The Pienaars had lived lives of dispersal, and their dead bodies were relocated across national and continental borders to be turned into museum objects. Nancy Mykoff's chapter illustrates that circulated life narratives can serve as an educational and comparative tools, as they enable students to identify and establish connections between life experiences across time, nations and continents. Mykoff concludes that such texts can have great value for teaching history in a transnational perspective. Drawing from her own teaching experiences, she shows how 19th century ex-slave narratives and migrant memoirs from the U.S., dealing with the trafficking of humans, their unjust treatment, and social exclusion, can make the experience of violence in transnational lives ingenious and powerful in an educational setting. Edy Seriese's unique archival project titled Aangespoeld ('Washed up') saves for posterity the personal narratives of Indonesians who were partially assimilated to, but also rejected by, Dutch society. Seriese allows the archive's 'inhabitants' to connect in significant ways. As a signifier for the lives and cultural heritage of these Indonesians she uses the figure of Jan Johannes Theodorus Boon (1911-1974), alias Tjalie Robinson. Boon was of Dutch-Indonesian parentage and a prolific writer who in 1958 founded the journal *Tong Tong* in the Netherlands. Thus Seriese offers an innovative, comparative approach to understanding the wider significance of transnational, (post)colonial lives.

The fourth and final section of this volume, "Positionings," includes two studies that stretch the borders of transnational Life Writing, as they point out how transnationalism as a phenomenon can be a matter of fabrication and construction.

Individuals manoeuvre themselves through, within and across different milieus, adapting to and accommodating social norms as a way to survive, to interact, and also to advance. Culture, gender and class differences accentuate these experiences, causing some to create their own hybrid 'positions' as a means to allow their characters to flourish and their integrity to remain intact. The two chapters in this section focus on writers who responded to the challenges of being a transnational subject, both playing with and rejecting the expectations that this caused. Monica Soeting's study of the work of Dutch writer Cissy van Marxveldt centers on one specific meaning of the term transnationalism, namely the cosmopolitan outlook of the higher classes to feel at home in many cultures, classes and countries as a result of their financial means and higher education. Van Marxveldt transgressed, or wished to transgress, social borders in order to be acknowledged as a member of the upper middle class with a cosmopolitan taste, the ability to speak different languages, and a sophisticated knowledge of the international literary canon. For Van Marxveldt transnationality was a status symbol and immaterial value, and an important aspect of her complex practice of self-fashioning as a writer and as a member of the social elite. Van Marxveldt's cosmopolitanism and social mobility did not only intersect with class but also with gender, as social mobility required adopting the middle class epitome of women as nurturing wives and mothers, despite the cosmopolitan quality of their lives. Sjoerd-Jeroen Moenandar highlights the ambivalence towards transnational identity in Hafid Bouazza's autobiographical essay *A Bear in Fur Coat* (2001/2004). In this ironic and playful text Bouazza, an author who was born in Morocco and moved to the Netherlands in the late 1970s, criticizes the labels of 'Moroccan-Dutch' or 'migrant writer' which have been imposed on him. Moenandar demonstrates how Bouazza finds a home in language as a transnational space which moves beyond the cultural dichotomies of Moroccan-Dutch, barbaric-civilised, rational-irrational, and Muslim-non-Muslim.

Two threads of the volume bind the case studies together. One is its strong connection to the Netherlands. Not all, but the majority of the chapters are in one way or another linked to a country that makes for a particularly well-positioned stepping stone into the transnational arena: the long-winded Dutch involvement in global histories of exploration, slavery, colonisation and decolonisation, international trade and migration constitutes the backdrop, or even the setting, of many of the case studies presented. The second thread running through all chapters is the practice of constructing identities, as carried out by the subjects themselves as well as the researcher. Each case study seeks to tease out and analyse the "various ways transnational settings and dynamics affect the construction, negotiations and reproduction of identities."[12] How do the subjects engage in self-narration and emplot their life narratives? How do they position themselves vis-à-vis nation states, and their borders? Some may fashion themselves as crossing boundaries easily, as cultural mediators or brokers. Others also present themselves as being implicated in the European colonial project, framed by a colonial discourse that is appropriative and imperialist. The ways in which they present the nation's others may hint at how inclusive or exclusive their sense of nation is. The subjects may

12 Stephen Vertovec, "Transnationalism and Identity," *Journal of Ethnic and Migration Studies* 27, no. 4 (2001): 573.

embrace a colonial ideology or discourse, but also profess a more progressive view of world citizenship. This suggests that we could detect various national, colonial, and global layers of citizenship, some more progressive than others. This collection therefore offers a diversity of methodologies to analyse sources that were perhaps originally selected, processed, and framed in a national framework, but are now being employed in a much more inventive, comprehensive and creative fashion. As the Afterword by Giles Scott-Smith points out, this produces not only surprising but also challenging results for the practices of history itself, and its potential to subvert ruling paradigms.

In all processes and practices of (self-)narration, of course, class, language, gender, and race and their concomitant discourses play a role. Thus it is not only imperative to look at the subjects' affiliations and loyalties in terms of nation. Subject positions are never just based on (trans)nationality, but are established in an intersectional manner.[13] The chapters written by Barbara Henkes, Sjoerd-Jeroen Moenandar, Ciraj Rassool and Monica Soeting especially show that transnationality intersects with gender, class, race and ethnicity. The case studies we present here, of transnationality and its intersections with class, language, gender, race, and other markers of difference, aim to reframe national and literary histories. The life stories, in combination with others, provide an intimate access to narrated experiences – published texts, archives, oral histories – of living through the 19th and 20th centuries, and to complex processes of identity construction. As a collection of life-histories they contribute to a more complicated view of the ambivalent and complex histories in which, paradoxically, national identity has become a dominant discourse in a globalizing world.

Bibliography

Bauerkämper, Arnd, and Grzegorz Rossoliński-Liebe, eds. *Fascism without Borders: Transnational Connections and Cooperation between Movements and Regimes in Europe from 1918 to 1945*. Oxford, New York: Berghahn Books, 2017.

Beck, Ulrich. *Power in the Global Age: A New Global Political Economy*. Cambridge, UK: Polity Press, 2005.

Bickers, Robert. *Empire Made Me: An Englishman Adrift in Shanghai*. New York: Columbia University Press, 2003.

Buettner, Elizabeth. *Empire Families: Britons and Late Imperial India*. Oxford: Oxford University Press, 2004.

Caine, Barbara. *Biography and History*. Basingstoke: Palgrave Macmillan, 2010.

Cammaerts, Bart. "ICT-Usage Among Transnational Social Movements in the Networked Society: To Organise, to Mobilise and to Debate." In *Media, Technology, and Everyday Life in Europe: From Information to Communication*, edited by Roger Silverstone, 53-72. Aldershot, UK: Ashgate, 2005.

13 Kimberlé Crenshaw, "Mapping the Margins: Intersectionality, Identity Politics, and Violence against Women of Color," *Stanford Law Review* 43, no. 6 (July 1991): 1241-1299.

Crenshaw, Kimberlé. "Mapping the Margins: Intersectionality, Identity Politics, and Violence against Women of Color." *Stanford Law Review* 43, no. 6 (July 1991): 1241-1299.

Deacon, Desley, Penny Russell, and Angela Woollacott, eds. *Transnational Ties: Australian Lives in the World.* Canberra: Anu Press, 2010.

Deacon, Desley, Penny Russell, and Angela Woollacott, eds. *Transnational Lives: Biographies of Global Modernity, 1700-present.* London: Palgrave Macmillan, 2010.

Drieënhuizen, Caroline. "Social Careers Across Imperial Spaces: An Empire Family in the Dutch-British World, 1811-1933." *The Journal of Imperial and Commonwealth History* 44, no. 3 (June 2016): 397-422.

Dwork, Debórah. "Flight and Exile." In *A Companion to Nazi-Germany*, edited by Shelley Baranowski, Armin Nolzen, and Claus-Christian W. Szejnmann, 449-464. Hoboken, NJ: Wiley-Blackwell, 2018.

Gamson, William A. and Micah L. Sifry. "The #Occupy Movement: An Introduction." *The Sociological Quarterly* 54, no.2 (March 2013): 159-163.

Goodfellow, Samuel Huston. "Fascism as a Transnational Movement: The Case of Inter-War Alsace." *Contemporary European History* 22, no. 1 (February 2013): 87-106.

Herr, Ranjoo Seodu. "Can Transnational Feminist Solidarity Accommodate Nationalism? Reflections from the Case Study of Korean 'Comfort Women'." *Hypatia: A Journal of Feminist Philosophy* 31, no. 1 (Winter 2016): 41-57.

Herr, Ranjoo Seodu. "Reclaiming Third World Feminism: Or Why Transnational Feminism Needs Third World Feminism." *Meridians: Feminism, Race, Transnationalism* 12, no. 1 (March 2014): 1-30.

Jolly, Margaretta, ed. *Encyclopedia of Life Writing: Autobiographical and Biographical Forms.* 2 vols. London: Routledge, 2001.

Leurs, Koen. *Digital Passages: Migrant Youth 2.0. Diaspora, Gender & Youth Cultural Intersections.* Amsterdam: Amsterdam University Press, 2015.

Mainas, Efstathios D. "The Analysis of Criminal and Terrorist Organisations as Social Network Structures: A Quasi-Experimental Study." *International Journal of Police Science & Management* 14, no. 3 (September 2012): 264-282.

Malet, David Samuel. *Foreign Fighters: Transnational Identity in Civil Conflicts.* Oxford: Oxford University Press, 2013.

Mentan, Tatah. *Dillemmas of Weak States: Africa and Transnational Terrorism in the Twenty-First Century.* Aldershot: Ashgate, 2004.

Pakes, Francis J. *Comparative Criminal Justice.* New York: Routledge, 2014.

Renders, Hans, Binne de Haan, and Jonne Harmsma, eds. *The Biographical Turn: Lives in History.* London/New York: Routledge, 2016.

Schaffer, Kay and Sidonie Smith. *Human Rights and Narrated Lives: The Ethics of Recognition.* New York: Palgrave Macmillan, 2004.

Schechter, Patricia Ann. *Exploring the Decolonial Imaginary: Four Transnational Lives.* London: Palgrave Macmillan, 2011.

Seidman, Gay W. "Gendered Politics in Transition: South Africa's Democratic Transitions in the Context of Global Feminism." In *Globalizing Institutions: Case Studies in Regulation and Innovation*, edited by Jane Jenson and Boaventura de Sousa Santos, 121-144. London: Routledge, 2018.

Smith, Sidonie and Julia Watson. *Life Writing in the Long Run*. Michigan: Michigan Publishing Services, 2016.

Smith, Sidonie and Julia Watson. *Reading Autobiography: A Guide for Interpreting Life Narratives*. Minneapolis/London: University of Minnesota Press, 2010.

Tames, Ismee. "Transnational Approach to Resistance: Turntable the Netherlands." Working Paper. Amsterdam: Institute for War, Holocaust and Genocide Studies, 2016.

Vertovec, Stephen. "Transnationalism and Identity." *Journal of Ethnic and Migration Studies* 27, no. 4 (2001): 573 – 582.

Whitlock, Gillian. *Soft Weapons: Autobiography in Transit*. Chicago: University of Chicago Press, 2006.

SECTION 1

ARCHIVAL TRACES

Mieke Bouman (1907-1966) and the Jungschläger/Schmidt trials

Ernestine Hoegen

Introduction[1]

"Woman Defense Lawyer Threatened by Mob, Flees from Indonesia," reported the American newspaper *The Dispatch* on 21 September 1956. "(A) woman defense attorney in two highly controversial cases in Indonesia left that country by plane today after being threatened by a mob earlier this week. The attractive Dutch woman, Mrs Mieke Bouman, (...) was besieged in the courthouse for several hours. She finally got out through a side door, climbed a six-foot wall and escaped." This was the latest instalment in a saga that had featured in newspapers around the world for the previous eighteen months, and that had preoccupied lawyers, politicians and diplomats from many countries besides Indonesia and the Netherlands.

The Western-oriented international press was delighted with Mrs Bouman-here was an 'attractive' Dutchwoman who could climb six-foot walls and who had taken over the high-profile cases of subversion suspects Jungschläger and Schmidt in Indonesia when her Dutch lawyer-husband had jumped ship some eighteen months before. The fact that she was not herself a qualified lawyer, but a classics teacher, linguist and translator, added to her appeal. She again caught the eye of in particular the American, Indonesian and Dutch media in January 1957, when she travelled to the United States to campaign for the release of Schmidt, who was appealing his sentence to life imprisonment-Jungschläger had died in prison. A year later, she and her husband fulfilled their ambition of sailing from the Netherlands to the Mediterranean, and eventually settled on the Spanish Balearic Island of Ibiza. Hers was a restless life, which took her to many different countries, and led to a career that ranged from classics teacher and translator, to defence lawyer, public speaker, and finally landowner.

In Mrs Bouman's life, there was a notable moment when she stepped out from the wings onto the public, and eventually international stage – in biographical terms, she moved from being 'representative' for the dwindling number of Dutch women still living in post-colonial Indonesia in the 1950s, to being 'unique.'[2] In

1 The author would like to thank Hessel and Lot Bouman, Eveline Buchheim, Pamela Guldie, Michiel Köhne, Hans Renders and the editors of this volume for their valuable suggestions and comments to earlier versions of this contribution.

2 Hans Renders, "Roots of Biography," in *Theoretical Discussions of Biography: Approaches from History, Microhistory, and Life Writing*, eds. Hans Renders and Binne de Haan (Leiden/Boston: Brill, 2014), 37.

the following, I will map the trajectory of Mrs Bouman's life, and pinpoint the many geographical, social and cultural borders and boundaries she crossed. These 'coded crossings' included the geographical demarcations between nations as well as social and cultural delineations within colonial and post-colonial Indonesian society signalled by language, race, class and gender.[3] Furthermore, in her role as attorney, she challenged and crossed several boundaries within the social field of the Indonesian legal world, which has its own distinctive institutions, professions and codes of conduct.

For a fuller understanding of Mrs Bouman's life in terms of her transnationalism and her agency, we cannot circumvent the question of her personal motives. *Why* did she – a Dutch linguist, with no legal training whatsoever – take on the role of defence attorney in such highly politicised criminal trials? What fuelled her ambition, and drove her to eventually take her campaign for the release of the defendants to America? The excavation of these layers of subjectivity, concealed in personal letters, Mrs Bouman's court files and her notes and preparatory texts for speeches, reveals both the scope and the limits to her transnationality. Although unfazed by gendered boundaries, or by social, cultural or legal 'rules of play,' she was also very much a child of her imperial times, a European woman imbued with Dutch colonial attitudes on the 'guiding' or leading role of the West in relation to the former colonies, in particular where law and human rights were concerned. In the 1950s, Indonesia was still in the violent throes of decolonisation, and in the frenzied arena of the subversion trials, with Dutch nationals in the dock and the Indonesians in positions of power, national frameworks were firmly reiterated. For the Dutch defendants, it was their individual right to a fair trial that was at stake. But for the Indonesians, the trials were all about settling old colonial scores and ridding themselves of the Dutch for once and for all.[4] It is precisely here, at the outer edges of Mrs Bouman's transnationality, that the very boundaries she claimed to be crossing come sharply into focus.

Transnationalism and agency

Transnationalism and agency are by no means undisputed theoretical concepts, and depending on the scholarly discipline, the methodological starting points and the subject-matter of the research, they have been understood, developed and applied in many different ways.[5] The underpinning discipline of this paper is that of the biographical method, which has its roots in historiography, and takes as its

---

3 Sarah Panter, Johannes Paulmann, and Margit Szöllösi-Janze, "Mobility and Biography, Methodological Challenges and Perspectives," in *Jahrbuch für Europäische Geschichte / European History Yearbook*, ed. Sarah Panter (Berlin: De Gruyter Oldenbourg, 2015), 9.

4 This point is elaborated elsewhere, see Ernestine Hoegen, "De nigo-processen door de ogen van *De tolk van Java*," in *Wegen der vrijheid: Liber Amicorum voor Willem Witteveen*, eds. Carinne Elion-Valter, Bart van Klink, and Sanne Taekema (The Hague: Boom Juridisch, 2019), 63-70.

5 For an overview of transnationality and agency in the disciplines of international relations, anthropology and migration studies see Stefan Köngeter and Wendy Smith, "Transnational Agency: Migrants, Movements and Social Support Crossing Borders," in *Transnational Agency and Migration: Actors, Movements, and Social Support*, eds. Stefan Köngeter and Wendy Smith (London and New York: Routledge, 2015), 12-41.

starting point the study of individual lives.[6] This "methodological and theoretical shift towards the individual perspective . . . has encouraged a shift of focus away from large structures, towards human agency."[7] But how does one avoid the pitfall of conceptualising transnational actors as "'heroes' acting autonomously with regard to larger structural settings," when these agents move through, have connections with, and draw on multiple social worlds?[8] As Köngeter and Smith argue, "one major challenge for theorizing agency in transnational contexts is the question of how to conceptualize the interdependency of agency and social worlds with heterogeneous national frames of reference."[9] In the transnational context, a relational understanding of agency is called for. Drawing on elements of Bourdieu's theorem, that capital is crucial to agency, and Sewell's concept of the 'schema,' *i.e.* the knowledge to make use of resources, Köngeter and Smith conclude that "transnational actors gain agency through the translation of capital (be it social, economic or cultural) to other different social worlds by making use of schemas that emerge in transnational social fields."[10] This conception of agency is particularly fruitful in our case study of Mrs Bouman, as we shall see below.

Moving across social worlds

Until 6 May 1955, Maria Sophia ('Mieke') van den Berg (1907-1966) had lived the life of a typical Dutchwoman in colonial and post-colonial Indonesia.[11] In 1935, she and her husband, Herman Adriaan Bouman (1909-1968), had arrived from the Netherlands in what was then the Netherlands East Indies – now Indonesia – and settled in Semarang, on the North-East coast of Java, where Herman had been offered a job as an attorney in a successful law firm. Upon arrival, the young couple encountered a strongly segregated colonial society, in which one's position and standing was determined by the accumulation of the colour of one's skin, class, gender, education, religion, profession, social networks and demeanour.[12] On all counts, Herman Bouman scored maximum points: white, European mid to upper class, male, Christian, a lawyer with access, and social ties, to the most influential colonial circles, and a respectable man. As 'wife of' Mieke Bouman's position was at the time, to a large extent, a derivative of Herman's. However, as Buchheim has argued in line with Callan and Ardener, "even though the wife was mostly dependent on the status of her husband, she could by her attitude and demeanour

6 Hans Renders, Binne de Haan and Jonne Harmsma, "The Biographical Turn: Biography As Critical Method in the Humanities and in Society," in *The Biographical Turn, Lives in History*, eds. Hans Renders, Binne de Haan and Jonne Harmsma (London/New York: Routledge, 2017), 3-11.

7 Kaarle Wirta, "Rediscovering Agency in the Atlantic: A Biographical Approach Linking Entrepreneurial Spirit and Overseas Companies," in *The Biographical Turn, Lives in History*, eds. Hans Renders, Binne de Haan and Jonne Harmsma (London/New York: Routledge, 2017), 119.

8 Panter, Paulmann, and Szöllösi-Janze, "Mobility and Biography," 5.

9 Köngeter and Smith, "Transnational Agency," 25-26.

10 Köngeter and Smith, "Transnational Agency," 27; Pierre Bourdieu, *Outline of a Theory of Practice* (Cambridge: Cambridge University Press 1977); William H. Sewell, Jr., "A Theory of Structure: Duality, Agency and Transformation," *The American Journal of Sociology* 98, no. 1 (July 1992) 18.

11 For a comprehensive biography of Mrs Bouman-van den Berg, see Ernestine Hoegen, *Een strijdbaar bestaan: Mieke Bouman en de Indonesische strafprocessen* (Amsterdam: Unieboek | Het Spectrum, 2020).

12 Eveline Buchheim, "Passie en Missie: Huwelijken van Europeanen in Nederlands-Indië en Indonesië 1920-1958" (PhD diss., University of Amsterdam, 2009), 27.

positively or negatively influence both her own and her husband's position."[13] Ambitious of her own accord, Mrs Bouman had no intention of following the traditional line of staying at home and having children, but started out on a career of her own, as a teacher of classical languages at a grammar school in Semarang.

The invasion of Java by the Japanese in March 1942 signified the beginning of the end of colonial life in the Netherlands East Indies. Both Herman and Mieke spent the next few years in Japanese captivity, Herman in a prisoner of war camp in the Japanese Alps and Mieke in a camp for women and children in Semarang. After the war, they picked up their married life in Wellington, New Zealand, where Herman worked for the RAPWI (Recovery of Allied Prisoners of War and Internees) and Mieke organised classes for the European children that had been evacuated to New Zealand.

In 1947, the couple returned to an Indonesia in the violent throes of decolonisation, and discovered that not only Indonesian society, but also the Indonesian legal world had changed drastically in the intervening years. Already under the Japanese occupation the Dutch had been ousted from all prominent positions within the Ministry of Justice, the judiciary and the office of the Procurator General, and the two separate judicial hierarchies for Indonesians and Europeans had been merged into one.[14] After the war, only the free profession of advocacy remained open to Europeans, and in the light of the substantial business interests the Dutch retained in Indonesia, there was still plenty of legal work for Herman. The couple settled in Jakarta, where Herman opened new law offices, and Mieke found work as a translator and language teacher, as well as editor at the Dutch radio news service.

In early 1951, when the Dutch radio news service was discontinued and Mieke Bouman was out of a job, she went to work as a linguist and translator for her husband's law offices. This was still in line with what was expected of a European wife living in the former colony in the 1950s, whose primary role was to support her husband in his life and his work. All this was to change radically on 6 May 1955, the day Herman Bouman left his home in Jakarta and quietly slipped out of the country, leaving Mieke Bouman behind to take over his role as attorney in the two cases he was defending at the time.

The context of the Jungschläger/Schmidt cases

In the months leading up to Herman Bouman's flight, he and his wife had been working together full-time on the defence of two Dutch nationals, who had been imprisoned under suspicion of committing subversive activities directed against the Indonesian Republic.[15] Leon Jungschläger, formerly head of the Netherlands Forces Intelligence Service (NEFIS), and Henry Schmidt, a former officer of the Royal Dutch East-Indies Army (KNIL, *Koninklijk Nederlandsch-Indisch Leger*), were charged with leading a paramilitary organisation referred to as the NIGO (Netherlands-Indonesian Guerrilla Organisation) and plotting to undermine the young Indonesian Republic. At the time of their arrest, in December 1953 and

13 Buchheim, *Passie en Missie*, 31; Hillary Callan and Shirley Ardener, eds., *The Incorporated Wife* (London/Dover N.H.: Croom Helm, 1984).

14 Daniel S. Lev, "Judicial Unification in Post-Colonial Indonesia," in *Indonesia* no. 16 (1973): 1-37.

15 Between December 1953 and January 1954, a total of 34 Dutch nationals had been arrested on charges of subversion. In this paper, the focus is on the two prime suspects.

January 1954 respectively, relations between Indonesia and the Netherlands were extremely explosive, and the Boumans were convinced that the trials were political by nature, and nothing more than a punitive expedition against the Dutch.[16] Herman Bouman began describing them as "pure frame-ups," and spoke of an Indonesian "Fourth Estate," in which the police force responsible for investigating the cases was directly controlled by the prime-minister.[17] On 17 February 1955, the very first witness to be heard in the Jungschläger trial accused Herman Bouman of having attempted to bribe him. The public prosecutor opened an investigation against Bouman, repeatedly bringing him in for questioning, and searching his office and his house for evidence. It was clear that Herman Bouman was now in no position to carry on as defence attorney for Schmidt and Jungschläger, and in consultation with the Foreign Office in The Hague, the Dutch High Commission started a frantic search for a replacement. Meanwhile, Bouman had decided not to wait around for his arrest, which brings us to that fateful day in May when he quietly slipped out of the country.

Mrs Bouman takes over

Despite newspaper reports to the contrary, a careful analysis of the available sources shows that Mieke Bouman consciously and purposefully made herself available to take over Herman's position as attorney.[18] In a letter written by Herman on the morning of his departure, which Mieke personally handed to High Commissioner Van Bylandt on 9 May 1955, he wrote about future provisions for asylum for "my wife, who wants to carry on working at the defence for as long as possible."[19] In a cable to the Foreign Office in The Hague of that same day, Van Bylandt reported that "Mrs Bouman remains available and is prepared to act not only as translator but also as co-defender." Most significantly, when Herman left Indonesia on 6 May 1955, he and Mieke had already procured powers of attorney for Mieke from most of the defendants.[20] The couple had foreseen a prolonged absence of Herman Bouman, although not necessarily a permanent one. The plan was for Mieke to carry on acting on behalf of the suspects until a suitably qualified

---

16 Many factors contributed to these strained relations, among them the festering issue of sovereignty over West New Guinea and the aftermath of a failed coup by former Dutch army captain Raymond Westerling and his subsequent escape from Indonesia. See Hans Meijer, *Den Haag-Djakarta: De Nederlands-Indonesische betrekkingen 1950-1962* (Utrecht: Aula/Het Spectrum B.V., 1994).

17 Letter H.A. Bouman to L.Th. Vervloet (advisor to Bouman at the Dutch Ministry of Foreign Affairs in The Hague), 15 November 1954, Digitale bronnenpublicatie Nederlands-Indonesische Betrekkingen 1945-1969 nr. 7129 (attachment), http://resources.huygens.knaw.nl/indonesischebetrekkingen1945-1969. For the power struggles going on at the time between the Indonesian police, the prosecution service and the judiciary, see Daniel S. Lev, "Judicial Unification."

18 See, for example, the Dutch language Indonesian daily paper *De Nieuwsgier* of 6, 17 and 18 May 1955, and the Dutch language *Het Nieuwsblad voor Sumatra* of 20 May 1955, registering Mrs Bouman's 'surprise' at her husband's departure.

19 Letter H.A. Bouman to High Commissioner Van Bylandt of 6 May 1955, Dutch National Archives, The Hague, 2.05.189, inventory nr. 109.

20 Copies of these powers of attorney are kept in the Dutch National Archives, The Hague, 2.05.189, inventory nr. 109.

lawyer of international repute had been found to take over. As time went by, and no replacement materialised, Mieke Bouman's ad interim position became a permanent one.

In itself, there was nothing unusual about a woman acting within the legal arena in the 1950s. At the time, there were already many emerging Indonesian women lawyers, and indeed one of these, Mrs Erna Razak, had for a while been Herman Bouman's co-defence lawyer in the Jungschläger case, until she, too, withdrew.[21] Neither did Indonesian procedural law require legal qualifications or registration at the bar to act as defence attorney. What wás striking was that, since the transfer of sovereignty per ultimo 1949, public space for *European* women had been steadily diminishing, and most of them had retreated into the domestic domain of their own homes. Colonial life had developed into an ex-pat life and married European women did not, as a rule, hold down jobs or participate actively in the public realm.[22] By taking on the defence of Jungschläger and Schmidt, Mrs Bouman was crossing newly demarcated lines of Indonesian post-colonial society. Moreover, she was challenging both views of women and their capacities, as well as 'colonial' attitudes about the 'feminine' nature of Indonesians, that were still deeply entrenched in Dutch society. "I have never concealed the fact that I would rather have had a man and then a fully-fledged lawyer appointed as attorney," wrote defendant Schmidt in 1961.[23] This was because a "woman – however strong and resolute she may be – is still a woman and more vulnerable than a man." Others considered her gender an advantage where it came to dealing with the Indonesians. "Perhaps it is because she is a woman, that Mrs Bouman . . . has such a fine intuition . . . which according to us gave her a valuable head start on her male colleagues, considering that in the Indonesian society so many affairs are settled with the heart instead of with the head."[24]

In the courtroom, Mrs Bouman was considered to be crossing other lines with her forceful attitude and challenging style. She did not attempt to disguise her contempt for the way the proceedings were conducted, and she was uncompromising and determined in her dealings with all the other actors in the court, including the judge and the prosecutor. Although her style was in no way different from her husband's combative courtroom tactics, they were at the time perceived to be 'unladylike.' In court, she was regularly reprimanded by the Indonesian judge for being overbearing and argumentative, and the Indonesian press described her as rude. By contrast, much was made in the Dutch press of her perceived bold, gutsy and challenging – *i.e.* 'masculine'–behaviour.

---

21 Mrs Erna Razak also represented one of the other defendants, Caton, in the so-called Badjanegara trials.

22 Buchheim, *Passie en Missie*, 201-202. A notable exception was Julia Jaarsma-Adolfs (1899-1975), a Dutch national of mixed Dutch-Javanese descent, who started practicing law in the Dutch East Indies in 1927, and was still doing so in Indonesia in the 1950s. *De Indische courant* 28 March 1927; *Het Parool* 7 June 2016.

23 H. Schmidt, *In de greep van Soekarno: Achtergronden van een proces tegen een Nederlander* (Leiden: A.W. Sijthoff, 1961), 107.

24 H.C. Beynon, *Nederland staat terecht in Indonesië: Achtergronden van de processen tegen Nederlanders in Djakarta* (Utrecht: A.W. Bruna & Zoon, 1956), 135-136.

On 8 March 1956, Mieke Bouman gave her closing statements in the Jungschläger trial, arguing that there was no evidence to support the claim that there was such an organisation as the NIGO, never mind for Jungschläger's involvement. Outside the courtroom, a crowd demanded the death sentence, and afterwards stormed the courtroom. Mrs Bouman was pushed and spat on as she left the courthouse. Newspapers from, among others, Indonesia, South-East Asia, Australia, Europe and the United States of America reported on these events, including lead articles in the Saturday editions of 10 March 1956 of the *New York Times* and the *New York Herald Tribune*.

The final months of the trials

As Jungschläger awaited sentencing in prison, Mrs Bouman continued to represent Schmidt in court. The abuse from Indonesian crowds continued whenever she appeared at the courthouse, and her long-time Indonesian chauffeur, intimidated, handed in his notice. Privately, she was becoming increasingly isolated as one-time friends and acquaintances started avoiding her, for fear of themselves being implicated or arrested.

On 19 April 1956, just a few days before verdict was to be passed in his case, Leon Jungschläger died of a cerebral haemorrhage. Reports of his death were carried across the world, and his body was flown home to the Netherlands, to his hometown of Maastricht, where thousands thronged the streets on the day of his burial.[25]

It was another five months before the Schmidt case finally drew to a close. In her closing statements, given on 10 September 1956 in a four-hour address, Mrs Bouman concluded that the indictments, the NIGO and the evidence were all fabrications and that her client should be acquitted. A week later, Schmidt addressed the court one final time. Outside, hundreds of Indonesians demanded the death sentence, and after Schmidt had been driven away, the crowd stormed the court house. Mieke Bouman, two representatives of the Dutch diplomatic mission and a journalist were still inside, and as the journalist held off the crowd, Mrs Bouman hid in a back room.[26] As recounted in the introduction to this paper, those trapped in the court house eventually made their escape by scrambling over a back wall, while the crowd vented their rage on Mrs Bouman's car, which was parked at the front.[27] There was nothing more Mieke Bouman could do for Schmidt in Indonesia, and a few days later, she boarded an early morning flight to Rome, leaving Indonesia for good.

On Sunday 14 October 1956, the day Schmidt was handed a life sentence by the Indonesian court, Mrs Bouman landed at Schiphol airport in a blaze of publicity. The Dutch public treated her to a heroine's homecoming, and she was personally knighted by the queen. Already, preparations were being made for her to go to America, to make a grand tour of eminent legal institutions, in the hope of

25 On 11 May 1956, the regional paper *Limburgsch Dagblad* reported that tens of thousands of people watched the burial procession pass through the streets of Maastricht.

26 The journalist was Willem Mooyman of the Dutch-language newspaper *De Nieuwsgier.* The other men were mr. E. Bonn, legal adviser to the Dutch diplomatic mission, and mr. H. Menke, head of the political department of the Dutch diplomatic mission. *Javabode,* 18 September 1956.

27 *Javabode,* 18 September 1956.

bolstering Schmidt's appeal against his life sentence.[28] Herman Bouman had grave misgivings about his designated role in all this. "I don't like it at all that (Mieke) is determined to stay involved in the Schmidt case" wrote Herman to his elder brother. "I'm going to end up with my nose in a pool of mud, which disgusts me and in which I occupy the worst possible position as husband of Madam."[29] The Dutch government, reluctant to further antagonise the Indonesians, was equally unenthusiastic.

The American tour

Mrs Bouman was convinced that the only way justice could be achieved for Schmidt, was by getting his case referred to either the United Nations or to the International Court of Justice, and that to do so, the support of the United States of America was vital. To achieve this, she gave a total of twenty speeches about the trials to bar associations, universities and organisations across the US during January and February of 1957. These included the Federal Bar Association in New York, the Common Wealth Club in San Francisco and the Academic Women's Organisation in Yale, New Haven, Connecticut. Besides that, she gave thirteen press conferences, four television interviews and three radio interviews. During her speeches, she appealed for the establishment of a supra-national, independent legal order to deal with cases such as these, where the individual rights of defendants were at risk of being sacrificed for the sake of what Moyn has called the desire for "collective liberation from empire."[30]

Back in the Netherlands, there was one more important public engagement for Mrs Bouman, and that was to receive an honorary doctorate from professor dr. B.V.A. Röling of Groningen University for the "character" and "personal courage" she had shown in serving the interests of the rule of law.[31] Not long after this ceremony, Mieke and Herman Bouman abruptly withdrew from public life. It had always been their dream to sail to the Mediterranean, and they had bought a suitable yacht in England before their US trip. In the spring of 1957, they set off down the coasts of the Netherlands, Belgium, France, Spain and Portugal, round the rock of Gibraltar and to the Mediterranean. After roaming the seas, they finally settled on Ibiza, where they used the money the Dutch government had paid them for their work on the trials to buy an estate and to build a house. Mieke died there in July 1966, Herman two years later in Amsterdam.

28 The trip was financed by the Jungschläger Committee, a Dutch organisation that had been set up in support of Leon Jungschläger, and that had switched its efforts to campaigning for the release of Schmidt after Jungschläger's premature death.

29 Letter of H.A. Bouman to H.J. Bouman, Rome, 6 October 1956, private collection Bouman family.

30 Samuel Moyn, *The Last Utopia: Human Rights in History* (Cambridge, MA/London: The Belknap Press of Harvard University Press, 2010), 85.

31 "Redevoering uitgesproken bij gelegenheid van de promotie honoris causa tot doctor in de rechtsgeleerdheid van Mevr. M.S. Bouman-van den Berg op 6 mei 1957," *Jaarboek der Rijksuniversiteit Groningen* (1957): 50-54. Incidentally, professor Röling had been one of the judges in the Tokyo Tribunal.

On Mrs Bouman's transnationalism and agency

In the above, we have mapped Mrs Bouman's geographical crossings between the Netherlands, Indonesia, New Zealand, the United States of America and Spain. She not only lived and worked in these countries, but also spoke and wrote their languages fluently. Within the Indonesian context, she crossed the newly emerging socio-cultural boundaries of a society in the throes of decolonisation, where space for European women was rapidly diminishing, by stepping out into the public arena. Regarding the scope of her transnationalism, Mrs Bouman saw herself as having risen above, or transcending the dichotomies of the post-colonial Dutch-Indonesian context. This cosmopolitan position, with its focus on world citizenship, was a prerequisite for her self-appointed role as a campaigner for a universal concept of justice, applicable to each and every individual, whatever the country of origin. To her American audiences she said: "I have been trying all along to look at things as if they had happened not in Indonesia, but somewhere else, and as if the people involved were not Dutch, but say French, Scandinavian or something else."[32] In every speech she stressed that she was not hostile to Indonesia or the Indonesians. "I have lived there and been happy there for nearly all of my adult life. I have many good friends there." But in her view, the trials of Jungschläger and Schmidt had been what she termed "mock trials": fake trials with trumped up charges and false testimonies ordered by the highest echelons in Indonesian government, intended purely as propaganda against foreign citizens and foreign capital that was still a powerful factor in Indonesia. Her message in America was that it was the duty of the Western, developed world, to signal such injustice, and to provide guidance to developing nations on morals, law and justice. This statement marks the limits to Mrs Bouman's transnationalism by accentuating how 'the Western', 'the European', or Europeanism, was still – or again – her point of reference, and how she remained firmly 'rooted' in particular localities and networks.[33] The 'locality' was the Western world, in particular Europe, and the 'network' was her social circle of primarily well-educated, successful, mid- to upper-class Europeans.

Regarding Mrs Bouman's agency, there were several key components. First of all, her husband Herman's flight from Indonesia created the opportunity for her to step into his shoes as attorney. Much appears to have been down to circumstance: if Herman had not been forced to withdraw from the cases, or if the Dutch High Commission had succeeded in finding a suitable replacement for him, Mrs Bouman would never have been able to take on the role she did. As it was, she was the ideal candidate to step in: she was the only person besides Herman who knew the cases inside out, she spoke fluent Indonesian, and she had the determination, commitment and ambition to fulfil the task. Furthermore, there were no legal obstructions to her acting as defence attorney. The only 'drawback' was the fact

---

32 Mrs M.S. Bouman-van den Berg, "The Jakarta Trials" and "Shall Justice Be Assured Foreigners Residing in Asia," transcripts of speeches held in January/February 1957 in the US (Amsterdam: NIOD Institute for War, Holocaust and Genocide Studies) nr. 419, inventory nr. 34.

33 Sidney Tarrow, "Rooted Cosmopolitans and Transnational Activists," in *Strangers at the Gates: Movements and States in Contentious Politics*, ed. Sidney Tarrow (New York: Cambridge University Press, 2012), 181-199. As quoted by Sarah Panter, Johannes Paulmann and Margit Szöllösi-Janze, "Mobility and Biography," 6-7.

that she was a woman. This meant ignoring, or overcoming, prevalent, primarily Dutch attitudes that women were 'more emotional' and 'more fragile' than men, and therefore less capable of doing the job.

Despite the initial misgivings of the Dutch High Commission and the Dutch government about her taking up the role of defence lawyer for Jungschläger and Schmidt, Mrs Bouman managed to complete the task. In doing so, she set the international legal community alight, and drew substantial international press coverage. Furthermore, she successfully pressurised the Dutch High Commission in Indonesia and the Dutch government in The Hague into drawing international diplomatic and media attention to the trials. The effusive welcome that Mrs Bouman received upon returning to the Netherlands from the Dutch general public, who saw her as a heroine and a brave fighter for the rights of individual Dutchmen in their former colony, as well as the knighthood and the honorary doctorate, all served to further strengthen her position vis-à-vis her critics within the Dutch government. Conversely, as her status rose in the Netherlands, it was accompanied by a loss of status in Indonesia, something referred to as the "transnational status paradox" by Nieswand.[34] Mrs Bouman had failed to secure the freedom of her clients, and in the process had offended not only the Indonesian court officials but also national Indonesian sensibilities. Where the translation of her European social and economic capital to the pre-war colony of the Dutch East Indies had automatically guaranteed agency, this was no longer the case after the independence of Indonesia. Mrs Bouman was a new-comer to legal practice, and the 'schemas', *i.e.* the conventions she was familiar with, were not the conventions of the newly-emerging social field of Indonesian legal practice. Here, she encountered the limits to her agency.

Personal motives

The above analysis of Mrs Bouman's transnationalism and agency still leaves us with the question *why* she took on the role she did. What was it that incited and drove her? What were the origins of her apparent state of readiness, her desire, intention and ambition to take over as defence counsel, when the opportunity arose? Did the balance between Herman and Mieke Bouman, in which Herman had adopted the superior role of the lawyer and Mieke the ancillary one of the willing assistant, perhaps start tipping irreversibly some time *before* his flight, with Mieke Bouman readying herself for action well before Herman knew his days in Indonesia were numbered?

Revisiting the available sources, we find evidence that Herman Bouman had been suffering from severe strain well before his flight from Indonesia. A cable written by Dutch High Commissioner Van Bylandt to the Dutch foreign ministry seems to suggest that Bouman was suffering from some kind of breakdown.[35] In this scenario, with Herman increasingly suffering from tension and fear as the

34 Boris Nieswand, *Theorising Transnational Migration: The Status Paradox of Migration* (New York: Routledge, 2011), 150. As quoted by Köngeter and Smith, "Transnational Agency," 26.

35 Cable High Commissioner Van Bylandt to the Dutch Ministry of Foreign Affairs 12 May 1955, Digitale bronnenpublicatie Nederlands-Indonesische Betrekkingen 1945-1969 nr. 4214, http://resources.huygens.knaw.nl/indonesischebetrekkingen1945-1969.

cases built up, it seems probable that the workload will have started shifting from him to his wife well before his flight. This explains why the couple had already arranged powers of attorney for Mrs Bouman, and why she was so well-prepared for her public task when the time came. Furthermore, a notarial deed of 1 February 1955, detailing the sale of his law practice including his inventory and assets such as cars to his law firm partners, confirms that Herman Bouman had been planning his departure well before May 1955.[36]

Why, then, did Mieke Bouman wish to stay behind in Indonesia, instead of accompanying her husband back to the Netherlands as she was expected to do? What was the source of her confidence and what had triggered her ambition? Self-sufficiency in the absence of a 'man about the house' was a pattern that she was familiar with. In her teenage years, her parents had split up and she had lived with her two younger sisters and mother in an all-female household. This experience was repeated, albeit under entirely different circumstances, during her internment in camp Lampersari during WWII, which had primarily women and children as inmates. Within the context of the prison camp, the women organised and ran their own society, and Mrs Bouman played an active part in this. For the duration of the war, she hid a fully operational Bakelite radio receiver from the Japanese, thus keeping the self-appointed Dutch camp leaders informed of international developments.[37] It should be noted, however, that both in her youth, and during the war, these all-female environments had been forced on her by circumstance. By contrast, her decision to stay behind on her own in Indonesia, rather than accompany Herman to the Netherlands, was a matter of personal choice. Did she, perhaps, have ulterior motives? Delving ever deeper into the Boumans' personal correspondence, we come across an incident that had occurred in 1936.[38] During an evening with friends, the 'light-hearted and facetious' conversation had turned towards the role of women in contemporary society. Herman proceeded to make a highly derogatory remark, suggesting that the woman's only function was to serve the sexual needs of the man. This was an observation he was to rue for the rest of his life. "Mieke saw this as an attack on her, convinced herself that I see no other qualities in her, and regularly revisits this subject," wrote Herman to his elder brother Harro in 1964. "If today I were to observe that the potatoes are not salty enough, then I can be sure that this evening I will be served a peppery dish of (my remark from 1936)."[39]

This sheds new light on the deeper motives fuelling Mrs Bouman's ambition and her grounds for taking over as defence attorney. It was not (only) a matter of wanting to continue – or complete – her husband's work, or of commitment

---

36 Amsterdam: NIOD Institute for War, Holocaust and Genocide Studies 419, inventory nr. 36.

37 Lennie van Empel and Gon Boissevain, *Lampersari Concentration Camp on Java 1941-1946: The Secret Diary of Lennie van Empel and Memoirs of Gon Boissevain*, trans. Nick Walker (Amsterdam: Walker Publications, 2008).

38 In biography, this is referred to as a 'biographical turning point,' an event or incident that occurs in a subject's *private life* – i.e. a highly personal experience – that subsequently influences his or her public actions. Hans Renders and Sjoerd van Faassen, "Biographies as Multipliers: The First World War As Turning Point in the Lives of Modernist Artists," in Hans Renders, Binne de Haan and Jonne Harmsma, "The Biographical Turn," 91.

39 Letter H.A. Bouman to H.J. Bouman, 12 December 1964, private collection Bouman family.

to the individual causes of Jungschläger and Schmidt, men whom she had got to know well during her many visits to their prison cells, and whose plight she had taken to heart. There is evidence that Mrs Bouman fostered a deep-seated sense of inferiority and frustration at the contemporary position of women and harboured a specific resentment against her husband Herman on this point. She had a score to settle, and a point to make. Mrs Bouman had an agenda, and she wanted to prove that she was equal, and perhaps even better, than any man. This implies that when the opportunity arose for Mrs Bouman to reverse the gender roles between her and her husband, she seized it with both hands. The seeds for her emergence onto the public stage had been sown a good twenty years before the cases were to start.

To conclude

In this case study of Mrs Bouman and her role in the subversion trials of Dutchmen Jungschläger and Schmidt, we have analysed her life in terms of transnationalism and agency. A detailed excavation of her life, her actions and her personal convictions has revealed the complexity, the many paradoxes, and also the limits to her border-crossings. Using among others her prolific language skills, her influential social networks, her prior knowledge of the court files due to her work as translator, and her personal conviction that the defendants stood unjustly accused, she took over as attorney where her husband had left off, and later continued her campaign in the United States. But where Bouman saw herself as a cosmopolitan, and as championing universal human rights, the available texts of her speeches reveal that she remained firmly rooted in a European or Western locality, where it was considered to be up to the 'developed,' Western world to provide guidance to decolonising countries such as Indonesia on morals, law and justice. In this respect, her transnationalism was curbed by her prevalent Dutch conceptions and attitudes. Ultimately, however, it would seem that it was not primarily her outrage at the treatment of the Dutch defendants that drove her to her actions and her 'coded crossings.' A derogatory remark about the role of women made by her husband back in 1936 had triggered what would develop into a deep sense of personal aggrievement, and it was this – albeit at the time probably subconscious – factor that to a large extent drove her actions. Interestingly, this crossing of perceived gender boundaries attracted far more attention in the Netherlands than in Indonesia, where women were already a regular feature in court. It goes to show how a seemingly mundane and highly personal experience can lead to a very public life, but also that what qualifies as transnational in one context, may be relatively unremarkable in another.

Bibliography

Beynon, H.C. *Nederland staat terecht in Indonesië: Achtergronden van de processen tegen Nederlanders in Djakarta.* Utrecht: A.W. Bruna & Zoon, 1956.

Bouman-van den Berg, M.S. "The Jakarta Trials" and "Shall Justice Be Assured Foreigners Residing in Asia," transcripts of speeches held in January/February 1957 in the US. Amsterdam: NIOD Institute for War, Holocaust and Genocide Studies, nr. 419, inventory nr. 34.

Bourdieu, Pierre. *Outline of a Theory of Practice*. Cambridge: Cambridge University Press, 1977.

Buchheim, Eveline. "Passie en Missie: Huwelijken van Europeanen in Nederlands-Indië en Indonesië 1920-1958." PhD diss., University of Amsterdam, 2009.

Callan, Hillary, and Shirley Ardener, eds. *The Incorporated Wife*. London/Dover N.H.: Croom Helm, 1984.

Empel, Lennie van, and Gon Boissevain. *Lampersari Concentration Camp on Java 1941-1946: The Secret Diary of Lennie van Empel and Memoirs of Gon Boissevain*. trans. Nick Walker. Amsterdam: Walker Publications, 2008.

Hoegen, Ernestine. "De NIGO-processen door de ogen van *De tolk van Java*." In *Wegen der vrijheid: Liber Amicorum voor Willem Witteveen,* edited by Carinne Elion-Valter, Bart van Klink, and Sanne Taekema, 63-70. The Hague: Boom Juridisch, 2019.

Hoegen, Ernestine. *Een strijdbaar bestaan: Mieke Bouman en de Indonesische strafprocessen*. Amsterdam: Unieboek | Het Spectrum, 2020.

Köngeter, Stefan, and Wendy Smith. "Transnational Agency: Migrants, Movements and Social Support Crossing Borders." In *Transnational Agency and Migration: Actors, Movements, and Social Support*, edited by Stefan Köngeter and Wendy Smith, 12-41. London and New York: Routledge, 2015.

Lev, Daniel S. "Judicial Unification in Post-Colonial Indonesia." In *Indonesia* no. 16 (1973): 1-37.

Meijer, Hans. *Den Haag-Djakarta: De Nederlands-Indonesische betrekkingen 1950-1962*. Utrecht: Aula/Het Spectrum B.V., 1994.

Moyn, Samuel. *The Last Utopia: Human Rights in History*. Cambridge, MA/London: The Belknap Press of Harvard University Press, 2010.

Nieswand, Boris. *Theorising Transnational Migration: The Status Paradox of Migration*. New York: Routledge, 2011.

Panter, Sarah, Johannes Paulmann, and Margit Szöllösi-Janze. "Mobility and Biography: Methodological Challenges and Perspectives." In *Jahrbuch für Europäische Geschichte/ European History Yearbook*, edited by Sarah Panter, 1-14. Berlin: De Gruyter Oldenbourg, 2015.

Renders, Hans, Binne de Haan, and Jonne Harmsma. "The Biographical Turn: Biography As Critical Method in the Humanities and in Society." In *The Biographical Turn: Lives in History*, edited by Hans Renders, Binne de Haan, and Jonne Harmsma, 3-11. London/New York: Routledge, 2017.

Renders, Hans. "Roots of Biography." In *Theoretical Discussions of Biography: Approaches from History, Microhistory, and Life Writing,* edited by Hans Renders and Binne de Haan, 24-42. Leiden/Boston: Brill, 2014.

Renders, Hans, and Sjoerd van Faassen. "Biographies as Multipliers: The First World War As Turning Point in the Lives of Modernist Artists". In *The Biographical Turn: Lives in History*, edited by Hans Renders, Binne de Haan, and Jonne Harmsma, 91-103. London/New York: Routledge, 2017.

Röling, B.V.A. "Redevoering uitgesproken bij gelegenheid van de promotie honoris causa tot doctor in de rechtsgeleerdheid van Mevr. M.S. Bouman-van den Berg op 6 mei 1957," In *Jaarboek der Rijksuniversiteit Groningen* (1957): 50-54.

Schmidt, H. *In de greep van Soekarno: Achtergronden van een proces tegen een Nederlander.* Leiden: A.W. Sijthoff, 1961.

Sewell, William H. "A Theory of Structure: Duality, Agency and Transformation." In *The American Journal of Sociology* 98, no.1 (1992): 1-29.

Tarrow, Sidney. "Rooted Cosmopolitans and Transnational Activists." In *Strangers at the Gates: Movements and States in Contentious Politics*, edited by Sidney Tarrow, 181-199. New York: Cambridge University Press, 2012.

Wirta, Kaarle. "Rediscovering Agency in the Atlantic: A Biographical Approach Linking Entrepreneurial Spirit and Overseas Companies." In *The Biographical Turn: Lives in History*, edited by Hans Renders, Binne de Haan, and Jonne Harmsma, 118-128. London/New York: Routledge, 2017.

Colonialism, class, and collaboration: A wartime encounter on Java

Eveline Buchheim

The Japanese occupation of Indonesia between 1942 and 1945 brought large numbers of Japanese military and civilians to the then Dutch colony.[1] This thoroughly reshuffled how Europeans (among which many Dutch), Indonesians and Japanese coexisted. Right from the start of the occupation, everyday life went through significant changes: living conditions, power relations and loyalties all shifted substantially. The Japanese military quickly erased Dutch colonial influence from society. Of the total European population in 1942 of 300,000, around 100,000 civilians were put in internment camps. Most of those who were interned were white Dutch or Eurasians who were identified as being Dutch. White Dutch women rarely could remain outside the internment camps; often those outside the camps were on more or less friendly terms with the Japanese occupiers. The Dutch-Belgian Marie-Thérèse Brandenburg van Oltsende-Geyssens, widow of the Dutch planter Frederik Brandenburg van Oltsende, was one of these women. During the Japanese occupation she continued to live on her affluent property on Jalan Raden Saleh in Batavia/Jakarta. Many Japanese nationals visited her house, and she had a special connection with one of them, Minoru Sakata, employed at the Japanese Propaganda Department.[2] Although this definitely raised eyebrows post-war, and both British and Dutch authorities examined her case, she was never sentenced for collaboration with the enemy. In this article I zoom in on their connection, both in its own right and in relation to larger networks, in order to 'unhinge' the common views on wartime Dutch-Japanese contacts. This case clearly demonstrates that ". . . it is impossible to segregate the public from the intimate, the economic from the cultural or the political from the personal."[3]

Since the 1990s, research on colonial networks has focused more on relations between colony and metropole, but other types of connections – between different colonies, or between representatives of those colonies – have also been given consideration. These "'. . . imperial webs' . . . functioned as systems of exchange, mobility, appropriation, and extraction, fashioned to enable the empire-building

1 The author would like to thank the reviewers and the editors of this volume for their careful reading and critical commentary on earlier versions of this chapter. Special thanks to Takashi Sakata for access to his private archive, the collaboration on this research and the translation of the Japanese sources.

2 All Japanese names are given in English order.

3 Desley Deacon, Penny Russell, and Angela A. Woollacott, eds., *Transnational Lives: Biographies of Global Modernity, 1700-present* (Basingstoke: Palgrave Macmillan, 2010), 5.

power to exploit the natural resources, manufactured goods, or valued skills of the subordinated group."[4] Looking at Marie-Thérèse's and Minoru's networks as imperial webs is helpful in analysing how they set up their common network. Both Minoru's Japanese connections and Marie-Thérèse's bond with the former colonial elite were central, and combining their social capital made it possible for them to navigate the war period successfully.

Since the end of the war, connections between Dutch and Japanese citizens under the Japanese occupation of Indonesia have been remembered in a rather unbalanced way. In the Netherlands, in particular, there was a common assumption that enmity between Dutch and Japanese citizens was dominant, and that personal contacts were limited. In the context of the decolonisation war that started right after the end of the Japanese occupation, this dominant narrative gained more ground. But over time, there has been more attention for deviant histories, often related to (intimate) connections between Dutch and Japanese citizens, and sometimes to cases of what the Dutch considered to be collaboration. Personal documents are an essential source if we want to understand what happened on the ground at the time, especially if different actors produced them. The motives behind Marie-Thérèse's strategies became clearer after her personal letters resurfaced in a private archive. At the time officials were not completely aware of her actions or reasons. Marie-Thérèse presented her life history as she saw fit, changing the narrative to suit her goals. Only by analysing the different discourses can her (re)constructed life story be unveiled, and we can then grasp how the entangled histories of the two world wars and the process of decolonisation influenced her decisions.[5]

Focusing on the connections between Marie-Thérèse, Minoru and their larger network, I argue that transnational networks in which Japanese and Dutch worked together have been largely overlooked. I want to reveal hitherto neglected layers of the relationships that existed between members of the former colonial elite on Java and the Japanese occupier. Analysing their connections on the basis of archival sources and private documents, I demonstrate that Japanese-Dutch connections were often more complex than has been assumed. It transpires that times of war are pre-eminently befitting transnational networks because people from different places come into contact, and this can stimulate female agency. These wartime transnational networks were quite different from the usual colonial networks, because they challenged the alleged strict borders between who was considered friend and who foe. As we will see, not every Dutch national considered the Japanese occupiers exclusively as an enemy.

The house on Jalan Raden Saleh in Batavia/Jakarta, which contained a well-known art collection, was an important asset for Marie-Thérèse as a signifier of her colonial position. The loss of this important place after her arrest in May 1940 robbed her of her possessions and of her social status, and without access to her villa she lost the most important part of her cultural capital. The house represented prestige and functioned

4 Tony Ballantyne and Antoinette Burton, *Bodies in Contact: Rethinking Colonial Encounters in World History* (Durham/London: Duke University Press, 2006), 3. See Tony Ballantyne, *Webs of Empire: Locating New Zealand's Colonial Past* (Vancouver: University of British Columbia Press, 2015).

5 See the introduction to this volume.

Figure 1: Lavishly decorated room at Jalan Raden Saleh 47. Private archive by courtesy of Takashi Sakata.

as the infrastructure she needed to safeguard her position. This was the case in colonial times and it would function like that under the Japanese occupation as well.

It becomes clear, especially by scrutinising the wartime actions and statements of Marie-Thérèse, that she broadened her opportunities considerably in making creative use of expected gender roles while at the same time amplifying unconventional gender roles. I argue that in particular her talent to oscillate between these two extremes made it possible for her to not only navigate wartime in a for her favourable way, but also that she additionally managed to free herself from post-war blame.

I will introduce Marie-Thérèse and Minoru, explain their background and delve into the different narratives of their meeting on Java somewhere in 1942. Subsequently I will map their transnational network, and demonstrate how both, albeit in different ways, could benefit from these connections. In analysing the sources, it becomes clear that Marie-Thérèse and Minoru not only made clever use of the people around them, but also that they were both interested in broader international networks. These networks give us an additional insight into their political sympathies. Since both had been active internationally from early on in their lives, they probably felt at ease functioning in a cosmopolitan environment. Marie-Thérèse was born in Belgium, and arrived in the colony via the Netherlands. Minoru left Japan at a young age to work in China. Marie-Thérèse was scrutinised by post-war authorities because of suspected collaboration with the enemy, and she fought like a lion to vindicate her honour and safeguard her property. The biggest disappointment for Marie-Thérèse was that after the war she never received the social rehabilitation she envisioned. Minoru too, faced the legal consequences of his wartime connections, especially related to the annulment of his marriage with Marie-Thérèse. Their last contact dates from 1956.

A journey from Leuven to Batavia

On 20 February 1893 Marie-Thérèse Geyssens was born in Leuven, Belgium, as the daughter of a day labourer. Unfortunately, next to nothing is known about her early years and her upbringing or education. At the age of 18 she followed her sister to Brussels to work as a seamstress. Marie-Thérèse was engaged to Frederik Brandenburg van Oltsende on 25 August 1916, and the couple married in Amsterdam on 9 May 1917. It is unclear how the two, apparently from completely different backgrounds, met in besieged Brussels. Around 1921 they moved to Java together for the first time, where Frederik had been born. Until his retirement from the army in 1903, Frederik's father, Paul Justus Brandenburg, worked as a lieutenant colonel in the Indies. In 1909 he became the director of the plantation Pasir Nangka, and in 1929 Frederik succeeded his father. Because of his pedigree, Frederik was a well-respected member of the colonial elite. He was a member of several commissions related to agriculture and journalism, besides which he was politically active.[6] His spouse fulfilled her role as a colonial wife with grace and enthusiasm; she was often lauded for her qualities as a hostess.[7] Their acquaintances and friends reflect the different circles in which they moved, involving a broad range of people from politicians to businessmen, and journalists to artists.

In May 1940, after the German army had occupied the Netherlands, their destiny changed completely overnight. They were arrested on alleged membership of the pro-German National Socialist Party (NSB) and completely fell from grace. Marie-Thérèse was interned in the Banjoebiroe Camp where German women and children were sent. The term internment camp was only used for a short time; the facilities were soon renamed "protection camps." This was in line with the rhetoric that the people were kept there for their own protection. Of course, like interned Indonesians or others facing residential restrictions, there were no charges – this was merely an administrative issue.[8] Frederik was said to be one of the founders of the NSB, but unfortunately there are hardly any sources to verify his role. In a clipping in the Nationalist Socialist weekly *Volk en Vaderland* from 1942 Frederik was listed as a member of the NSB, and one of the "victims of stupidity and terrorism of the democratic rulers who were interned by the Dutch officials."[9] If nothing else, their imprisonment makes clear that they also had high-ranking enemies. The internment of the couple lasted until September 1941. In that period they were never formally accused, charged or tried. Frederik died shortly after

---

6 A few examples: in 1936 Frederik was part of the initiative 'Defensible Indies,' a committee that aimed to strengthen the military force in the Indies (*De Indische Courant* 18 September 1936); he was a member of the commissariat of the press agency Aneta, and played a role at Aneta after the sudden death of its founder Berretty; he acted as chair for the Committee to promote trade in tea from the Indies (*Het Nieuws van den Dag voor N.I.*, 5 July 1939).

7 See *Bataviaasch Nieuwsblad* of 10 September 1936 for an article that describes the important role of the couple in "Batavian society" and names Marie-Thérèse as "the perfect host."

8 For more information on the internment of Germans and NSB members in May 1940 see C. van Heekeren, *Batavia seint Berlijn: De geschiedenis van de Indische Duitsers in Nederlandse gevangenschap* (The Hague: Nijgh & van Ditmar, 1983).

9 On 13 March 1942 a list with the names of 500 men was published in the weekly magazine for the Nationalist Socialist movement (NSB) in the Netherlands, *Volk en Vaderland: Weekblad der Nationaal-Socialistische Beweging in Nederland.* The title of the article is "The list of honor, the interned in the Indies." The article states that NSB had 4000 members in the Indies.

his release, according to the public prosecutor because he was critically ill, but according to his wife Dutch officials murdered him.[10] His death was discussed in the newspapers, and although vehemently denied by the authorities, the rumour of the alleged murder continued to circulate. Marie-Thérèse was released around the same time, on the assumption that, now that her husband had died, she was harmless. Her release did not go unnoticed either and provoked uproar. The right hand of the Governor-General, P.J.A. Idenburg, who had befriended the couple, hosted her in his house and yet another scandal was born.[11] For Idenburg, this hospitality proved costly indeed, since in October 1941 he was denied the post of Minister for Colonial Affairs because of his connection to the Brandenburg van Oltsende couple.[12] In hindsight, we can assume that the marginalisation from her colonial network left Marie-Thérèse with a strong hatred against the Dutch authorities. The experience of internment was a bitter pill for her, and it instilled a strong fear for a similar experience in the future.

As soon as the Japanese military occupied Java, Marie-Thérèse tried to regain access to her house on Jalan Raden Saleh 47. During her absence, and until February 1942, the house had been used as the temporary residence for the Governor-General Tjarda van Starkenborgh Stachouwer. Making use of a Japanese business partner of her husband, her charm, and persistence, she managed to not only convince the Japanese officials that she was entitled to the right to regain her house, she also managed to convince them to let her house – brimming with art by French and Dutch painters of the 17th, 18th and 19th centuries – become a museum.[13] Marie-Thérèse stated that it was because of her collection that she came in touch with Minoru who, apparently, was assigned to help her make a catalogue of the works in both Japanese and English.[14]

During the Japanese occupation, Marie-Thérèse easily adjusted to the new rulers and presented herself, and even her late husband, as a "friend of Nippon." Obviously, after the end of the war she reversed that narrative and denied all sympathy for the Japanese occupiers. In a letter to Minoru in 1944, who had returned to Japan, she explicitly mentions her work for the Japanese cause: ". . . But this is not a motive to forget the people here [on Java] that cooperated so strongly with you and your country to get victory for two years. I am still waiting to continue my cooperation and to get new orders."[15] The letter also gives us insights into their common plans, when she writes: "When you think that it will take much more time before I can start [the procedure to go to Japan], then it is better that you come here again as quickly as possible."[16]

---

10 *Soerabaijasch Handelsblad,* 17 October 1941.

11 *Bataviaasch Nieuwsblad,* 9 October 1941.

12 C. Fasseur, "Idenburg, Petrus Johannes Abram (1896-1976)," *Biografisch Woordenboek van Nederland,* accessed 12 November 2013, http://resources.huygens.knaw.nl/bwn1880-2000/lemmata/bwn2/idenburg.

13 *Java Shinbun,* August 1943; 400 Indische Collectie, Inventory 4025, Memorandum van Mevrouw M. Th. Brandenburg van Oltsende-Geyssens betreffende de internering van NSB'ers in mei 1940 en hun latere behandeling, 1947, Amsterdam: NIOD, Institute for War, Holocaust, and Genocide Studies.

14 Until now the catalogue has not been found. The photographs that show the works of art in the villa are now being researched.

15 Letter from Marie-Thérèse in Batavia to Minoru in Japan, 21 June 1944, Private Sakata Archive, Ishinomaki, Japan.

16 Ibid.

From May 1940 onwards, Marie-Thérèse's fate in the Indies changed rapidly. It went from a life in the spotlight as a member of the colonial elite, via internment in which she ceased to be of significance, to a more or less luxurious life behind the walls of her grand villa during the Japanese occupation. She considered the internment between May 1940 and September 1941 the ultimate humiliation, betrayed by her influential friends and without any possibility of defending herself against the accusations. She had considered her social status secure and took her elite position completely for granted. In 1942, with the Japanese occupation imminent, Marie-Thérèse became confident again that her life could change for the better and she hoped that the new regime would benefit her.

Broadening horizons

Minoru Sakata[17] was born in Aichi prefecture in central Honshu on 14 November 35 Meiji (1902) as the eldest son of seven children in a landowning farming family. It was the year of the Anglo-Japanese Alliance that "marked the 'arrival' of Japan in international society,"[18] and Minoru turned the possibilities that came with this expansion to good account. Without doubt his ambitions and aspirations as a young man can be placed in the context of the changes that Japan went through in this period.

Since his mother suffered from weak health, Minoru was sent to a Buddhist temple as a young child during the day. The monk's wife in this nursery came from India and she taught him English. He had a strong appetite for foreign languages; later in life he also learned Chinese, Korean, Indonesian and some Dutch. He graduated from Okazaki Middle School in 1919, after which he was trained in sericulture at *Sanshi Koshujo*, a school for sericulture in Okazaki. Between 1920 and 1922, he worked for the Koto Koshi trading firm in Shantung, China. After returning from China, in 1922, he was conscripted into the second Company of the eighteenth Infantry Regiment in Toyohashi.

After his military service he married Humi Yamamoto, and the couple had 5 children, two daughters and three sons. The eldest daughter, Kaeko (1927), died young. A boy, Noboro, was born in 1929, and in 1932 a daughter, Mayumi was born, followed by two more sons, Shigeru in 1933 and Masaru in 1935. Around this time Minoru had different jobs, working for the Mainichi Shinbun, and also for Hearst Metrotone News as its Far East representative.[19] In Osaka, Minoru was involved with the Osaka film club, and later in Nagoya he became even more active in the photographic art scene, as he was one of the initiators of the Nagoya photographic avant-garde. In his photographic work Minoru developed an original surrealist style, and his photos are still being exhibited in Japan. In this period he started giving lectures for different photography associations, he wrote

17 Sakata is the family name; I mainly use his given name in the text. The biographical information in this paragraph is based on family records, the summary of Minoru's Military Record, his biography by Joe Takeda in Anne Wilkes Tucker, *The History of Japanese Photography* (New Haven: Yale University Press, 2003), and information from interviews with three of his sons.

18 Marius B. Jansen, *The Making of Modern Japan* (Cambridge: Belknap Press, 2002), 439.

19 Minoru Sakata, "Shashin no bunkateki shimei" (cultural responsibility of photography), *Shashin Bunka* 22 (April 1941), 480-484.

theoretical essays about photography and he published a book *Zókei Shashin (Zókei Photography)*.[20] In 1941 Minoru was conscripted under the Civilian Mobilisation Plan and placed under Army Control in the 16th Army. Like many other artists, he was sent to Java as a member of the Propaganda Department. It is not completely clear what Minoru's tasks were; apparently he had to investigate cultural facilities on Java under the direct supervision of Major Ikuki Adachi, who was attached to the Batavian Military Government.

Early 1942 Minoru and Marie-Thérèse met in Batavia. According to Minoru the two fell in love, after having met at a party of the Italian opera singer Nunu Sanchioni.[21] Marie-Thérèse had a different story and linked their connection to the writing of the catalogue for her art collection. Minoru has not written much about his assignments and nowhere in his documents do we find any reference to the writing of a catalogue for the art collection. Instead, we have several indications of other texts that he translated into Japanese for Marie-Thérèse. Among them the wartime version of a *Memorandum* that chronicled her life history and which formed the basis for a series of articles in the Japanese newspaper *Jawa Shinbun*.[22] Whatever the true nature of their connection in Batavia, it was apparently quite intense between 1942 and 1944, and in analysing the different sources some form of intimate bond between them cannot be denied. After returning to Japan in 1944, on 5 August Minoru divorced his first wife Humi, with mutual consent. Although their marriage had already shown cracks before Minoru left for Java, the main reason for their divorce was his intended marriage with Marie-Thérèse. On 8 September 1944 the marriage between Minoru and Marie-Thérèse was registered in the *Koseki Tohon* (Family Registry). Minoru presented a power of attorney that expressed her wish to marry him. The local Japanese officials accepted this document and registered the marriage.

The common network of Marie-Thérèse and Minoru

As we have seen, the main actors made different statements about their liaison at different points in time and in different contexts. Of the two, Minoru has the most consistent story; he presents his connection to Marie-Thérèse as a sentimental one from the beginning and sticks to that story until the end. Marie-Thérèse's written expressions are more aloof; only in a personal letter from 1944 does she allude to a common life with Minoru, but neither of the stories necessarily unveils the real reasons behind their actions, let alone allows us to assess them. Their motivations are fluid and might have changed over time.

In hindsight, it is impossible to pinpoint the real reason for the marriage. One plausible reason could be that it was a ploy with which she could remain outside the Japanese internment camp. On the other hand, from a letter Marie-Thérèse wrote to Minoru in June 1944 it seems likely that she was really trying to get to Japan with his help, and if that would not work she wanted him to get back to Java as soon as

20 Minoru Sakata, *Zōkei shashin, 1934-1941: Sakata Minoru sakuhinshū (Structure in photography: Minoru Sakata's anthology)* (Nagoya: Arumu, 1988).

21 Nunu Sanchioni was an Italian opera singer who came to Java in the 1930s after marrying a German citizen. She returned to Italy after the end of the Second World War.

22 A series of four articles appeared in the newspaper *Jawa Shinbun* in August 1943.

Figure 2: A picture of Marie-Thérèse and Minoru taken at Jalan Raden Saleh 47 between 1942 and 1944. Private archive by courtesy of Takashi Sakata.

possible.[23] This at least suggests the intention of wanting to spend time together. Whatever the wartime intentions had been, after the war Marie-Thérèse completely denied that she had ever wished for, or consented to, marriage with Minoru.

An analysis of the intersecting and competing drives of Marie-Thérèse and Minoru indicates that both benefitted from their connection, albeit in different ways. For Marie-Thérèse, good connections with the Japanese occupier were vital, for only with Japanese help could she continue to live in her former residence under the occupation. A special relationship with one Japanese individual, and especially with a man, could provide better possibilities to achieve protection. Her strong resentment for what the Dutch officials had done to her is also an important cause for her rapprochement with the Japanese occupiers. For Minoru, other issues were at stake. Being sent to Java provided possibilities to leave his daily routine in Nagoya behind where living conditions had deteriorated as a result of the war. Leaving for Java gave him the opportunity to explore new horizons. Both shared the ability to make the best of a given situation, and that might have given their cooperation an additional boost.

The photo albums and negatives that Minoru brought back with him to Japan in 1944 offer rare glimpses of their connection on Java.[24] The pictures convey a sense of confidence, of a common life, maybe even of friendship and intimacy, and clearly contradict Marie-Thérèse's written sources. At the same time these snapshots make

23 Letter from Marie-Thérèse in Jakarta to Minoru in Japan, 21 June 1944, Private Sakata Archive, Ishinomaki, Japan.

24 These are in the Private Sakata archive in Ishinomaki, Japan.

us realise that although they capture some kind of affection, they cannot give us the complete story or a clear answer of the real purposes behind their relationship.

The colonial elite and its direct surroundings were Marie-Thérèse's habitat before the war on Java, where she felt at ease. Her network was diverse and consisted of politicians, businessmen and to some extent artists. Minoru's network in Japan was also varied, he engaged with intellectuals and artists but (inter)national businessmen were also part of his circle. Apparently Minoru also knew politicians, among them the rather controversial figure Mitsuru Touyama, one of the founders of Gen'Yousha (The Dark Ocean Society), an ultranationalist group that promoted imperialist expansion and was in favour of fascism.[25] Minoru seemed attracted to the ultra-nationalistic ideas of Touyama. It is possible that a common sympathy for nationalistic ideologies was an interest Marie-Thérèse and Minoru shared.

Marie-Thérèse's house on Jalan Raden Saleh, where the two spent their time, functioned as a contact zone in which their pre-war networks came together and transformed into a new one. Here the members of the network – as Pratt phrased it – could "meet, clash and grapple with each other, often in contexts of highly asymmetrical relations of power . . ."[26] In mapping their common network here I focus on three main sources: first the reports in the NEFIS (Netherlands East Indies Intelligence Service) archive, which illustrate how officials viewed Marie-Thérèse's wartime behaviour right after the end of the war. The second source is the *Memorandum* that she wrote in 1947 about her life between the 1930s until the date of writing, which reflects how she wanted to present her actions post-war. She wrote it to be used in the court case with the Nederlands Beheersinstituut (NBI: Netherlands Custodian of Enemy and Collaborator Property), which was responsible for locating and administrating enemy property after the war. This institute confiscated all her belongings in 1947 when she was considered an enemy of the state because of her marriage to Minoru, the proof for which could be found in the Japanese Family Registry, something that Marie-Thérèse vehemently denied.[27] The private Sakata archive with wartime telegrams and letters is the third source, which contains exchanges between Minoru and some of his colleagues, and between him and Marie-Thérèse.

Marie-Thérèse figures in the NEFIS archive because she was scrutinised for her collaboration with the enemy and activities for the Kenpeitai, and later her alleged marriage to Minoru was added to the list of accusations. Right after the war, the indications for her sympathy for the Japanese, although undeniable, seemed not to have been taken too seriously and she could remain under the radar. She tried to show her patriotism by donating large sums of money and goods to the Red Cross. She was well aware that her wartime behaviour would have raised suspicion and knew that she had to act. But on 11 December 1945 the twenty-third Indian Division, which suspected her of collaboration with the Japanese enemy, arrested

---

25 玄洋社 in Japanese.

26 The concept 'contact zone' was coined by Mary Louise Pratt in "The Arts of the Contact Zone," *Profession* 91 (1991): 33-40. See also Mary Louise Pratt, *Imperial Eyes: Travel Writing and Transculturation* (London: Routledge, 2010).

27 Eveline Buchheim, "Victim, Accomplice or Culprit? Marie-Thérèse Brandenburg van Oltsende's Relations with the Japanese Occupier," in *Under Fire: Women and World War II,* eds. Eveline Buchheim and Ralf Futselaar (Amsterdam: Verloren, 2014), 127-140.

her. Investigations at the time suffered from unqualified personnel and there were time constraints that might have helped with the dropping of her case.[28] She was released again in December 1946.[29] After being officially cleared, she left for the Netherlands, but in a list of cleared persons the qualification "traitor" was still attached to her name.[30] Once evidence on the Family Registry was sent from Tokyo to the Netherlands, she was accused of being an enemy of the state.

The NEFIS archive gives several clues about her network during the war. One of the interesting sources is a book with business cards owned by Marie-Thérèse that was confiscated in her house at Jalan Raden Saleh right after the war. Unfortunately, the object itself is not present in the archive, but the report states that the book contained many business cards with names and addresses of German, Japanese and Indonesian nationals,[31] which indicates that a diverse range of people visited her house. In a list with Japanese names, we find individuals from different walks of life, among them military officials, journalists and film distributors. Although Marie-Thérèse insisted that her house functioned as a museum for Japanese visitors, NEFIS officials stated that it was a "centre of amusement where huge parties were organised for Japanese nationals."[32] The report also mentioned a few Japanese men, other than Minoru, with whom she apparently had amorous connections. In these allegations, gender and more specifically expected gender roles of Dutch women play a prominent role. While the Dutch officials were suspicious of her collaboration, Japanese officials also suspected Marie-Thérèse of spying for the Dutch. According to NEFIS, Marie-Thérèse's Dutch contacts were all alleged collaborators and former NSB members. The NEFIS reporter concludes that "Marie-Thérèse was a very shady character who without doubt was capable of collaboration (both horizontal and vertical),"[33] another indication that the assessment of her behaviour is heavily gendered.

The next source that allows an insight into Marie-Thérèse's network is the *Memorandum* which she wrote to disprove all the allegations made against her. Here again we see how gendered strategies are employed, albeit with a different objective. Marie-Thérèse presents herself as an old, sickly, and helpless female who unwittingly became the victim of misunderstandings and slander. The document lists a total of around 100 different names and Marie-Thérèse especially drops names that could convince the reader of her social status before the war. As could be expected, she rarely mentions Japanese names. The only one that would be

28 Lisette Schouten, "Netherlands East Indies' War Crimes Trials in the Face of Decolonization," in *War Crimes Trials in the Wake of Decolonization and Cold War in Asia, 1945-1956: Justice in Time of Turmoil,* ed. Kerstin von Lingen (London: Palgrave Macmillan, 2016), 195-220.

29 In December 1945 the newspaper in Batavia mentioned that a member of the Australian bureau for war crimes arrested Marie-Thérèse. Procureur-Generaal van het Hooggerechtshof van Ned. Indie (Mr. H. W Felderhof) aan de Procureur-Generaal bij het Bijzonder Gerechtshof in Amsterdam, 20 April 1948, in: National Archive, The Hague, Ministerie van Justitie: Centraal Archief van de Bijzondere Rechtspleging (CABR) 2.09.09, Inv .nr. 107765. Dossier nr. 12581.

30 National Archive, The Hague, Netherlands Forces Intelligence Service (NEFIS) catalogue reference number 2.10.37.02, inventory 15, BJS 2.

31 NEFIS report dated 15 November 1945 in NL-HaNA, NEFIS 2.10.62 inventory 2537.

32 NEFIS report dated 3 November 1945 in NL-HaNA, NEFIS 2.10.62 inventory 2537.

33 National Archive, The Hague, Netherlands Forces Intelligence Service (NEFIS), catalogue reference number 2.10.37.02, inventory 15, dossier BJ 228. The term 'horizontal collaboration' referred to sleeping with the enemy.

impossible to omit is Minoru's name, but she gives a very limited account of their connection. Especially the section that covers the Japanese occupation gives few details. If she mentions Japanese nationals she only uses derogatory expressions like "Jap." Evidently, after the war she sought to downplay her connections with Japanese citizens, and her main objective was to gloss over her relationship with Minoru. Instead, she made sure that the subtext gave a consistent impression of her patriotic attitude. She described her contact with Minoru in a very detached way, and although on different occasions she branded him as a "good Japanese," she also carefully stresses his negative 'Japanese' features like cruelty and his fitful conduct. Between the lines, she basically makes her opportunistic attitude clear. She consented to be on friendly terms with him only because he seemed a "good Japanese" who was sympathetic to Westerners, and besides she saw him as a good contact to keep her outside the internment camps.

The last sources that can give us an insight into the wartime network are the letters and telegrams from the Sakata archive.[34] From these, again another picture of Marie-Thérèse's intentions arises. In a letter to him she clearly expresses her feelings, and her wish to leave for Japan during the war becomes clear. These plans are a bit awkward because it was virtually impossible to go to Japan voluntarily during the war as a civilian of an occupied territory. It still remains unclear whether she wanted to use Minoru as a means to be able to go to Japan, or that she genuinely felt sentimentally attached to him. Minoru was much more explicit about his warm feelings for her, not only in the post-war interrogations where he described their amorous connection, but also how he mentioned later to his sons that Marie-Thérèse had been important for him.[35]

The letters and telegrams clarify why we can speak of Japanese-Dutch collaboration on different levels. The correspondence indicates contacts with many Japanese, mostly army officials with whom Minoru discussed assignments and plans for the future. But it also gives an insight into Marie-Thérèse's contribution. The telegrams written by Japanese military officials mention chemicals that Marie-Thérèse provided with the help of a Dutch pharmacist, apparently for the production of luminous powder. Here the combination of her Dutch and his Japanese contacts becomes clear. Because of the information in the letters and telegrams we have to assume that Marie-Thérèse's actions were known, or even approved of, in Japanese military circles. In Marie-Thérèse's letter to Minoru from 1944, similar articles are mentioned. From these sources, it also transpires that the Japanese officials were on friendly terms with her, and they ponder what presents would be suitable to thank her for what she did. Also, the plans for Marie-Thérèse's transfer to Japan are discussed. This source focuses less on the influence of Marie-Thérèse's gender, but more on the importance of her class and wealth.

These three different sources show how diverse the network around Jalan Raden Saleh 47 was, and what actions Marie-Thérèse deployed to be useful for the Japanese cause. To what extent this was mainly for pragmatic reasons, or ideologically driven, cannot be known exactly, but it becomes clear that a mix of

34 It is interesting to try to understand why Minoru kept the specific material that he did in his archive. This topic will be addressed in a future publication.

35 Interview by Takashi Sakata and the author with Masaru and Shigeru Sakata, Nagoya, 23 August 2015.

personal sympathies, survival strategies and shared ideologies resulted in a well-matched connection from which Marie-Thérèse and Minoru both could profit. And although they can by no means be considered big fish, their actions and their network give an impression of how on different levels Japanese and Dutch citizens worked together during the war. Marie-Thérèse's villa definitely functioned as a meeting place to establish new circles in which she could be at the centre of attention, like in the Dutch colonial era. She knew that her money was an important asset to remain an interesting party, which can explain the tenacity she deployed to regain full control of her belongings.

Micro histories and colonial history

Reconstructing the shared wartime network of Minoru and Marie-Thérèse is complicated because they were not very eager to reveal their connections or their nature. This was already the case during the war, when an intimate connection between a Japanese man and a Dutch woman raised eyebrows, and certainly afterwards when controversial wartime loyalties had to be downplayed. Right after the war, Marie-Thérèse tried to deemphasize the importance of her contact with Minoru and she employs her pre-war status and racial prejudice to explain the improbability of a personal connection. She does not shy away from denigrating him in the most humiliating way: ". . . Sakata, a poverty-stricken man of insignificant lineage . . . , who was also extremely ugly, almost disfigured . . . "[36] For Minoru, after the war there seemed less at stake in recognizing his connection with her and probably more to gain. This might explain why he still tried to get in touch with Marie-Thérèse, through personal postcards and letters written to her and to her lawyer Mr. A. Van Doorninck up to 1956. From her side, there was complete silence; this was especially painful since she still owed him money for the court case in which annulment of their marriage was arranged. For Marie-Thérèse the most important goal seemed to be to remain in control of her social position and her belongings, and as long as individuals seemed helpful she was ready to engage with them.

Following her arrival in the Indies and becoming part of the colonial elite, Marie-Thérèse had relied on her network to express and affirm her position in colonial society. After her arrest and the expulsion from her habitual circles she learned the hard way that networks are volatile and that the ones that used to be useful can easily become destructive.[37] During the war she actively converted her villa at Jalan Raden Saleh 47 into a contact zone. It was here that, together with Minoru, she reconfigured existing networks and established new ones. It is unclear whether Minoru expanded his networks as part of his assignments for the Propaganda Department, or that personal interests drove him. Marie-Thérèse managed to navigate the asymmetric power relations during the war in a very skilful way, deploying different gender strategies to reach her goal; when necessary she would present herself as a weak, vulnerable old woman, while alternatively acting as a tough businesswoman.

---

36 In NEFIS report from 1949, National Archive, The Hague, Nederlands Beheersinsitituut (NBI) catalogue reference number 2.09.16.16. Inventory: 47094.

37 Ballantyne and Burton, *Bodies in Contact*, 3, points at the fragility of networks.

Even though the archival material is far from complete, we can still deduct how both used parts of their former networks and connected them in a new transnational constellation. Focusing on micro histories from different types of sources it has been possible to provide a new perspective on Japanese-Dutch connections during the Japanese occupation of Indonesia. The relationship between Marie-Thérèse and Minoru turned out to be more entangled than she wanted us to believe, and as we have seen their alliance during the war was fruitful and both apparently benefitted from it. Besides, Marie-Thérèse was very able to adjust to changing circumstances, and she demonstrated a large degree of agency in her discourses and deeds. This might have been because of her character, it might have been related to her skilful navigation of class, gender, and cultural capital, it might even just have been a matter of chance. The transnational biographical perspective taken here seems a productive way to figure out how these three aspects are connected with each other. As such this story adds to a more complicated view of connections between Japanese occupiers and members of the colonial elite.

Bibliography

Ballantyne, Tony and Antoinette Burton, *Bodies in Contact: Rethinking Colonial Encounters in World History.* Durham, London: Duke University Press, 2006.

Ballantyne, Tony. *Webs of Empire: Locating New Zealand's Colonial Past.* Vancouver: University of British Columbia Press, 2015.

Buchheim, Eveline. "Victim, accomplice or culprit? Marie-Thérèse Brandenburg van Oltsende's relations with the Japanese occupier." In *Under Fire: Women and World War II,* edited by Eveline Buchheim and Ralf Futselaar, 127-40. Amsterdam: Verloren, 2014.

Deacon, Desley, Penny Russell, and Angela A. Woollacott, eds. *Transnational Lives: Biographies of Global Modernity, 1700-present.* Basingstoke: Palgrave Macmillan, 2010.

Fasseur, C. "Idenburg, Petrus Johannes Abram (1896-1976)." In *Biografisch Woordenboek van Nederland.* Accessed 12 November 2013. http://resources.huygens.knaw.nl/bwn1880-2000/lemmata/bwn2/idenburg.

Heekeren, C. van. *Batavia seint Berlijn: De geschiedenis van de Indische Duitsers in Nederlandse gevangenschap.* The Hague: Nijgh & van Ditmar, 1983.

Jansen, Marius B. *The Making of Modern Japan.* Cambridge: Belknap Press, 2002.

Pratt, Mary Louise. "The Arts of the Contact Zone." *Profession* 91 (1991): 33-40.

Pratt, Mary Louise. *Imperial Eyes: Travel Writing and Transculturation.* London: Routledge, 2010.

Schouten, Lisette. "Netherlands East Indies' War Crimes Trials in the Face of Decolonization." In *War Crimes Trials in the Wake of Decolonization and Cold War in Asia, 1945-1956: Justice in Time of Turmoil,* edited by Kerstin von Lingen, 195-220. London: Palgrave Macmillan, 2016.

Tucker, Anne Wilkes. *The History of Japanese Photography.* New Haven: Yale University Press, 2003.

"The *Voortrekkers*, on their way to Pretoria, 1952"

Doing race in life writing from South Africa to the Netherlands

Barbara Henkes

In this essay I want to explore how a series of letters from a Dutch migrant woman can help us to understand how practices of race – its meaning and performing in daily life – changed when moving from the post-war Netherlands to apartheid South Africa.[1] Subsequently I shall introduce Mrs Beusekom (1928) and the way she reports on her experiences during her travel and after her arrival in Pretoria in 1952. Her observations, as they are presented in the weekly letters she wrote to her parents in Amsterdam, may help to further develop new lines of inquiry that facilitate a transnational perspective on 'doing race' and different forms of racism in the postcolonial 1950s.[2] This is indeed a correspondence between relatives who are all registered as Dutch nationals and who experience white Dutchness as a matter of course. However, the correspondence shows how in the process of migration and settlement in a different national context new meanings are attached to Dutchness. Crucial for this unhinging of a national framework is the difference in proximity of the colonised and racialised subjects, recognizable as 'people of colour' in the Netherlands and South Africa. For Dutch newcomers in South Africa, it was often the first time that they had to deal with daily encounters across the colour line.[3] As long as the colonial 'other' was at a distance from their Dutch back yard, 'race' remained an abstract entity. The category 'race' only became urgent during a stay in distant Dutch colonies or elsewhere outside Europe.

---

1 I want to thank Victor van Bentem for transcribing the handwritten letters. I would also like to thank Timothy Ashplant and Richard Johnson for their detailed and constructive feedback on the first draft of this contribution.

2 When referring to 'doing race' I want to emphasize that race and ethnicity are not things that people or groups have or are, but rather sets of actions that people do. Cf. Hazel Rose Markus and Paula M. L. Moya, eds., *Doing Race: 21 Essays for the 21st Century* (New York: W.W. Norton & Company, 2010).

3 The notion of 'colour line,' to indicate racial segregation and racist exclusion, gained fame after W. E. B. Du Bois' repeated use of it in his book *The Souls of Black Folk* (New York: New American Library, Inc, 1903), where he stated that the worldwide problem of the twentieth century was going to be "the problem of the color-line." Later Du Bois expanded his approach to include discrimination beyond that of simply 'white' versus 'black.'

Upon arriving in South Africa the proximity of people of colour was immediate and it was soon perceived as an immediate threat to whiteness and European civilisation. We can therefore explain different forms of doing race and racism in both countries and in the life stories of Dutch migrants in terms of 'contact zones': the concept Mary Louise Pratt introduced to indicate a social space where actors from different cultural backgrounds meet, clash, and grapple with each other, in a context of highly asymmetrical relations of power. [4] By examining how the white Mrs Beusekom was doing race in apartheid South Africa, we gain insight into the transfer and impact of a colonial gaze that European migrants brought with them to the African continent.[5] How did Mrs Beusekom negotiate her involvement in racialised inequalities and the naturalness of white privileges in letters to her family in the Netherlands? And is it possible to connect these "narratives of whiteness," as Melissa Steyn calls them,[6] to different forms of doing race in both countries?

In order to answer such questions, we need to rethink the notion of human agency in our histories of apartheid and other (post)colonial regimes. Migrant letters from South Africa to the Netherlands invite an approach to human agency that acknowledges how European imperialism frames the experiences of individual actors along the global colour line. At the same time these individual experiences facilitate a search for mutual complicity of the actors in articulating racialised inequalities and strengthening the powers that produce and reproduce them. This approach brings me to the possibilities of what became known as *Alltagsgeschichte*: a history of everyday life that may help us to analyse the negotiations of historical actors, certainly in times of violent forms of exclusion and repression along the colour line.

History of everyday life & human agency

Alltagsgeschichte, or the history of everyday life, emphasises exploring the capacity of historical subjects to act in and on their immediate social worlds.[7] When looking at the conditions to act, it is important to examine the often conflicting responsibilities, loyalties and identifications that were at stake in a specific time and place.[8] Especially now that historiography seems to be moving from grand

---

4 Mary Louise Pratt, "Arts of the Contact Zone," *Profession* 91 (1991): 33-40.

5 The colonial gaze, determined by a set of conventions for viewing colonial realities, underwrote colonial power. It turned 'people of colour' into observed objects, and authorised the official discourses of European viewers, whose representations determined and fixed the status and stature of colonised subjects.

6 Melissa Steyn, *Whiteness Just Isn't What It Used To Be: White Identity in a Changing South Africa* (Johannesburg: SUNY Press, 2001).

7 During the deployment and elaboration of the *Alltagsgeschichte* concept, I was inspired, among others, by the "Forum" contribution in *German History* 27, no. 4 (2009) 560-579 based on a panel discussion on 'Everyday life in Nazi Germany' with Elissa Mailänder Koslow (Kulturwissenschaftliches Institut Essen), Gideon Reuveni (University of Melbourne), Paul Steege (Villanova University), and Dennis Sweeney (University of Alberta), moderated by Andrew Stuart Bergerson (University of Missouri, Kansas City). And also by Andrew I. Port, "History from Below, the History of Everyday Life, and Microhistory," in *International Encyclopedia of the Social and Behavioral Sciences,* ed. J. Wright, volume 11, 2nd ed. (New York: Elsevier, 2015),108-113.

8 See also Martijn Eickhoff, Barbara Henkes, and Frank van Vree, "De verleiding van een grijze geschiedschrijving: Morele waarden in historische voorstellingen," *Tijdschrift voor geschiedenis* 123, no. 3 (2010): 322-339.

narratives of oppression and resistance to more ambiguous and ambivalent stories, we need to find ways to move back and forth between different domains of involvement in (un-)doing race. [9] In this contribution I focus in particular on doing race and different forms of racism involved.

The first domain in which human agents become involved in doing race concerns formal, political institutions and their articulation of national interests in connection to racialised categories. The racialised practices involved are indeed state oriented, although the political and the cultural in this domain can be strongly intertwined, for instance when church and state are inextricably linked in their shared orientation towards a white, or ethnically homogeneous Christian nation-state. This was the case with the Dutch Reformed (NG) Church in South Africa that maintained a strong bond with the Nasionale Party and its state policies of apartheid.[10]

In the case of migration from the Netherlands to South Africa, the individual migrants were part of transnational and global migration policies after the Second World War. The Dutch government stimulated emigration in order to relieve postwar society of its assumed overpopulation and prevailing unemployment. This policy seamlessly matched the nationalist South African government's ambition to fortify the Afrikaner population by attracting specific white immigrants from the so-called Germanic countries: Germany, the Netherlands, and Scandinavia. After all, these countries were – in the eyes of the Afrikaner Nationalist – the cradle of the white Afrikaner people. The migrants from these European countries were supposed to strengthen the white population in general and in particular the Afrikaner cultural and political domain. Simply by emigrating, Dutch migrants became part of apartheid policies of the South African government and its self-presentation as the promotor of a modern, civilised and white nation.[11] But how, as a historian, to move on from this general observation? How to open up more ambivalent and complex histories with multiple repertoires, varying from denial to acceptance or rejection of racist practices?

Arriving in South Africa during the 1950s, Dutch migrants took with them in their baggage a colonial version of global history and a 'cultural archive,'[12] which moulded the way they perceived themselves and acted upon their new surroundings. Once arrived at their destination, the dominant discourse of racial exclusion seamlessly connected to deeply rooted images and ideas about Western civilisation versus African barbarism, and an essentialist inequality between blacks and whites. This dichotomy between the 'white We' and 'black Them' was further enhanced by the colonial footprint left by the Dutch in South Africa. The historical ties between the two countries were highlighted in various ways in the 1950s, during mutual visits by dignitaries, by signing a cultural agreement between the two countries, by simultaneous celebrations of the arrival of the Dutchman

---

9 Paul Steege, referring to the work of Peter Fritzsche, *Life and Death in the Third Reich* (Cambridge MA: Belknap Press, 2008), in his contribution to the panel discussion (Forum) on "Everyday life in Nazi Germany" in *German History*, 562.

10 Erica Meijers, *Blanke broeders, zwarte vreemden: De Nederlandse Hervormde Kerk, de Gereformeerde Kerken in Nederland en de apartheid in Zuid-Afrika 1948-1972* (Hilversum: Verloren, 2008).

11 Barbara Henkes, "Shifting Identifications in Dutch-South African Migration Policies (1910-1961)," *South African Historical Journal* 68, no. 4 (2016): 641-669.

12 Edward Said, *Culture and Imperialism* (New York: Knopf, 1993).

Jan van Riebeeck in the Cape three centuries earlier, and by stressing the ethnic similarities ('*stamverwantschap*') between the Christian and 'Caucasian' Dutch and Afrikaners.[13]

National and global *civil societies* can be defined as a second domain in which race was and is (un)done. This domain encompasses both national and international organisations working either against apartheid regime or in support of it, in addition to organisations that took a more ambivalent stance. The latter applied, for example, to the Catholic Church, while the national and international Dutch Reformed Church for a long time maintained their strong bond with the Nasionale Party and its State policies of apartheid. In that respect there is an overlap between the first and second domain. In 1950s South Africa the organised protests against the exclusion of the black majority grew. In the Netherlands and worldwide it took another decade – in spite of the 1948 proclamation of the Universal Declarations of Human Rights by the United Nations – before the anti-apartheid movements became prominent. Only after 1960 were anti-apartheid movements outside of (South) Africa able to present a 'counter' narrative that stressed equality and universal human rights against racial exclusion.[14] In the 1950s, this organised critical voice was still easy to be ignored by the vast majority of Dutch migrants in South Africa and their families and friends in the Netherlands. When after 1960 the South African, Dutch and worldwide anti-apartheid movements grew into a 'global civil society,'[15] this development did not necessarily made organised criticism more accessible to Dutch migrants in South Africa. On the contrary, many of them felt threatened as former Dutch citizens by the Dutch anti-apartheid movements and it reinforced their identification with the South African apartheid policies, while distancing themselves from their critical Dutch connections. This process was reinforced by the South African regime framing the anti-apartheid movements in Cold War terms as a 'red' menace, aligned with the communist movement, undermining 'Western' civilisation.[16]

A third domain of (un)doing race comprises social formations – some more permanent, some less – such as passengers on the same migrant ship, family networks, colleagues, neighbours, or members of national (Dutch) Associations abroad. Within these communities, networks or associations one became acquainted with current local practices of racial exclusion, humiliation and violence that were taken for granted and reproduced. Those who tried to express doubts or criticism risked being excluded and marginalised as a '*kafferboetie*.'[17] However, there were

---

13 Barbara Henkes, "The 1952 Celebrations of Jan van Riebeecks [sic] Tercentanary in the Netherlands and South Africa: 'Stamverwantschap' and the Imagination of a White, Transnational Community," in *Imagining Communities. Historical Reflections on the Process of Community Formation,* eds. Gemma Blok, Vincent Kuitenbrouwer, and Claire Weeda (Amsterdam: Amsterdam University Press, 2018), 157-177.

14 Barbara Henkes, Caspar Dullemond, and James Kennedy, "Inleiding: Kerk en apartheid in transnationaal perspectief," in *"Maar we wisten ons door de Heer geroepen": Kerk en apartheid in transnationaal perspectief*, eds. Caspar Dullemond, Barbara Henkes, and James Kennedy (Hilversum: Uitgeverij Verloren, 2017), 7-22.

15 Håkan Thorn, *Anti-Apartheid and the Emergence of a Global Civil Society* (London: Palgrave, 2006).

16 Sue Onslow, "Introduction" and "Chapter 1," in *Cold War in Southern Africa: White Power, Black Liberation*, ed. Sue Onslow (New York: Routledge, 2009).

17 Boetie means brother in Afrikaans, so we may translate this term as 'brother of the kaffirs (blacks),' or in terms of that time: nigger lover.

Figure 1: Kruger Park, 1952. A Dutch migrant family is visiting the wildlife park with the African staff in the background. Private collection.

Figure 2: Johannesburg, 1954. "Elisabeth gets the coal" (with a Dutch migrant's daughter by her side). Private collection.

circumstances in which these kinds of informal networks could provide for a platform for the articulation of more critical views.

That brings me to a fourth domain of involvement concerning the individual agent and the moments when he or she is doing or undoing 'race.' Those moments were often related to 'contact zones', where 'black' and 'white' met and at the same time were separated by the colour line. It was there that one 'chooses' to participate, watch, ignore, muddle through, resist, or some combination of those attitudes over time. The painful considerations that were made in this respect cannot be separated from the dynamics between the previously mentioned domains of (un)doing race.

Figure 3: Johannesburg, 1954. Caption in the familyalbum of Dutch migrants: "What is Master doing now?" (Making a picture while the domestic worker Elisabeth is polishing his shoes). Private collection.

Figure 4: Koppies, March 1956. Caption in the familyalbum of Dutch migrants: "Aupa warms his tea on the slow combostion stove and is busy preparing his milliepap (porridge). (Daugther) Hanneke is waiting for her share. Rover (dog) must watch." Private collection.

The movement back and forth between these different domains of responsibility and identification is decisive for the, often ambivalent, ways individual actors dealt with race as a category and a practice. A rejection or even tentative criticism of the dominant racist discourse in the 1950s, had an irrevocably effect on one's own position and also on the positions of those for whom one felt responsible. Feelings of responsibility and loyalty could range from the well-being of one's own family, to the success of one's business, or the development of a church community. At the same time these responsibilities could interfere with a moral and political engagement for equal human rights and with those who were racialised, marginalised and excluded from society as a whole.

In relation to these four domains of analysis I look for an approach to human agency that acknowledges how structures of power and the people who inhabit them, limit the space for manoeuvre available to individual actors. Yet, at the same time this approach must leave room for mutual complicity of the actors in producing and strengthening those same structures of power. This is why I am looking for overlapping and intertwining practices of (un)doing race. The fact that different practices are often part of the same biographical trajectories makes it even more urgent to depict everyday life as an ambiguous space of intersubjectivity, interpretation, and interpellation.

Elissa Mailänder Koslow has mentioned that everyday life in history writing is both an *analytical concept* and a *methodological approach* that relates experience to agency.[18] A focus on the everyday allows me to reconstruct how individuals, like Mrs Beusekom, appropriate or reject ideas and practices that are prevailing in their immediate environment, in order to position themselves in wider socio-political landscapes. It calls for a close examination of the means by which people endow their world with meaning and it invites researchers to interrogate rules, practices, objects and spaces of everyday life that have become self-evident for the people involved. By doing so we may be able to question familiar or 'normal' practices in the context of their times (like racial segregation) and to negotiate 'normality' and 'abnormality' in our analyses.[19]

I am not the first to stress that it does not really matter whether the main actors in our histories are the so-called 'rank & file' or 'the elites' in power – a problematic distinction anyway. Researching the history of everyday life during the apartheid era is not a matter of *whom* we choose to be our historical subjects (whether politicians in the public sphere, freedom fighters in hiding, or housewives 'hidden' in the private sphere); it is about *how* we interpret their negotiating with the situations in which they found themselves.[20] In what ways were they doing or undoing race at the intersections of class, gender, age, religion and nationality? Small, seemingly insignificant experiences can provide us with unexpected insights into the larger picture of social networks and cultural meanings relating to power and violence that otherwise may be easily overlooked.

First encounters with the 'dark' continent

I intend to develop the above argument on the basis of the weekly letters Mrs Beusekom wrote to her parents in Amsterdam after her departure to South Africa. She was one of the approximately 33.000 Dutch migrants who settled in South Africa between 1946 and 1960. In October 1952 Mrs Beusekom, her husband and their one-year old child were waved goodbye by family and friends. From the port of Rotterdam, they reached Southampton, where they transferred to the *Bloemfontein Castle* which would bring them to Cape Town within three weeks.

---

18 Elissa Mailänder Koslow, "Forum: Everyday Life in Nazi Germany," *German History* 27, no. 4 (October 2009): 562.

19 See also Barbara Henkes, "Negotiating the '(Ab)normality' of (Anti-)Apartheid: Transnational Relations within a Dutch-South African Family," *South African Historical Journal* 65, no. 4 (2013): 526-554.

20 Mailänder Koslow, "Forum," 563.

A stopover in Lobito (Angola)[21] provided a first encounter with the African continent: "Yesterday . . . we really became acquainted with 'Dark Africa.' Well, it is pitch dark," according to Wendela Beusekom and she continued: "At 7 o'clock in the morning we entered the harbour. The quay was crowded with 'little blacks' (*zwartjes*) who looked grotesque in their worn clothes on bare feet, which were grey with dust." Although Mrs Beusekom probably had never been in the company of a black African before, her image of the African continent and its inhabitants was already formed by stereotypes in Dutch (children's) books, advertisements, exhibitions, and stories that circulated in Dutch society.[22] The inequality between the white Europeans on the top deck looking down on the black dockers below on the quays, is mirrored in the diminutive *little* blacks. The city, "which is said to be one of the most important ports of Africa," was disqualified as "an awful place to live for Europeans."[23] It was the first time that Mrs Beusekom used the notion of Europeans. In the letters she wrote before during the crossing, she introduced her fellow passengers in terms of class and nationality. Especially the "annoying" or "arrogant" Germans could do no good, with the Nazi-occupation of the Netherlands still fresh in mind. But in sight of the African continent this would radically change.

After Mrs Beusekom had taken a stroll in the company of her spouse, she writes about "the stink of rotten sardines" on the beach where "ragged, screaming, begging, laughing and screaming blacks" were moving about. At the same time, she added her admiration for the "upright" posture and "smooth" pace of the African women. Her experiences are framed in a (post)colonial discourse that is characterised by a mix of restraint and admiration for the "(noble) savage." Mary Louise Pratt introduced the notion of 'colonial gaze' for such situations in which people of colour were turned into observed objects. These kinds of representations determine and fix their status as colonised subjects, one that is closely linked to the 'naturalness' of white supremacy.[24] Her letters show how the perspective from which Mrs Beusekom experienced her first encounter with the African continent and its black population, was already fixed long before she had ever set foot on African soil. Her personal observations were clearly framed by a version of whiteness and European-ness in opposition to the African 'other.' This framing might have been strengthened by the pre-war colonial experiences of her own family and that of her family-in-law in the Netherlands Indies, now Indonesia.

Lobito formed a 'contact zone,' in which the white Europeans on board gazed upon black Africans in a context of highly asymmetrical relations of power.[25] This was further articulated when the *Bloemfontein Castle* departed. At the time the ship cast off from the quays, the passengers, following the example of the crew, threw cigarettes, pennies, menu cards and other insignificant little things down on the

21 Angola was then still under Portuguese rule.

22 Jan Nederveen Pieterse, *White on Black: Images of Africa and Blacks in Western Popular Culture* (New Haven/London: Yale University Press, 1998 [1992]); G.P.F. Buddingh and W.E. Westerman, *Werkmap racisme in kinder- en schoolboeken* (Voorburg: Protestantse Stichting tot Bevordering van het Bibliotheekwezen en de Lectuurvoorlichting in Nederland, 1979).

23 Letter Mrs Beusekom, 7 October 1952.

24 Mary Louise Pratt, *Imperial Eyes: Travel Writing and Transculturation* (London/New York: Routledge, 1992).

25 Pratt, "Arts of the Contact Zone," 33-40.

quay. The sight of the romping "cheerful negroes" who eagerly "as children" threw themselves on the ground in order to get something, made her and other passengers "laugh their heads off."[26] Thus, with this repeated ritual that the crew and the dockers knew only too well, the preconceived notions of black Africans as primitive and childlike were confirmed and strengthened. The stopover in Lobito marks a turning point, or a *rite de passage*, by which the different European nationalities and classes on the ship turned into one white, European community in sight of black Africans.

Compared with Lobito, Mrs Beusekom described their arrival in Cape Town in very different terms: there the famous Table Mountain – just as it was depicted in tourist brochures and travelogues – rose from the sea with a sunlit city at its feet. About blacks on the quay there was no word in Beusekom's report of their arrival. On the contrary, she wrote back home that she immediately felt at ease with the Europeanness of the city.[27] Even more so as they were welcomed by a representative of the Dutch Bank of South Africa, the new employer of Mr Beusekom. He took them to the station by taxi and provided Mr Beusekom with the necessary British pounds to cover the travel expenses. Indeed, they had arrived in a 'white settler society' that glorified a white, European 'culture'–albeit at the expense of a multitude of African and Asian experiences. The image of Europeanness, as reflected in her letters, was perfectly in line with the representation of South African society in the pamphlets that were made available to aspiring Dutch and other European migrants before they left.

In April 1952, six months before the departure of the Beusekoms, both the Netherlands and South Africa had celebrated the Jan Van Riebeeck Tercentenary. The arrival of this Dutch captain and his ships from the United East India Company (Verenigde Oost Indische Compagny -VOC) at the Cape coast was then presented as the beginning of modern and civilised South Africa. Also, heroic stories about the *Great Trek* of the white, Dutch-speaking Boers or *Voortrekkers*, who founded the Boer Republics of the Transvaal (1852) and the Orange Free State (1854) were part of the image of the 'natural' connections between white, nationalist South Africa and the Netherlands.[28] Before their departure, the Beusekom family was photographed. 'The *Voortrekkers*, on their way to Pretoria, 1952', reads the caption in the photo album of Mrs Beusekom's parents.

The Beusekom's, echoing the so-called Voortrekkers, would travel from Cape Town through the Cape Province and the Orange Free State to the Transvaal to install themselves in the 'Boer capital' Pretoria. However, the narrative of the Great Trek was not confined to a heroic story about independent spirits of Dutch descent who cultivated the interior of South Africa; a violent tale of bloody confrontations with cruel, 'unreliable', black 'tribes' was also included. Both were decisive for how Mrs Beusekom approached her new environment.

---

26 Letter Mrs Beusekom, 7 October 1952. Another Dutch migrant on the same ship describes the same scene in similar words (travelogue Pim de Valk, private collection Barbara Henkes).

27 Letter of 13 October 1952.

28 See for instance the widely-read oeuvre of the Dutch author Louwrens Penning (1854-1927), whose books were reprinted long after his death. Referred to by Wilfred Jonckheere, *Van Mafeking tot Robbeneiland: Zuid-Afrika in de Nederlandse literatuur 1896-1996* (Nijmegen: Van Tilt, 1999).

Race: seeing and looking away

From their first class compartment in the Blue Train from Cape Town to Pretoria, Mrs Beusekom observed the imposed segregation between black and white, which she described as "quite extreme": even the smallest stations in the desert had separate waiting rooms for blacks and whites, whereby the designated place for black train passengers was no more than a "hutch" (*hok*).[29] Within two days of their arrival in Pretoria, this critical perception of everyday, so-called 'petty' apartheid seems to have faded, when one reads her letters. Mrs Beusekom mentions the "masses of Negro labourers" working on a new building opposite her hotel window. "They are very lazy and silly and playful. Suddenly one of them starts clapping his hands and singing and dancing – and then the others come up to him, grinning. But the whites remain patient: they poke them to start working again and smile along with them."[30] To the newly arrived Mrs Beusekom, blacks and labourers merged into one category. Her description of how the black construction workers arrived at work on their bicycles and were dressed "just like Dutch workers" in blue overalls also shows how categories of class and race intersected and strengthened each other.

In her letters, she simultaneously expresses her awareness of the great poverty that prevails amongst black South Africans, and her conviction that this poverty was due to their own fault "because they are lazy and dirty and prefer to sleep in the sun and to laugh and chat endlessly with each other."[31] In this way she creates an association between a number of categories such as blacks, labourers, poverty, laziness, laughter and filth. Initially, Mrs Beusekom perceived black South Africans as the poor working class. Raised in a well-to-do Dutch family, she was used to connecting class inequality to a *moral* distinction between those who were able to take up responsibilities leading to material success, and others who lacked this sense of responsibility which inevitably led to poverty. This liberal discourse of personal responsibility was projected onto the 'patient' (*geduldig*) and disciplined (white) supervisors versus the undisciplined, dancing (black) workers. Because Mrs Beusekom could situate the undeniable poverty among blacks within this discourse of personal responsibility, she was able to accept and legitimise both her own privileged position, and the apartheid policies (in terms of 'the native problem') during her stay in South Africa. Moreover, for those whom she had left behind in the Netherlands, Mrs Beusekom was able to present the extreme poverty of the black population and racial inequality as a 'normal' condition. A condition in which she became actively engaged as soon as she, as a white European, had entered the Union of South Africa.

Within a short time, Mrs Beusekom lived her life according to the apartheid system and accepted racial inequality as natural and before long as justifiable. A week after her arrival she wrote with enthusiasm about a visit to the Burgerspark: "This is for whites only (*alleen vir Blankes*), she wrote in Afrikaans – and there are the most wonderful flowers, palm trees and a playground for children. It is remarkable how plants like phloxes, which we know in the Netherlands, bloom

29 Letter Mrs Beusekom, 15 October 1952.
30 Letter Mrs Beusekom, 17 October 1952.
31 Letter Mrs Beusekom, 17 October 1952.

much more exuberantly over here."[32] Although she first mentions the most notable difference between the Vondelpark, next door to her parental house in Amsterdam, and the Pretorian park (for whites only), Mrs Beusekom quickly moves on to the symbol of innocence par excellence: flowers. The lilac phloxes and red bougainvillea brought her back to a 'safe story' about the beauty of cultivated nature from which the forced absence of blacks could be left out.[33] A few months later she wrote that she still had to get used at the fact "that you can walk anywhere in the parks and sit on the grass. I always expect fences and prohibiting signs that are everywhere in Holland."[34] Her simultaneously observing and ignoring racial exclusion in the public space made it possible for her to neglect the prohibiting signs that were everywhere in South Africa: signs that did not apply to her, nor to the people she knew and cared for.[35] By carefully separating 'seeing' and 'acknowledging' (the impact of what one is seeing), historians of everyday life have argued that *knowing* is an undertaking rather than a condition.[36] Mrs Beusekom's letters underline this finding. They show her need and capacity to ignore information about the humiliations along the colour line that might cause discomfort, not only on the part of her family in Amsterdam but also for herself and her husband.

Her life writings provide us with an insight into local practices of exclusion and humiliation which were the result of racialised policies, on the British ship, together with the other European passengers and crew or when she was confronted with racial segregation in her daily surroundings in South Africa. We can follow how Mrs Beusekom, like so many white European newcomers, adjusted and acted according to these local practices, not only when visiting the Pretorian Burgerpark – as mentioned before – but also and more specifically in the house, when dealing with domestic staff. This is a theme that is often and in detail mentioned in her many letters. Her experiences with black domestic servants show how race was done at all levels in the public and private sphere, and how race took shape in different ways at the intersection of class, nationality, gender and age.

Troubled encounters in the intimate sphere

As soon as the Beusekom family exchanged their hotel in Pretoria for a rented flat, Mrs Beusekom was faced with a 'boy' who worked in and around the block: Johannes's work was included in the rent. He wiped the floor and cleaned the bathtub every morning. It did not take long before 'the little housemaid' (*het meidje*) Christien was hired for three times a week to do the laundry and the ironing, to polish the shoes and the silver, to clean the vegetables and to do the dishes.[37] With the black domestic staff, fear of infection and theft also entered the

32 Letter Mrs Beusekom, 17 October 1952.

33 Richard Johnson, "Two Ways to Remember: Exploring Memory as Identity," *Nothing Bloody Stands Still: Annual Magazine of the European Network for Cultural and Media Studies* (1991): 26-30.

34 Letter Mrs Beusekom, 12 March 1953.

35 The simultaneous recall and forgetting of confrontations with racial inequality is also addressed by Bill Schwarz, *Memories of Empire, Volume I: The White Man's World* (Oxford: Oxford University Press, 2011), 198-205.

36 Steege, Forum on "Everyday life in Nazi Germany," 566.

37 Letter Mrs Beusekom, 20 June 1953. Activities that came close to the intimate body parts, like doing the beds and cooking the meals, remained – for the time being – Mrs Beusekom's domain.

household. Once more the notion of 'contact zone' helps to explain the negotiations and collision taking place when people have to live and work together, in a context of highly asymmetrical relations of power.[38]

The family had only just taken up residence in their flat, when Mrs Beusekom saw how 'the boy' crouched down with the child who wanted to stroke Johannes's hair. She wrote to her parents: "I can't tell you how quickly I had to wash his hands" after he had touched this "crooked frizzy head."[39] Also the physical proximity of Christien caused inconveniences. At first, Mrs Beusekom wrote she would never entrust her child to the care of a black nanny. Soon enough, however, she reversed this decision: when she and her husband went for an outing in the evening, Christien was asked to look after the child. Everyday life in practice was apparently stronger than the fears of contamination that accompanied the racial discourse.[40]

One and a half years after their arrival in Pretoria and after the second child was born, the family moved from the flat to a house in the Muckleneuk neighbourhood. Christien came to live in. In one of her letters Mrs Beusekom describes 'the maid's hutch' (*bediendenhok*) in the back of the garden, without electricity.[41] Her initial perception of the extreme, 'abnormal' inequality between 'black' and 'white' provisions – when observing the 'hutch' the black train travellers were assigned to – had by then been replaced by the 'normality' of this abnormal inequality in her everyday practice. It clarifies how we can acknowledge for the ways individual immigrants from Europe negotiated their experiences, and at the same time it shows the mutual complicity of these actors in producing and strengthening a racialised frame, and the (post)colonial power structures that produced and reproduced it.

In reaction to her mother's questions, Mrs Beusekom wrote that Christien's husband ("if she has one at all"[42]) and her children lived in Lady Salborne, a township on the fringe of Pretoria. "Obviously," Mrs Beusekom explained to her mother, it was impossible for Christien's children to stay with their mother: "No way. It is impossible. . . . *Kaffers* never live in the city or in the vicinity of whites." By then the 'negroes' in her letters were replaced by *kaffers*, the Dutch and Afrikaans equivalent for 'niggers.' Mrs Beusekom continues to explain, using the passive form that shows an interesting deletion of agency in her letters: "There are several so-called locations around the city where they live. No whites are allowed over there. This is the way it is organised everywhere. Imagine that they could dwell in the midst of the Africans: they would get a fit. Besides, I think this situation is quite alright . . . . They are so different from us."[43] The 'they' she mentions seems

38 See also Ena Jansen, *Soos familie: Stedelike huiswerkers in Suid-Afrikaanse tekste* (Pretoria: Protea, 2015) and Jacklyn Cock, *Maids & Madams: A Study in the Politics of Exploitation* (Johannesburg: Ravan Press, 2001 [1980]).

39 Letter Mrs Beusekom, 16 January 1953, later supplemented by a similar description by Mr Beusekom in a letter of 13 July 1953.

40 Letters Mrs Beusekom, 12 February 1953 and 9 June 1953. As Christien regularly went home to see her children and kin in the township, fears for contamination continued.

41 Letter Mrs Beusekom, 23 March 1954.

42 This addition indicates that Mrs Beusekom did not link the absence of the father of Christien's children to the apartheid policies that enforced a separation between the black workers and their families; rather it seems as if she sees it as a freely chosen difference in 'lifestyle' or culture. Cf. Cock, *Maids & Madams*, 49-54.

43 Letter Mrs Beusekom, 7 April 1954.

to change the subjects it refers to: at first 'they' applies to the white population (*de blanken*), without herself being involved, as she avoids the 'we.' In the last sentence however the 'they' refers to the black population in opposition to 'us.' At that moment she herself enters the text as a moral agent in a white-I position.[44]

We do not know what her mother wrote or asked for in her letter, but in Mrs Beusekom's reaction and her presentation of the 'naturalness' of Christina's situation and that of all black South Africans, we can observe an undertone of defence. Judging by this tone, she was aware of other assessments of this situation and she seems to feel compelled to brace herself against criticism from the Netherlands. This brings me back to the question of how the naturalness of white privileges was negotiated in relation to the different responsibilities and loyalties that Mrs Beusekom experienced during her stay in South Africa. Her letters show a remarkable capacity to appropriate the dominant discourse on race-inequality and segregation. In order to understand this capacity we need to understand the responsibilities, she – in her position as a young, white, (pregnant) mother and housewife, newly arrived from the Netherlands – experienced concerning the well-being and status of her family. By going against the prevailing norms of apartheid she could compromise not only her own privileged position, but also that of her husband and children. Her astute observations are primarily employed in the pursuit of the career of her husband and the social success of their family unit. That caused her to focus on the 'appropriate' behaviour amongst white women in Pretoria. As far as race-discrimination was involved, she soon presented it as inevitable, necessary and 'normal' practice.

However, there were circumstances when she was able to formulate criticism, when apartheid policies interfered with, for instance, the health or well-being of her own family or other white families. Mrs Beusekom's personal fear of infectious diseases that could be transmitted via the maidservant, for instance, led to criticism of the poor health care for black South Africans. She found that it was virtually impossible to have her maidservant medically examined, let alone treated. And if she was examined, it was questionable whether the treatment was adequate. Mrs Beusekom had heard "disturbing stories of people who had taken their sick staff to the hospital and believed that nothing was done about it."[45] The realisation that the unequal healthcare for black and white could turn against her and her family offered a space for cautious criticism of the apartheid policies. The same was true of problems she and other housewives encountered when their staff was arrested, because they had forgotten to carry their passes with them. "Pretty inconvenient," she calls such experiences with apartheid measures when they disrupted the course of white household affairs.[46]

---

44 Hubert J.M. Hermans and Agnieszka Hermans-Konopka, *Dialogical Self Theory: Positioning and Counter-Positioning in a Globalizing Society* (Cambridge: Cambridge University Press, 2010).

45 Letter Mrs Beusekom, 8 September 1954.

46 Letter Mrs Beusekom, 4 December 1952. In it she refers to a meeting with a woman who had to cancel all her guests for a dinner party at the last minute, because her cook was taken prisoner as he had forgotten to carry a proper pass with him. The Pass Laws of 1952 required that all black people over the age of 16 were to carry passes, and that no black person could stay in an urban area more than 72 hours unless allowed to by Section 10.

Figure 5: Housemaid with the baby daughter of a Dutch immigrant family, Cape Town 1955. Private collection.

These kinds of experience could be a starting point for contemplating the unjust and painful implications of state measures in the first domain of doing race by formal, political institutions. An acknowledgement of racist policies, however, would require some form of identification, which is not limited to the unfortunate white hostess, but also extends to the imprisoned black domestic. In the case of Mrs Beusekom and many other newcomers from Europe the power of the 'naturalness' and benefits of white privilege weighed too heavily during their stay in South Africa. Only after their return to the Netherlands, some room for criticism emerged, criticism that since the 1980s fitted within the dominant anti-apartheid discourse in the Netherlands.

Conclusion

Mrs Beusekom reports on her day to day experiences as a Dutch woman migrant in Pretoria. Her observations may seem rather trivial at first glance, but they hold considerable significance. Although she is classified as a 'white' woman, Mrs Beusekom feels at some distance from white South Africans when she and her family settle in Pretoria. This makes her an 'inside outsider' and turns her into a keen observer of the world around her and the ways race is 'done' in her immediate surroundings. But only as long as her observations do not interfere with the welfare of her nuclear family.

The letters she wrote from Pretoria to her parents in Amsterdam invite an approach to human agency that acknowledges how European colonialism framed the experiences of individual actors as well as the narratives they lived by. At the same time these narratives show the mutual complicity of the actors in producing and strengthening that frame and the postcolonial powers that produced and reproduced it. This brings me back to the aforementioned domains and an examination of how in her letters Mrs Beusekom negotiates her involvement in racialised inequalities and different forms of racism. In relation to the first domain, her letters reveal her familiarity with a colonial gaze and her quick adoption of the 'normality' of segregation and inequality along the colour line.

Dutch colonial history and the emigration policy of the Dutch government at the time provided her with a frame that facilitated her acceptance of a political culture of racial exclusion in South Africa. Mrs Beusekom's consent to inequalities along the colour line was embedded in wider (trans)national and global politics. In the 1950s the apartheid regime received the necessary support from abroad, certainly also from the Dutch government. The South African government was one of the few that had supported Dutch colonial warfare against the struggle for independence in Indonesia at the end of the 1940s.[47] Support for the South African government was also part of Cold War policies. The apartheid regime stressed the fact that communists supported the anti-apartheid movement and other movements against colonial rule on the African continent. Mrs Beusekom's 'everyday' racism and her acceptance of white supremacy was part of this grand narrative of whiteness that was ingrained in the colonial make-up of imperial societies like the Netherlands. In the 1950s she was still able to ignore the rise of the universal human rights discourse and black power that civil societies worldwide placed on the political and cultural agendas. Only after her return to the Netherlands was she confronted with these developments, when from the 1960s and 1970s the Dutch anti-apartheid movement rose to become a well-established political factor. To what extent these developments fundamentally changed Mrs Beusekom's perspective on white supremacy is difficult to say. However, when I asked her more than half a century later to tell about her experiences in South Africa, it became clear that the self-evidence of her former ways of 'doing race' could no longer be sustained.

As mentioned before: Mrs Beusekom's ways of doing race were intertwined with the colonial history of the Netherlands and the 'naturalness' of white supremacy that accompanied this history. This might have been strengthened by the social formations she was part of: her family and family-in-law who had been involved in the colonial practices in the Netherlands Indies, now Indonesia. She, her husband and some Dutch and English friends in South Africa had their criticism towards the South African authorities, as evidenced in letters on the 1953 elections, when the Nationalists were re-elected.[48] Their criticism, however, was not more than a grumble indoors and it concerned mainly the policies of the National Party that were aimed against 'the British' and institutions that were not (yet) run by Afrikaners, like her husband's employer, the Dutch Bank of South Africa.

A rare critical remark concerning racism was never connected to the domain of civil society and organised protests against the apartheid regime, nor did Mrs Beusekom's letters ever show a sign of contemplating any involvement in protests against the exclusion of the black population. The second domain of involvement

---

47 Maarten Kuitenbrouwer, "Drie eeuwen Nederlandse betrokkenheid bij Zuid-Afrika: 1652-1952," in *Nederland tegen apartheid,* ed. Carry van Lakerveld (Amsterdam:SDU 1994), 39.

48 Letters Mr and Mrs Beusekom, 20 March-30 April 1953.

in (un)doing race, through civil societies that acted in favour or in disapproval of the government, was beyond her reach as a housewife who tended to adapt to the prevailing political and cultural discourse. Therefor I move on to the third domain of involvement in doing race through more or less permanent social formations.

Mrs Beusekom's letters show how she and her husband were part of a network of family and friends in the Netherlands, as well as a network of married couples who had emigrated from the Netherlands to South Africa. In the 1950s married women in both countries were primarily held responsible for the welfare of their families and the success of their husbands' careers. Led by these gendered responsibilities within their social networks in both countries, most women experienced little scope nor inclination to put their white privileges at risk because of a critical attitude towards racist practices they encountered. On the contrary, within the social networks in which Mrs Beusekom participated the fears of their black staff were shared and thereby heightened. In that domain existing ideas of white supremacy and the uncivilised 'other' were strengthened and confirmed by the exchange of narratives about smelling, unreliable or infectious maidservants and other anecdotes about the staff's 'stupid' behaviour that could be traced back to a lack of information about the maintenance of a European household.[49]

Coming back to the fourth domain of individual actors having to deal with racist exclusion in everyday life and the notion of human agency in times of overt oppression: Mrs Beusekom's letters show that we need an approach that is not so much about interpreting passive ways of *being*, but rather active forms of *doing*. We can make a start by carefully considering just how everyday practices relate to larger systems of meaning, power and repression. Among micro-historians and some biographers this approach is familiar: their kind of research shows how individuals are making their own histories in spite of being constrained by circumstances not of their own choosing, but sometimes, precisely because of those constraints.[50]

Ego documents such as letters and diaries are indispensable for analysing the process whereby the initial 'strangeness' of newcomers in South Africa quickly transformed into familiarity and identification with the dominant politics and culture of racial inequality. This may help us understand how the Nationalists in power were able to open up spaces for collaboration with non-supporters. If we are able to locate apartheid within everyday practices, a history of post-war Dutch migration to South Africa is less about people *being* racist, than about men, women and children *doing* racism in and across various domains under Apartheid.

---

49 One, rather innocent, but nonetheless telling example is when Mrs Beusekom writes her parents about how Christien is mixing up the kitchen cutlery (that should go in the kitchen cupboard) and the silver (that had to go in the china cabinet): "She does not see difference" (Letter, 20 July 1953).

50 Andrew Stuart Bergerson, contribution to Mailänder Koslow, Reuveni, Steege, and Sweeney, "Forum: Everyday Life in Nazi Germany," *German History* 27, no. 4 (October 2009): 570.

Bibliography

Bergerson, Andrew Stuart. "Forum: Everyday Life in Nazi Germany." *German History* 27, no. 4 (October 2009): 560-579.

Buddingh, G.P.F. and W.E. Westerman. *Werkmap racisme in kinder- en schoolboeken*. Voorburg: Protestantse Stichting tot Bevordering van het Bibliotheekwezen en de Lectuurvoorlichting in Nederland, 1979.

Cock, Jacklyn. *Maids & Madams: A Study in the Politics of Exploitation*. Johannesburg: Ravan Press, 2001 [1980]).

Du Bois, W. E. B. *The Souls of Black Folk*. New York: New American Library, Inc, 1903.

Eickhoff, Martijn, Barbara Henkes and Frank van Vree. "De verleiding van een grijze geschiedschrijving: Morele waarden in historische voorstellingen." *Tijdschrift voor geschiedenis* 123, no. 3 (2010): 322-339.

Fritzsche, Peter. *Life and Death in the Third Reich*. Cambridge MA: Belknap Press, 2008.

Henkes, Barbara. "Negotiating the '(Ab)normality' of (Anti-)Apartheid: Transnational Relations within a Dutch-South African Family." *South African Historical Journal* 65, no. 4 (2013): 526-554.

Henkes, Barbara. "Shifting Identifications in Dutch-South African Migration Policies (1910-1961)." *South African Historical Journal* 68, no. 4 (2016): 641-669.

Henkes, Barbara. "The 1952 Celebrations of Jan van Riebeecks [sic] Tercentanary in the Netherlands and South Africa: 'Stamverwantschap' and the Imagination of a White, Transnational Community." In *Imagining Communities: Historical Reflections on the Process of Community Formation*, edited by Gemma Blok, Vincent Kuitenbrouwer and Claire Weeda, 157-177. Amsterdam: Amsterdam University Press, 2018.

Henkes, Barbara, Caspar Dullemond and James Kennedy. "Inleiding: Kerk en apartheid in transnationaal perspectief." In "*Maar we wisten ons door de Heer geroepen*"*: Kerk en apartheid in transnationaal perspectief*, edited by Caspar Dullemond, Barbara Henkes and James Kennedy, 7-22. Hilversum: Uitgeverij Verloren, 2017.

Hermans, Hubert J.M. and Agnieszka Hermans-Konopka. *Dialogical Self Theory: Positioning and Counter-Positioning in a Globalizing Society*. Cambridge: Cambridge University Press, 2010.

Jansen, Ena. *Soos familie: Stedelike huiswerkers in Suid-Afrikaanse tekste*. Pretoria: Protea, 2015.

Johnson, Richard. "Two Ways to Remember: Exploring Memory as Identity." *Nothing Bloody Stands Still: Annual Magazine of the European Network for Cultural and Media Studies* I (1991): 26-30.

Jonckheere, Wilfred. *Van Mafeking tot Robbeneiland: Zuid-Afrika in de Nederlandse literatuur 1896-1996*. Nijmegen: Van Tilt, 1999.

Koslow, Elissa Mailänder, Gideon Reuveni, Paul Steege, and Dennis Sweeney. "Forum: Everyday life in Nazi Germany." *German History* 27, no. 4 (October 2009) 560-579.

Kuitenbrouwer, Maarten. "Drie eeuwen Nederlandse betrokkenheid bij Zuid-Afrika: 1652-1952." In *Nederland tegen apartheid,* edited by Carry van Lakerveld, 15-41. Amsterdam: SDU 1994.

Markus, Hazel Rose and Paula M. L. Moya, eds. *Doing Race: 21 Essays for the 21st Century.* New York: W.W. Norton & Company, 2010.

Meijers, Erica. *Blanke broeders, zwarte vreemden: De Nederlandse Hervormde Kerk, de Gereformeerde Kerken in Nederland en de apartheid in Zuid-Afrika 1948-1972.* Hilversum: Verloren, 2008.

Nederveen Pieterse, Jan. *White on Black: Images of Africa and Blacks in Western Popular Culture.* New Haven/London: Yale University Press, 1998 [1992].

Onslow, Sue. "Introduction" and "Chapter 1." In *Cold War in Southern Africa: White Power, Black Liberation*, edited by Sue Onslow. New York: Routledge, 2009.

Port, Andrew I. "History from Below, the History of Everyday Life, and Microhistory." In *International Encyclopedia of the Social and Behavioral Sciences,* edited by J. Wright, volume 11, 2nd ed., 108-113. New York: Elsevier, 2015.

Pratt, Mary Louise. "Arts of the Contact Zone." *Profession* 91 (1991): 33-40.

Pratt, Mary Louise. *Imperial Eyes: Travel Writing and Transculturation.* London/New York: Routledge, 1992.

Said, Edward. *Culture and Imperialism.* New York: Knopf, 1993.

Steyn, Melissa. *Whiteness Just Isn't What It Used To Be: White identity in a Changing South Africa.* Johannesburg: SUNY Press, 2001.

Schwarz, Bill. *Memories of Empire, Volume I: The White Man's World.* Oxford: Oxford University Press, 2011.

Thorn, Håkan. *Anti-Apartheid and the Emergence of a Global Civil Society.* London: Palgrave, 2006.

SECTION 2
NETWORKING

Sleepwalking to a poem

A theory of Adrienne Rich's translations from the Dutch

Diederik Oostdijk

In 1961, the American poet Adrienne Rich (1929-2012) accompanied her husband, the Harvard economics professor, Alfred Conrad, to the Netherlands, with their three young sons. Not yet the feminist poet and political activist, Rich nevertheless had an established poetic voice, having won the Yale Younger Prize granted by W.H. Auden and various other accolades. Yet she described her recent development as a creative mind as "frustrating." She was "forced to work, even to think in fragments of time," she admitted on a Guggenheim application, a situation that was caused by her having to raise "young children, with only intermittent outside help." Conrad had given "every kind of support" for her "to remain alive as an artist."[1] Yet the same issue kept reemerging, as it was not a practical problem, but a deeply embedded cultural problem. The transformation of Rich from a neat, polite Audenesque poet to the radical feminist poet for which she is now mostly known has been well documented. This narrative often takes Conrad's suicide in 1970 as a departure point, Rich's coming out as a lesbian as the next step, and her many poems and essays contributing to the second feminist wave – addressing pervasive issues of patriarchy and "compulsory heterosexuality,"[2] a term which she coined – as the culmination.

In this essay, I will trace how her stay in the Netherlands and the translation project she embarked on in 1962 translating Dutch poetry to English both reflect the early stages and helped to occasion the dramatic turnaround in her life that would happen in the following decade. Rich's transformation was not a sudden course of action, but a slow process that announced itself between the lines of her poetry, and despite a seemingly perfect family life and stellar early career. It was a change at a snail's pace, in fact: a slowly kindling fire that once burning could not be put out. It was also a process of which Rich was both conscious and unconscious, a subconscious process that I will liken to the state of sleepwalking, which is also the title of Rich's most important translation from the Dutch. She translated the poem by Chr. J. Van Geel (1917-1974) as part of a series of Dutch poems she translated for an aborted book project for which she had received a

1 Adrienne Rich to Henry Allen Moe, 9 April 1959, Adrienne Rich Papers, Schlesinger Institute for Advanced Study, Radcliffe College.

2 Adrienne Rich, *Blood, Bread, and Poetry: Selected Prose, 1979-1985* (New York: Norton, 1986), 23.

Bollingen fellowship in 1962. Although the anthology was never published, nine translated poems – by Martinus Nijhoff, Hendrik de Vries, Gerrit Achterberg, Leo Vroman, and Van Geel – would appear in *Necessities of Life* (1966) and two more by Achterberg in *Leaflets* (1969), a volume that also included other translations. The 1969 volume shows traces of Rich's disintegrating marriage with Conrad as well as an increasingly violent diction reflecting both an inner, personal as well as outer, American political turmoil that was about to explode.

In 1989, more than two decades after publishing her translation of Van Geel's poem and when that turbulent phase of her life had quieted down considerably, Rich published an original poem with almost the same exact title–"Sleepwalking Next to Death"–in her volume *Time's Power*. It alludes to Van Geel's poem, especially in the beginning and at the end, but it is also clearly a product of Rich's own imagination. Looking at these two sleepwalking poems – Rich's translation of Van Geel's poem from 1966 and her own poem from 1987 – I aim to assess what they tell us about Rich's own personal theory of translation. I use the term "theory" lightly here, and perhaps even slightly ironically. Rich did not have a scientifically bonafide hypothesis on how translations ought to be written, but she did strongly believe in the act of translation, and developed a working procedure as the basis of her action. Like sleepwalking and change, translation was one of the "most important leitmotifs"[3] in Rich's career, as Sandra Bermann has argued. "Our Whole Life" (1969) from *Leaflets* starts with the premise that "Our whole life a translation," she has a poem called "Translations" in *Diving Into the Wreck* (1973), and the title of the opening poem of *Midnight Salvage* (1999) is called "The Art of Translation."[4] More than just an activity to make foreign-language poets available in English or as a means of inspiration for her own poetry, Rich evidently also regarded translating as a metaphor for a life skill to be mastered: the perennial approximation of finding words commensurate with the experience of being alive.

It is evident that translation was and is an important vehicle for transnationalism albeit "insufficiently studied within contemporary literary and cultural studies," as Ignacio Infante has argued. Jahan Ramazani's groundbreaking study *A Transnational Poetics* (2009), for instance, hardly even mentions the word translation, and his monolingual focus on English to study transnationalism in English and American poetry may ironically give off the erroneous impression that transnationalism does not occur across languages. This chapter traces the "interlingual dimensions" of Rich's Dutch translations and the influence these had on her own poetic development, treading the "critical space" that Infante and others have since opened up.[5] A multilingual approach to American poetry and the adoption of translation as a method for studying transnationalism allows us to see how European and American literary traditions intersect and overlap. Yet they also, more broadly, "problematize the validity of the notion of a 'predominantly English-speaking country' for the scholarly study of literature in and of the United

3 Sandra Bermann, "Re-Vision and/as Translation: The Poetry of Adrienne Rich," in *Translating Women,* ed. Luise von Flotow (Ottawa: University of Ottawa Press, 2011), 97.

4 Adrienne Rich, *Collected Poems:1950-2012* (New York: Norton, 2016), 324.

5 Ignacio Infante, *After Translation: The Transfer and Circulation of Modern Poetics Across the Atlantic* (New York: Fordham University Press, 2013), 6.

States."[6] Although this larger social concern will not be the focus of this essay, Rich was acutely aware of this emphasis of English-only while the United States always was and still is multilingual. In her later poetry, she frequently alludes to and incorporates the Spanish that was spoken all around her in California.

To tease out the influence of Rich's Dutch translations on her English-language poetry requires a finicky and in-depth approach, but I am aware that these translations do not occur in a political vacuum either. There are many social, political, and commercial factors that impinge on the process of translation, from the choices that are made whether or not to translate a text, who funds it, and to where and when the translations are published. The fact that Rich received a grant from the Bollingen Foundation to start up her translation project and that the Guggenheim Foundation funded her travels to Europe underlines this. Together with the Ford Foundation, these non-profit organisations sponsored American art and artists during the height of the Cold War in part to strengthen the Western Alliance, by fostering cultural exchange among Western nations and promoting Western values. These pro-American networking institutions were all "deeply involved and invested in cultural diplomacy," and sought to "use culture as a weapon to prevent war and against Soviet totalitarianism," as Greg Barnhisel has argued about the Ford Foundation.[7] Although Rich profited from these pro-American organisations, she ultimately veered away from their implicit political goals. Rich was aware of the "ethical-political" dimension of translation, and increasingly saw translation as "a site for negotiating towards democracy, equality, and justice in the age of globalisation," echoing what theorists on that topic, such as Judith Butler, Jacques Derrida, Gayatri Spivak, and Maria Tymoczko, have argued for more broadly.[8]

Rich shared a penchant for translating poetry with many of her contemporaries and near-contemporaries, including Robert Lowell, James Merrill, and W.S. Merwin, but it is important to see her not merely as a representative of her postwar generation or the American culture which surrounded her. Rich's reasons for choosing which poets to translate from which language appear stubbornly intuitive and radically personal. Despite winning Guggenheim and Bollingen fellowships, Rich was not involved in the cultivation of relationships for employment or business. Instead she fostered a network of likeminded writers and artists who could help her develop artistically. In this sense, this chapter follows Birgit Mara Kaiser's insistence of studying a transnational poetics alongside Derrida's concept of singularity. If a transnational methodology seeks to unhinge and get beyond national frameworks, it is crucial to be sensitive to narratives, such as Rich's, that "undermine or destabilize unified, homogenous notions of collective and subjective identities." Moreover, Rich was going through an ontological crisis between the years she worked on her Dutch translation of Van Geel's poem and the publication of "Sleepwalking Next to Death." By definition, such a crisis is

6 Ibid., 3.

7 Greg Barnishel, *Cold War Modernists: Art, Literature, and American Cultural Diplomacy* (New York: Columbia University Press, 2015), 185.

8 Xie Shaobo, "Translation and Globalization," in *The Routledge Handbook of Translation and Politics*, eds. Fruela Fernandez and Jonathan Evans (London: Routledge, 2018), 92.

singular and "resists generalization," to quote Kaiser, even if it occurs against a sociocultural and gendered background that affected many.[9]

Bermann has detected three phases of Rich's approach to the concept of translation, which show how that notion transformed in Rich's mind and also grew in importance. While Anglo-American influences dominated her early career, "translation and poetic imitation contribute[d] remarkably to the project of feminist re-vision" in the 1960s and 1970s. From the 1980s onwards, she widened her scope of translation, opening up her poems "to a plurality of national and transnational issues and persons."[10] Rich became increasingly interested in human rights issues, for instance, in Israel and Central and South America, but also in wars that kept occurring in the latter half of the twentieth century. The sleepwalking diptych bridges the second and third phase, but why did Rich sleepwalk back to that Dutch poem she translated twenty years earlier? To answer this question, I will examine how Rich published these poems and how they deviate from Van Geel's original, but I will also delve into Rich's archive at the Schlesinger Library of Radcliffe College. For someone so dedicated to rewriting history through 're-vision' and fighting patriarchal institutions, Rich's entire oeuvre, both poetry and prose, has become an archive too: one that was carefully constructed and importantly institutionalised. Rich's papers offers snippets of the "intimate and personal," "materials that archive emotion and feeling" as opposed to "institutionalized cultural memory," to quote Cvetkovich on how queer archives deviate from regular ones.[11]

Van Geel's title must have haunted Rich like a dream, and the poem became an imperative to change her life and poetry, as another poem by a foreign poet had a decade earlier. When coming across Rainer Maria Rilke's "Achaischer Torso Apollos" translated by J.B. Leishman and Stephen Spender at a Harvard Square bookstore in her early twenties, she suddenly realised that poetry "could be a fierce, destabilizing force," she later reminisced: "No one had ever said it quite so directly. At twenty-two it called me out of a kind of sleepwalking." It was as if "a wave" was "pulling you further out than you thought you wanted to be," she went on to say before quoting Rilke's famous, final sentence of that poem: "*You have to change your life.*"[12] Initially thinking that Rilke might be female considering the German-language poet's feminine sounding name, Rich latched on to this kindred spirit's poem in translation for the same reason why she would begin to translate herself later on. Translations provided voices from another world that could tell her who she was, or who she could be, as no other source of information could, barring perhaps dreams. The verb "sleepwalking" in the Harvard bookstore anecdote is not accidental. It reverberates throughout Rich's writing career, and always refers to a new or renewed alertness to the possibilities of life: in poetry, in politics, in partnerships. For Rich, sleepwalking ineluctably connects to a compulsion to change, another word that haunts the titles of her volumes of poetry and her poems.

9 Birgit Mara Kaiser, "Opening," in *Singularity and Transnational Poetics*, ed. Birgit Mara Kaiser (London: Routledge, 2014), 6.

10 Bermann, "Re-Vision and/as Translation," 99, 109.

11 Ann Cvetkovich, *An Archive of Feelings: Trauma, Sexuality, and Lesbian Public Cultures* (Durham: Duke University Press, 2003), 269.

12 Adrienne Rich, *What Is Found There: Notebooks on Poetry and Politics* (New York: Norton, 1993), 191.

"Sleepwalking (next to death)" by Chris Van Geel is the longest translation in *Necessities of Life*, and it also closes the volume. "Sleep, horns of a snail" the curious opening line of the poem, then unfolds in a surrealist and somnambulist journey in which the lovesick speaker walks out of a house, and into a garden:

> Out of the black and white bed, floors of red glaze,
> mornings in the careful garden
> on paths suitable rubbish slowly buried
> and without urgency overgrown with grass
> with ivy and sometimes a flower
> just as we dream
> to see unseen, to listen unattended.[13]

The speaker continues his crepuscular journey through the dunes, down to the sea, all the while pondering youth and ageing, sleep and waking, and life and death, until he wakes up, and returns home to sleep. The original poem by Van Geel called "Slaapwandelen" first published in the Dutch magazine *Vrij Nederland* on 22 December 1962, was republished in a radically revised and condensed version in the Dutch journal *Tirade* in 1967, which was reprinted several times. Rich translated the 1962 *Vrij Nederland* version of Van Geel's poem, which markedly differs from the later one. Photocopies of the *Vrij Nederland* version can be found in Rich's archive at the Schlesinger Library in Cambridge, Massachusetts. Whereas the original "Sleepwalking" presents a disorganised clutter all over two magazine pages, the later one sparsely spreads over twenty-four pages, making a much more measured impression. In the later version, many of Van Geel's observations look like haiku, devoid of nearly all effusive emotion, whereas the original poem resembles one longwinded, Romantic poem.

In an unpublished interview, Rich admitted that Van Geel gave her the "courage of freedom with images and language that no English or American poem had done." This was of course what poets always hoped for, she continued: "that one will find something usable, something one couldn't have found in one's native literature."[14] In 1987, twenty years after the publication of her Dutch translations, Rich curiously returned to Van Geel's poem, publishing a poem with the same title as her translation from Van Geel: "Sleepwalking Next to Death." This poem starts (and ends) with images that allude to Van Geel's poem, which Rich has italicised:

> *Sleep*　　*horns of a snail*
> 　　　　　　　　protruding, retracting
> What we choose to know
> 　　　　　　　　or not know
> 　　　　　　　　　　　　　　all these years
> *sleepwalking*
> 　　　　*next to death*[15]

---

13 Chr. J. van Geel, "Sleepwalking (next to death)" in Rich, *Collected Poems*, 214.

14 Adrienne Rich, untitled interview, Adrienne Rich Papers, Schlesinger Institute for Advanced Study, Radcliffe College.

15 Rich, *Collected Poems*, 669.

Rich intersperses her own lines which are "protruding" and "retracting" over the width of the page, suggestive of the passage of time as well as the waves of consciousness which make us only gradually aware of what is happening to our lives. In the second of eleven numbered parts of "Sleepwalking Next to Death," Rich explicitly refers to the process of adopting Van Geel's poem for her own creative endeavour. She repeats her own words that she interweaves in between Van Geel's image in the opening section of the poem, before evoking Van Geel himself:

> Knows, chooses not to know
> It has always
> been about death and chances
> The Dutch artist wrote and painted
> one or more strange and usable things
> For I mean to meet you
> in any landin any language
> This is my promise:
> I will be there
> if you are there[16]

Literally repeating the word "usable" from the interview I quoted above, Rich briefly reflects on how Van Geel ignited her creative process, before embarking on her somnambulist journey. Removed from the Dutch coastal area, it takes the reader to the border area between the United States and Mexico, in a poem that is thoroughly Americanised.

Rich's archive in Cambridge, Massachusetts shows what she salvaged from her Dutch translation project, but also what she abandoned. She finished many more translations from the Dutch besides Van Geel's poem, and the archive offers a glimpse into her working method as a translator which helps to establish how she transformed Van Geel's poem into her own. Translations exist of poems by Remco Campert, Jan Emmens, Henriëtte Roland Holst, Marsman, Jan Prins, which she completed but did not publish. Rich's initial plan to publish an anthology of Dutch poetry in English aimed to offer a broad and at the time much-needed overview of Dutch poetry for an English and American audience. After having returned to the States, Rich abandoned that idea and chose to include a section of "Translations from the Dutch" at the end of *Necessities of Life*, and to publish two additional Achterberg poems in *Leaflets*, significantly among her own poems and other translations. This already reflects a shift of Rich's focus as a translator. Whereas she initially aimed at comprehensibility and inclusiveness to represent all modern Dutch poetry, Rich gradually embraced a more idiosyncratic and personal interest in some Dutch poems that found their way among her own poems. As I will argue, they became almost indistinguishable as translations.

Rich's selection of Dutch poets to translate is perhaps most remarkable for the group she chose to omit. In the unpublished interview I quoted, Rich explained: "The young poets – Lucebert, Campert, Lehmann – seemed awfully familiar somehow, very interesting work, a lot of it, but the 19th and 20th century people seemed, many of them, so Dutch and yet so unlike the popular sense of

16 Ibid., 670.

the bourgeois, placid, flower-loving, beer-drinking Dutchman – full of the somber intensities, strange dreams and visions and solitudes – they seemed to have been waiting there for me all my life." Rich also stated elsewhere in the interview that "the younger generation" of Dutch poets "seemed to be influenced by Stevens, Williams, Cummings," and other American poets, an influence Rich herself sought to avoid at this juncture in her career. She culled most of the poems from two anthologies, *Stroomgebied* by Ad den Besten and *Dichters van deze Tijd* by Paul Rodenko, and a cheap *Prisma* dictionary which she used to spike her rudimentary Dutch. The two anthologies represented two polar opposites of postwar Dutch poetry where a similar battle was taking place as in the United States, with the former closer to what Robert Lowell called "cooked" and the latter being more akin to "raw." Rich herself gradually gravitated from "the cooked, marvelously expert," which often seems laboriously concocted to be tasted and digested by the graduate seminar" to the "raw, huge blood-dripping gobbets of unseasoned experience" that are dished up for midnight listeners."[17] Yet for her Dutch translations she ironically opted for more traditional poets, with the exception of Chr. J. Van Geel's poem.

Rich sought help from a few Dutch friends, including two poets: Judith Herzberg and Leo Vroman. Rich's relationships with both these poets deserve separate attention. Vroman was an expatriate Dutch poet living in Brooklyn at the time, and a friendship ensued which also led to Vroman dedicating an apocalyptic poem, "A Good Plan" to Rich. Judith Herzberg's life changing influence on Rich's life significantly was not a poetic or literary influence per se. Rich met Herzberg through their mutual friend Robert Lowell who had lived in Amsterdam in the early 1950s. Around Rich's age, Herzberg was a Holocaust survivor, which fascinated Rich, who was half-Jewish, and like Rich was a young mother with a brilliant and brilliantly successful husband. Herzberg too was forced to think in "fragments of time." While Rich boasted two volumes of poetry to her name in the early 1960s and would soon author a third, Herzberg still anticipated her debut volume, which happened in 1964 with *Zeepost*. The two bonded over many shared connections, as Rich and Herzberg recognised themselves in each other, as kind of transatlantic doubles.

Rich's feelings for Herzberg were deeper than that. As Herzberg admitted to me in an interview, Rich had a crush on her. These feelings were not openly expressed by Rich, and not reciprocated by Herzberg, and they were woefully out of place and inappropriate at the time, as both women were married. Yet those feelings subliminally entered into Rich poetry. In a valedictory poem, "To Judith, Taking Leave," written as she was departing from the Netherlands, Rich wrote:

> But this little piece of ground,
> Judith! that two women in love to the nerves' limit
> with two men–
>
> shared out in pieces
> to men, children, memories
> so different and so draining–

17 Christopher Grobe, *The Art of Confession: The Performance of Self from Robert Lowell to Reality TV* (New York: New York University Press, 2017), 53.

should think it possible
now for the first time
perhaps, to love each other
neither as fellow victims
nor as a temporary
shadow of something better[18]

"To Judith, Taking Leave," ostensibly a poem of female solidarity, celebrates the connection between women acknowledging their fragmented selves; but it is also a love poem. In a later interview, Rich admitted that "To Judith, Taking Leave" was an early lesbian poem, although she did not realize this at a time. The verb "love" crops up three times in this poem, and the noun "lover" once, but note how she uses enjambment to both acknowledge and rescind the kind of love she feels. "that two women / in love to the nerves' limit / with two men." When only reading the first line, genuine love between two women becomes all of a sudden a possibility, but the terse line that follows it – "with two men" – takes it all back, although the first meaning, of a lesbian relationship may still linger in the reader's mind. At this point in her life, Rich does not allow herself to feel what she really feels, the loneliest of feelings.

Rich and Herzberg remained lifelong friends, and although it is obvious that Herzberg changed Rich's life, she did not change her poetry, at least not directly. Rich translated "Opmaat," the first poem of *Zeepost*, but did not publish it, and I find the typescript translation, "Upbeat" the worst of all of Rich's Dutch translations. The dense textuality of Herzberg's original Dutch is a mismatch for the raw and expansive creative energy of Rich's poetry at the time. Yet it was Herzberg who pointed Rich to the poet, Chris Van Geel, who would help her find the poetic language and imagery that she was trying to articulate, which she seemed to have been waiting for all her life.[19] Van Geel was friends with Herzberg and her husband Huyck van Leeuwen. Herzberg also asked Van Geel if she could bring Rich along on an upcoming visit Van Leeuwen and she planned to Van Geel in the spring of 1963. Van Geel's knowledge of English was limited, and he apologised in advance to Herzberg that the meeting with Rich might be awkward because of the language barrier, as he was neither a diplomat nor a head of state.[20] The meeting went well enough, and over the years Van Geel and Rich occasionally corresponded with each other, with Herzberg serving as an intermediary when some kind of miscommunication occurred. Van Geel and Rich never became friends in the way Herzberg and Van Geel were friends, or the way Herzberg and Rich were friends. For Rich, Van Geel was purely a literary influence.

It was Herzberg who sent Rich Van Geel's poem "Slaapwandelen" from *Vrij Nederland* across the Atlantic,[21] a poem Herzberg characterised as a love poem composed of glittering fragments: "een uit schitterende scherfjes bestaand liefdesgedicht."[22] She also gave constructive feedback on Rich's translations, and

18 Rich, *Collected Poems*, 222.
19 Adrienne Rich, *Arts of the Possible: Essays and Conversations* (New York: Norton 2001), 133.
20 Judith Herzberg and Chr. J. van Geel, *Brieven 1962-1974* (Amsterdam: Uitgeverij Bas Lubberhuizen, 2018), 39.
21 Ibid., 99.
22 Judith Herzberg, "Van Geels poëzie speelt landgappertje met de dood," in *Chr. J. van Geel: Een Bundel over zijn Poëzie*, ed. Elly De Waard (Utrecht: Reflex, 1979), 47.

some of Herzberg's notes to Rich explaining various ambiguous meanings of Dutch words have survived in Rich's archive. Yet it was painfully ironic that it was Herzberg who handed Rich this bitter love poem about fragments of lost time. Van Geel's "Sleepwalking" was inspired by a brief love relationship Van Geel had with Nanette Salomonson. Like Herzberg, Salomonson was a Holocaust survivor, and she had been married to the painter Edgar Fernhout who himself was the son of a well-known Dutch painter named Charley Toorop. The relationship between Salomonson and Van Geel only lasted a few months, but she and her son had lived with Van Geel in his house in the dunes in Groet, which closely resembles the setting of his original poem "Slaapwandelen." The poet-painter was so distraught by Salomonson's abandonment that he poured out his longest, most personal, and most tortured poem. Despite the distraught and rambling journey of grief, the speaker nevertheless comes back to his senses, as the end of Van Geel's poem shows:

> Must I dejected and contemplating death
> now that above the sea a cloudless night
> empties the sky, let treason and false laughter
> prudently ring out until the morning?

> the threshold of the horizon shifts–
> and think with the thinkers of this earth:
> "Life is thus"– then am I crazed
> because my heart encloses what it held?
>
> Morning has broken and the sea
> is wide, I go back home to sleep.
> Path, dune, trees and sheep
> are rosy from the east, a rosy gull
> flies up under the rash sky.
> What's silent speaks aloud buried in sleep.[23]

Van Geel's original Dutch version of "Slaapwandelen" had ended as follows:

> Moet ik mistroostig en den dood betrachtend,
> nu boven zee een wolkenloze nacht
> de hemel leegt, verraad en valse lach
> voorzichtig klinken laten tot de ochtend
>
> de drempel van de horizon verzet
> en denken mat de denkenden op aarde:
> 'zo is het leven'–maar ben ik dan gek
> omdat mijn hart omsluit wat het bewaarde?
>
> De ochtend is gekomen en de zee
> is wijd, ik ga naar huis om te gaan slapen.
> Het pad, het duin, de bomen en de schapen
> zijn roze van het oosten, roze meeuw
> onder de roekeloze hemel stijgt.
> Verzwegen in de slaap klinkt mee wat zwijgt.

23 Rich, *Collected Poems*, 218.

However disorganised the first version of "Sleepwalking" looks, it resolves itself in a Petrarchan sonnet, a surprisingly conventional ending of Van Geel's poem which may not be perceptible to the casual reader. Rich fairly faithfully translates from the Dutch, but she also makes some unfortunate and peculiar choices. She does not try to keep Van Geel's alliteration, for instance in "verraad en valse lach" ("treason and false laughter"), she translates "roekeloos" as "rash" where "reckless" is closer to the Dutch meaning, and reflects the tormented feeling of the departed lover much better. She mistranslates the Dutch word "roze," meaning pink as "rosy." Funnily enough, she makes the same understandable mistake when translating Remco Campert's poem "Position" which was never published but can be found among her unpublished papers. Curiously, Rich corrected that mistake when making holograph annotations.[24] In "Sleepwalking" she does not correct the error, with the unfortunate result that the adjective "rosy" gives the poem a more sanguine feeling which the original Dutch version lacks and which conflicts with the hint of suicide that overshadows this morose sonnet.

Rich's carelessness was partly due to a limited command of Dutch, but faithfully rendering the Dutch poems into English became increasingly less germane as she delved deeper into Dutch poetry. She became more and more intrigued to "find something usable, something one couldn't have found in one's native literature," as she herself admitted. Harold Bloom famously argued that many poets respond to *The Anxiety of Influence* by misreading poets they love, and the same appears to be true for mistranslating. What Rich found "usable" for her own poetry is rendered immediately after Van Geel's enigmatic opening of the snail's horns in Rich's 1987 poem: "What we choose to know / or not know / all these years."[25] Van Geel's poem certainly conveys the idea of knowing and choosing not to know, but Rich foregrounds it, making it the essence of her poem. In the second part, she repeats this thought: "Knows, chooses not to know / It has always been about death and chance." More than just themes in Van Geel's poem, these concepts – knowing, chance, death – form motifs in Rich's life story. Her life with Alfred Conrad and her coming out were about knowing and choosing not to know, and quite literally, about death and chance.

After the opening, Rich takes up Van Geel's snail in the first part of her 1987 poem, sketching all sorts of scenarios as to what might happen to him. He "could have been eaten" or "crushed," or "could have dreamed it was a painter or a poet." Although these doom and dream scenarios are universal, Rich also quickly localizes or Americanises her poem. The snail could also have put "graffiti" up "with a spray-gun" or "ridden / in the back of the pick-up, handing guns."[26] It is clear that the snail is no longer just the mollusk, but a metaphor for human beings' development. This becomes the narrative that Rich develops in "Sleepwalking" without fully erasing the original meaning of the poem she translated by Van Geel, which still exists like pentimento in painting or palimpsest in writing. Rich's story takes us to the border area of Mexico and the United States where an American

24 Adrienne Rich, Typescript of "Position" by Remco Campert with Holograph Annotations, Schlesinger Institute for Advanced Study, Radcliffe College.

25 Rich, *Collected Poems*, 669.

26 Ibid., 670.

nurse heals and nurtures someone who flees over borders to reach the United States. The genders of the nurse and the refugee are not rendered, which is typical for the third phase of Rich's understanding of translation, as Bermann has pointed out.[27] Her lyrical "I" is no longer "a stable entity but as itself in movement, in transit – between spaces, languages, persons, times, genders."[28] Yet we can assume they are both female, as Rich briefly alludes to them as being similar to Ruth and Naomi, the much-tortured widows from the Bible, who are faithful to each other in their mutual grief. It is the kind of love she shared with Michelle Cliff, her Jamaican partner from the 1970s onwards, who migrated north like the immigrant she describes. This relationship is not ideal either. It is tense and full of recriminations, as "Sleepwalking Next to Death" shows,–"a process, delicate, violent, often terrifying to both persons involved," as Rich said elsewhere, but a process in which each dares to refine "the truths they can tell each other."[29]

Since the genders of the two characters in Rich's "Sleepwalking" remain undefined, the bodies traveling through space could apply to all relationships. Like Van Geel who stripped all the effusive verbiage of his poem in his final version, Rich's poem sings not just a tribute to the most lasting love relationship in her life, but also an acknowledgment of the "delicate, violent" nature of every love relationship, of being with someone. As a palimpsest, her "Sleepwalking" also contains other aborted, or failed relationships. It evokes Van Geel's love for Nanette Salomonson, hers for Herzberg, and for Michelle Cliff, as I have argued. Yet, perhaps most hauntingly, it also carries traces of Rich's relationship with her late husband Alfred Conrad. "Fifteen years of sleepwalking with you," Rich wrote to him in "The Blue Ghazals" in 1968, "wading against the tide, and with the tide."[30] Rich had *The Will to Change*, to quote the title of the volume in which this poem was published. Conrad could not accept the change that her life was taking at the time, while Rich already realised in that Cambridge bookstore when she read Rilke's translated poem that she had "to change" her "life."[31]

Sleepwalking in the unusual condition that a person finds himself in deep sleep, but can nevertheless perform complex, motoric functions.[32] This concept and Van Geel's poem appealed to Rich because it captured a central paradox in Rich's life and art. Van Geel's tortured love poem is a translation of Rich's own feelings of unrequited love, and a foreshadowing of Conrad's dramatic decision to drive into the woods in Vermont and take his own life when his marriage with Rich was falling apart. Rich herself sleepwalked back to this poem to meditate on what we allow ourselves to know about who we are and what choices we make and do not make, and the difficulties we have in sharing our lives with another, for whom we care and depend on for care. Ultimately, Rich was interested in translating life into her poetry rather than translating poetry. The final image of Rich's poem evokes Van Geel's enigmatic first line about the snail, and it captures Rich's hope that the lonely despair that Van Geel captures in his poem

---

27 Bermann, "Re-Vision and/as Translation," 108.

28 Ibid., 106-107.

29 Adrienne Rich, *On Lies, Secrets, and Silence: Selected Prose, 1966-1978* (New York: Norton, 1979), 188.

30 Rich, *Collected Poems*, 308.

31 Rich, *What Is Found There*, 191.

32 Sudhansu Chokroverty, Richard P. Allen, Arthur S. Walters, and Pasquale Montagna, *Sleep and Movement Disorders* (New York: Oxford University Press, 2013), 323.

is not the ultimate fate of the human condition. Rich asserts it is possible to travel with someone through life knowingly. It is possible to "travel / like two snails" as long as your "four horns" are "erect."[33]

In his influential book *A Transnational Poetics*, Jahan Ramazani notes "the surge of translation by poets" as contributing to the trend towards transnationalizing American poetry in the twentieth and twenty first centuries. Yet unfortunately he does not dwell extensively on why and how American poets translated so much, nor about how it intersects with other factors, including traveling abroad. Judging from Rich's case alone, however, it emerges that a renewed focus on translation as part and parcel of a transnational poetics is paramount. If we want to understand how transnational literature really works, it is vital to also examine "the transfer or figural correlation between different poetic forms written in different languages" and to "trace the processes of transnational circulation of these poetic forms and the particular historical conditions that determine these processes, as Ignatio Infante points out.[34] Translating helped broaden Rich's horizons at least as much as traveling did. Translating helped her to conceive of new poems, but also helped her to become more empathetic and reach out to oppressed women and men around the globe. Yet most importantly translating helped Rich to wake up to herself and what mattered most to her. Translation helped her realize that she should stop sleepwalking through life. She had to change her life.

Bibliography

Barnhisel, Greg. *Cold War Modernists: Art, Literature, and American Cultural Diplomacy*. New York: Columbia University Press, 2015.

Bermann, Sandra. "Re-Vision and/as Translation: The Poetry of Adrienne Rich." In *Translating Women*, 97-117, edited by Luise von Flotow. Ottawa: University of Ottawa Press, 2011.

Bloom, Harold. *The Anxiety of Influence: A Theory on Poetry*. Oxford: Oxford: University Press, 1973.

Chokroverty Sudhansu, Richard P. Allen, Arthur S. Walters, and Pasquale Montagna. *Sleep and Movement Disorders*. New York: Oxford University Press, 2013.

Cvetkovich, Ann. *An Archive of Feelings: Trauma, Sexuality, and Lesbian Public Cultures*. Durham: Duke University Press, 2003.

Grobe, Christopher. *The Art of Confession: The Performance of Self from Robert Lowell to Reality TV*. New York: New York University Press, 2017.

Herzberg, Judith. "Van Geels poëzie speelt landgappertje met de dood." In *Chr. J. van Geel: Een Bundel over zijn Poëzie*, edited by Elly De Waard, 47-50. Utrecht: Reflex, 1979.

---. *Zeepost*. Amsterdam: Van Oorschot, 1963.

Herzberg, Judith and Chr. J. van Geel. *Brieven 1962-1974*. Amsterdam: Uitgeverij Bas Lubberhuizen, 2018.

33 Rich, *Collected Poems*, 674.

34 Infante, *After Translation*, 183.

Infante, Ignacio. *After Translation: The Transfer and Circulation of Modern Poetics Across the Atlantic*. New York: Fordham University Press, 2013.

Kaiser, Birgit Mara. "Singularity and Transnational Poetics." In *Singularity and Transnational Poetics*, edited by Birgit Mara Kaiser, 3-23. London: Routledge, 2014.

Ramazani, Jahan. *A Transnational Poetics*. Chicago: University of Chicago Press, 2009.

Shaobo, Xie. "Translation and Globalization." In *The Routledge Handbook of Translation and Politics*, edited by Fruela Fernandez and Jonathan Evans, 79-94. London: Routledge, 2018.

Rich, Adrienne. *Arts of the Possible: Essays and Conversations*. New York: Norton 2001.

---. *Blood, Bread, and Poetry: Selected Pros e, 1979-1985*. New York: Norton, 1986.

---. *Collected Poems: 1950-2012*. New York: Norton, 2016.

---. *Leaflets: Poems, 1965-1968*. New York: Norton, 1969.

---. *Necessities of Life: Poems 1962-1965*. New York: Norton, 1966.

---. *On Lies, Secrets, and Silence: Selected Prose, 1966-1978*. New York: Norton, 1979.

---. Papers. Schlesinger Institute for Advanced Study, Radcliffe College.

---. *What Is Found There: Notebooks on Poetry and Politics*. New York: Norton, 1993.

Van Geel, Chr. J. *Uit de Hoge Boom Geschreven*. Amsterdam: Van Oorschot, 1967.

---. *Verzamelde gedichten*. Amsterdam: Van Oorschot, 1993.

W.E.B. Du Bois at Ons Suriname

Amsterdam transnational networks and Dutch anti-colonial activism in the late 1950s

Lonneke Geerlings

Introduction

In September 1958 W.E.B. Du Bois and his wife, Shirley Graham, spent three days in the Netherlands. The visit included a controversial lecture in The Hague, an interview on national television, and a reception at the Amsterdam association Ons Suriname [Our Suriname]. The visit gives the opportunity to examine the Netherlands as a contact zone of Black Atlantic networks, laying bare historical crosscuttings through a multi-biographical approach of the Du Boises, the Suriname-Dutch communist activists Otto and Hermie Huiswoud, the Dutch translator Rosey Pool, and the Dutch antiquarian Paul Breman. These individuals have been researched individually, but rarely in relation to each other, possibly due to methodological nationalism that renders transnational activism invisible.[1] The past decades there has been a growing interest in European Black History, with books focusing on Blackness, Blacks, and African Americans in Europe,[2] although it rarely focuses on the Netherlands exclusively.[3] This chapter explores how these individuals experienced a Black transnational consciousness and what the impact of national borders was on their activism.

Otto and Hermie Huiswoud and Ons Suriname

Ons Suriname originated in 1919, when about one hundred of Suriname citizens in Amsterdam organised themselves in the association called 'Suriname,' steadily growing as the Suriname community grew as well. As Ons Suriname entered the 1950s, the attention of its members shifted. The Netherlands was no longer the

1 Sarah Panter, Johannes Paulmann, and Margit Szöllösi-Janze, "Mobility and Biography, Methodological Challenges and Perspectives," in *Jahrbuch für Europäische Geschichte/ European History Yearbook*, ed. Sarah Panter (Berlin: De Gruyter Oldenbourg, 2015), 4.

2 Heike Raphael-Hernandez, ed., *Blackening Europe: The African American Presence* (London: Psychology Press, 2004); Darlene Clark Hine, Trica Danielle Keaton, and Stephen Small, eds., *Black Europe and the African Diaspora* (Champaign, IL: University of Illinois Press, 2009); Dienke Hondius, *Blackness in Western Europe: Racial Patterns of Paternalism and Exclusion* (Piscataway, NJ: Transaction Publishers, 2014).

3 Allison Blakely, *Blacks in the Dutch World: The Evolution of Racial Imagery in a Modern Society* (Bloomington: Indiana University Press, 2000).

Figure 1: The Du Boises sitting in a canal boat in Amsterdam, the Netherlands, 13 September 1958. From left to right: Michiel de Ruyter, Rosey Pool, Willy Breman, unidentified woman, W.E.B. Du Bois, Shirley Graham. Picture taken by Paul Breman. Source: UMass, W.E.B. Du Bois Papers.

imperial empire it had once been. Partly inspired by the Indonesian independence and global decolonisation, young Surinamers in the Netherlands acquired a new view on the relationship between the Netherlands and its colonies. A more radical group was founded, called Nieuw Suriname [New Suriname]. In 1948, after fierce debates they merged into 'Our Suriname.' It soon became a training ground for members of the Suriname government, society and cultural institutions.[4]

An important turning point for Ons Suriname was the arrival of Otto Huiswoud (1893-1961, also: Huiswood) in Amsterdam in 1947. Born in Paramaribo, Suriname, Huiswoud had moved to Harlem at the age of sixteen where he became a leader in the Black labor movement and, in 1919, co-founded the American Communist Party (CPUSA). In 1940, while on his way from the U.S. to Suriname on doctor's advice, the authorities searched his ship, and in Huiswoud's luggage they found "subversive literature": *The Negro* (1915) by W.E.B. Du Bois.[5] Upon arrival in Paramaribo Huiswoud was arrested, after which he spent two years in jail. He moved to the Netherlands in 1947, where he was granted access on the condition that he would abstain from political activities.[6] However, almost inevitably Otto Huiswoud came in contact with Ons Suriname. With his activist

---

4 *Vereniging Ons Suriname 18 januari 1919 – 18 januari 1989: Een aanzet tot de geschiedschrijving over zeventig jaren leven en strijd van Surinamers in Nederland* (Amsterdam: Vereniging Ons Suriname, [1990]), 24.

5 Tamiment Library and Robert F. Wagner Labor Archive, Hermina Dumont Huiswoud Papers and Photographs (TAM.354) 1.6: Correspondence.

6 Maria Gertrudis van Enckevort, "The Life and Work of Otto Huiswoud: Professional Revolutionary and Internationalist (1893-1961)," (PhD diss., University of the West Indies, Mona, Jamaica, 2001), 147.

experience, he soon became a prominent member and after 1954 served as a board member of the organisation.

Technically, Ons Suriname was not a political organisation, but a *gezelligheidsvereniging* (social club). However, under Huiswoud the board of the formerly moderate, elitist group (accused by young members of being led by "bourgeoisie"[7]) was gradually replaced by a new one, the members of which wanted to address societal issues and politics. Huiswoud placed the discontents of Surinamers in a global perspective of anti-racist activism and the current wave of decolonisation, and the association welcomed famous visitors such as Richard Wright and James Baldwin. Their search for an Afro-Suriname cultural heritage has been compared with the political thinking of Marcus Garvey.[8]

Huiswoud's wife Hermine ('Hermie') Dumont (1905-1998) was born in British Guiana, and migrated to New York in 1919, where she worked in different leftist organisations and became close friends with Langston Hughes. She had known W.E.B. Du Bois since 1924, when she worked in the office of the NAACP in New York. They did not hit it off immediately. "My impression then of Dr. DuBois was that he was inaccessible, cocky and aloof," she remembered years later. But after hearing one of his speeches on the Soviet Union in 1927, she considered him the person who convinced her "of the value of communism."[9] After her marriage to Otto Huiswoud in 1926 she joined the CPUSA and together they travelled across the Caribbean and to the USSR. After having operated transnationally for several decades, she moved to the Netherlands in 1951, after her husband had previously moved there in 1947.

The Du Boises and Rosey Pool

The famous sociologist W.E.B. Du Bois (1868-1963) barely needs any introduction. He is considered the 'Father of Pan-Africanism,' who wrote about the colour line in American society and coined the term 'double consciousness,' about the internal conflict that Blacks experience in American society. His outspokenness on racial issues made him a 'radical' in the eyes of the American government, while his internationalist ideas placed him outside of national structures. In late 1951 he was questioned by a McCarthy committee, and although he was not convicted, the American government considered him to be 'un-American' and confiscated his passport for the next eight years.[10] During the 1940s the gathering Cold War consensus drove him further to the left, and he became close to Shirley Graham, with whom he married shortly after his first wife Nina Gomer passed away in 1950.

Shirley Graham (1896-1977) was an author, playwright and activist. Her biographer Gerald Horne describes her as a "race woman"–a person who dedicated herself to improve circumstances of African Americans, then also called "negro

7 *Vereniging Ons Suriname,* 29.

8 Michiel van Kempen, *Een geschiedenis van de Surinaamse literatuur: Deel 4* (Paramaribo: Okopipi, 2002), 188.

9 Tamiment Library, 1.35: Women, Biographical Essays on ("Women I Have Known Personally"), "Shirley Graham Du Bois."

10 Gerald Horne, *Race Woman: The Lives of Shirley Graham Du Bois* (New York: New York University Press, 2000), 168.

uplift workers."[11] She was active in several leftwing groups and the NAACP during the Great Depression. After her marriage to W.E.B. Du Bois in 1951, however, she put her own career in the second place, solely focusing on editing the radical journal *Freedomways* and promoting the work of her husband. Because her husband was refused a passport, this 'power couple' became "virtual pariahs."[12] In 1958, however, Du Bois regained his passport, and together with Shirley Graham he made a grand journey through Europe, and to what many leftists and 'fellow travelers' considered promised lands: the USSR and China.

Although Black Atlantic networks mainly consisted of people of African descent, there were also small numbers of whites involved. One of those was Rosey E. Pool (1905-1971), a Dutch public intellectual of Jewish descent. Her political ideas were influenced by her involvement in the interwar labor movement. She also experienced anti-Jewish measures both in Berlin and Amsterdam, operated in a resistance group, and escaped from a Nazi transit camp. As a Holocaust survivor she deeply identified with people of African descent and was able to make transracial connections. "That piece of yellow cotton became my black skin," she wrote, referring to the yellow Star of David she had been forced to wear.[13] Pool possibly became involved with Ons Suriname through the artist Nola Hatterman (1899-1984), another white woman who was closely involved in the organisation and who became well-known with her paintings of Black Amsterdam citizens.[14]

It was, however, the 27-year old white Dutchman Paul Breman (1931-2008) who initiated the visit of the Du Boises and took care of most of the practical arrangements. Born in a middle-class family in the small town of Bussum, he became interested in African American poetry in the late 1940s and through this interest he stumbled upon Rosey Pool. "[W]ithout her it is unlikely that I would ever have become quite so deeply involved with black literature," he later recalled.[15] Soon he indulged in her network, and by the mid-1950s Breman maintained a vivid correspondence with Black writers and intellectuals such as Arna Bontemps, Waring Cuney, Langston Hughes, Harold Jackman, and NAACP-president Arthur Spingarn.

The involvement of these white, European people in Black arts and literature was quite uncommon. During the 1950s, European interest in Black culture was often limited and confined to a small group of either communists or *connaisseurs* – or a combination of these two.

---

11 Horne, *Race Woman*, 54.

12 Ibid., 100.

13 University of Sussex Library, Rosey Pool Collection (SxMs19): SxMs19/11/1/2: Documentation *Zielen vol soul*, "Mijn zwarte ziel . . . .".

14 Ellen de Vries, *Nola: Portret van een eigenzinnig kunstenares* (Amersfoort: Klapwijk & Keijsers, 2008); Myra Winter, "17 april 1953. Nola Hatterman vertrekt naar Suriname en ontwikkelt zich tot leermeesteres van een generatie Surinaams-Nederlandse beeldende kunstenaars. Een artistiek bemiddelaar tussen Nederland en Suriname," in *Cultuur en migratie in Nederland: Kunsten in beweging 1900-1980*, eds. Rosemarie Buikema and Maaike Meijer (The Hague: SDU Uitgevers, 2003), 263.

15 Chicago Public Library, Heritage Press Archives: 6.3: Paul Breman, *The Heritage Series of Black Poetry – 1962 to 1975: A Memoir* (London: private publisher, 2006), 6.3.

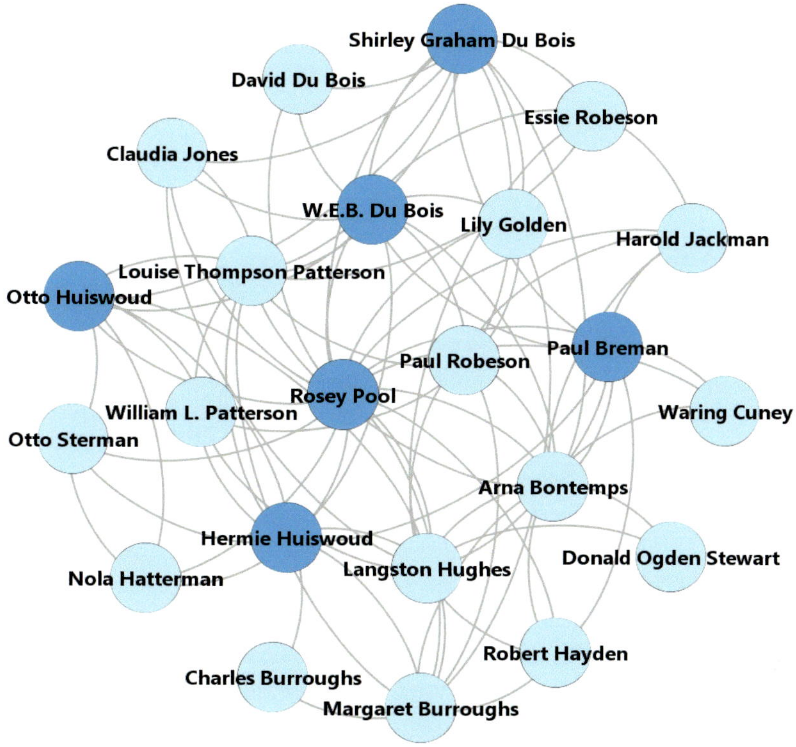

Figure 2: Network depicting the shared connections (light blue) of all individuals discussed in this chapter (dark blue). Visualised with Gephi, information based on archives of Rosey Pool and inventories of other personal archives.

Each of these individuals contributed the 'social capital'[16] that was needed: W.E.B. Du Bois generated publicity; his wife Shirley Graham took care that 'the Doctor' did not get exhausted and maintained their correspondence; Hermie and Otto Huiswoud had contacts in the Dutch Suriname community; Rosey Pool was a public intellectual in the Netherlands who had important contacts with Dutch television producers. Her former protégé Paul Breman was determined to make a name for himself and became an important initiator who had contacts with the The Hague Art Circle. Finally, the visit of the Du Boises to the Netherlands was made possible through its specific point in history.

Amsterdam was becoming an international, liberal playground,[17] laying the groundworks for the place to become what Mary Louise Pratt called a "contact zone," a social space "where cultures meet, clash, and grapple with each other."[18] The visit of the Du Boises in September 1958 formed different contact zones where people could freely discuss the implications of the Cold War, the African American struggle for civil rights, the decolonisation of Africa, and the debate

16 Pierre Bourdieu and Loïc J. D. Wacquant, *An Invitation to Reflexive Sociology* (Chicago: University of Chicago Press, 1992), 199.

17 James Kennedy, *Nieuw Babylon in aanbouw: Nederland in de jaren zestig* (Amsterdam: Boom, 1997).

18 Mary Louise Pratt, "Arts of the Contact Zone," in *Professing in the Contact Zone: Bringing Theory and Practice Together*, ed. Janice M. Wolff (Urbana, IL: National Council of Teachers of English, 2002), 4.

about the independence of Suriname. Despite popular beliefs, the late 1950s witnessed a temporal defrosting of the Cold War. The peaceful coexistence led to a more progressive public debate than before.[19] This defrosting directly led to Du Bois regaining his passport.[20] When Breman heard that the renowned scholar was able to travel again, he wrote to him and invited Du Bois and his wife to come to the Netherlands.

Transnational cultural spaces in the Black Atlantic web

Apart from Breman, these individuals shared a generational discourse and beliefs that were cemented in the interwar labor movement. The continuity of Popular Front activists (socialists, communists, 'fellow travelers,' etc.) into the postwar period has been of interest to scholars,[21] although research on *Black* activists remains a separate field of research.[22] A visualisation of these individuals' life lines and affiliations (see Figure 3) reveals historical patterns and transnational connections across the colour line. It makes clear that all but Breman (b. 1931) and his wife Willy had experience in socialist and/or communist movements and organisations. Based on shared contexts, contacts (see Figure 3), and emancipatory, anti-colonial, and leftist literature they read and produced, a transnational and interracial cultural space was created within Black Atlantic networks.[23] The transnational cultural space they generated could debouch into contact zones thanks to a sense of community, or,–to stay in the spirit of the times–'comradery.' The city of Amsterdam provided the background to create "spontaneous, possibly transitory communities that help to meet many of the material, social, and psychological needs that result from exile or alienation from the nation."[24] Encountering likeminded individuals during the Cold War gave a sense of belonging and togetherness.

The Du Boises in the Netherlands

The visit of the 'power couple' to the Netherlands was not an isolated event. The Du Boises were traveling through England, the Netherlands (a trip to Belgium was cancelled last minute), France, Czechoslovakia, the Soviet Union, and China. Before they departed for the continent they paid a short tribute to the grave of Karl

19 Hans Righart and Piet de Rooij, "In Holland staat een huis. Weerzin en vertedering over 'de jaren vijftig,'" in *Een stille revolutie? Cultuur en mentaliteit in de lange jaren vijftig*, eds. Paul Luykx and Pim Slot (Hilversum: Verloren, 1997), 17.

20 Gerald Horne, *W.E.B. Du Bois: A Biography* (Santa Barbara, CA: Greenwood, 2009), 182-183.

21 Herbert R. Lottman, *The Left Bank: Writers, Artists, and Politics from the Popular Front to the Cold War* (Boston: Houghton Mifflin, 1982).

22 Penny M. Von Eschen, *Race against Empire: Black Americans and Anticolonialism, 1937-1957* (Ithaca, NY: Cornell University Press, 1997); James Smethurst, "'Don't Say Goodbye to the Porkpie Hat': Langston Hughes, the Left, and the Black Arts Movement," *Callaloo* 25, no. 4 (Fall 2002), 1-14; Glenda Elizabeth Gilmore, *Defying Dixie: The Radical Roots of Civil Rights, 1919-1950* (New York: W.W. Norton & Company, 2009); Mary Washington, *The Other Blacklist: The African American Literary and Cultural Left of the 1950s* (New York: Columbia University Press, 2014).

23 Paul Gilroy, *The Black Atlantic: Modernity and Double-Consciousness* (Cambridge, MA: Harvard University Press 1995).

24 Shane Graham, "Black Atlantic Literature as Transnational Cultural Space," *Literature Compass* 10, no. 6 (June 2013), 509.

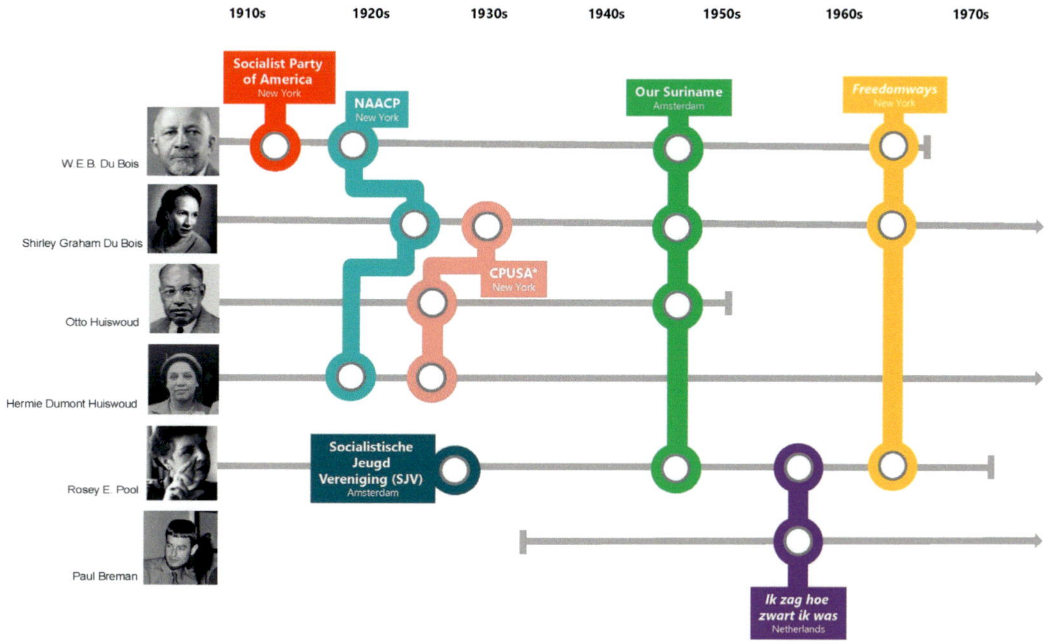

Figure 3: Crosscutting of life lines, showing common involvements in organisations. Made by author. CPUSA: Communist Party USA / Workers Party of America.

Marx in the north of London and then took a steamboat to the Netherlands. Upon arrival in Hoek van Holland they met Paul Breman, who "turned out younger than expected."[25] The communist newspaper *De Waarheid* sent a photographer to capture the arrival of the Du Boises in the Netherlands (see Figure 4). They embarked on a train to Amsterdam, where they were welcomed by Hermie and Otto Huiswoud and Paul's wife Willy Breman at the central station. Paul Breman had not told them when the Du Boises would be arriving, afraid that 'his' guests would be interfering too much with others. "Paul seemed surprised and slightly annoyed to see us," Hermie Huiswoud remembered. The Huiswouds had asked his wife Willy, "who was not aware of Paul's desire for exclusive contact with the DuBoises."[26] It was the first of many annoyances. The Huiswouds were appalled that the famous Du Boises "were to lodge in the attic apartment" in the house of Paul Breman's parents in Bussum. The 90-year-old "should not have been submitted to having to climb four flights of stairs to reach the attic perch," Hermie complained. She briefly considered to "kidnap" the Du Boises, "[b]ut since we became aware of the situation too late to do otherwise, we had to let the matter ride."[27] The Du Boises probably went to sleep early as they had a busy schedule (see Table 1).

25 Arthur and Elizabeth Schlesinger Library on the History of Women in America, Radcliffe Institute for Advanced Study, Harvard University, Papers of Shirley Graham Du Bois, 1865-1998 (MC 476): 15.4: 7.

26 Tamiment Library, 1.35.

27 Ibid., 1.35.

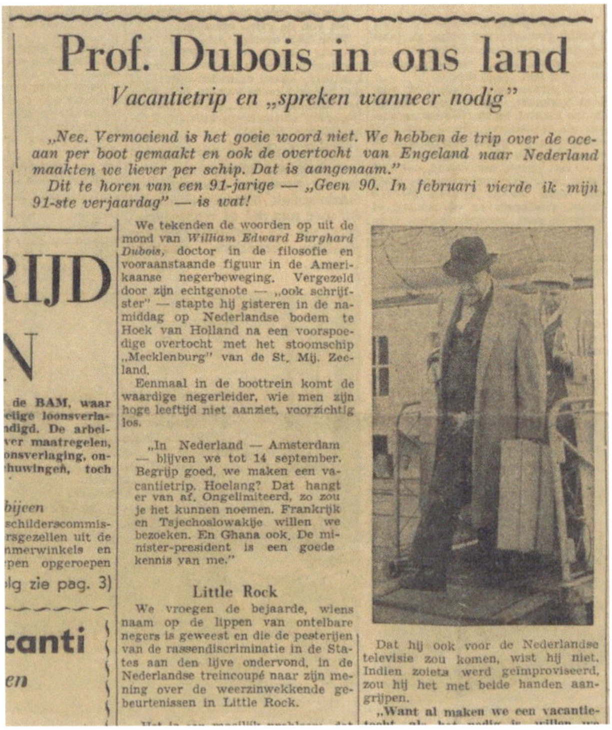

Prof. Dubois in ons land

Vacantietrip en „spreken wanneer nodig"

„Nee. Vermoeiend is het goeie woord niet. We hebben de trip over de oceaan per boot gemaakt en ook de overtocht van Engeland naar Nederland maakten we liever per schip. Dat is aangenaam."

Dit te horen van een 91-jarige — „Geen 90. In februari vierde ik mijn 91-ste verjaardag" — is wat!

We tekenden de woorden op uit de mond van *William Edward Burghard Dubois,* doctor in de filosofie en vooraanstaande figuur in de Amerikaanse negerbeweging. Vergezeld door zijn echtgenote — „ook schrijfster" — stapte hij gisteren in de namiddag op Nederlandse bodem te Hoek van Holland na een voorspoedige overtocht met het stoomschip „Mecklenburg" van de St. Mij. Zeeland.

Eenmaal in de boottrein komt de waardige negerleider, wie men zijn hoge leeftijd niet aanziet, voorzichtig los.

„In Nederland — Amsterdam — blijven we tot 14 september. Begrijp goed, we maken een vacantietrip. Hoelang? Dat hangt er van af. Ongelimiteerd, zo zou je het kunnen noemen. Frankrijk en Tsjechoslowakije willen we bezoeken. En Ghana ook. De minister-president is een goede kennis van me."

Little Rock

We vroegen de bejaarde, wiens naam op de lippen van ontelbare negers is geweest en die de pesterijen van de rassendiscriminatie in de States aan den lijve ondervond, in de Nederlandse treincoupé naar zijn mening over de weerzinwekkende gebeurtenissen in Little Rock.

Dat hij ook voor de Nederlandse televisie zou komen, wist hij niet. Indien zoiets werd geïmproviseerd, zou hij het met beide handen aangrijpen.

„Want al maken we een vacantie-

Figure 4: "Prof. Dubois in ons land. Vacantietrip en 'spreken wanneer nodig,'" De Waarheid, 10 September 1958, 1.

Figure 5: W.E.B. Du Bois and Shirley Graham Du Bois and other guests listen to Paul Breman in The Hague, 11 September 1958. Source: UMass, W.E.B. Du Bois Papers.

Date	Activity	Location	Attendants (apart from the Du Boises)
Tuesday Sep 9	Arrival by boat from London	Hoek van Holland	Paul Breman
	Arrival by train	Amsterdam, Central Station	Hermie and Otto Huiswoud, Willy Breman
	Overnight stay	Bussum, parental house Paul Breman	
Wednesday Sep 10	Interview national television (VPRO)	The Hague, Embassy of India	Interviewed by Indian ambassador in Netherlands, Z.E.J.A. (John) Thivy
	Dinner in honor of Dr. Du Bois	Probably in the Indonesian restaurant 'Deli,' Utrecht	Rosey Pool, Gordon Heath, Otto Sterman, Paul Breman
Thursday Sep 11	Travel from Bussum, via Utrecht to The Hague by car		Paul and Willy Breman
	Speech "The United States and War"	*Haagse Kunstkring,* The Hague	Paul Breman, Rosey E. Pool, Hermie Huiswoud, Otto Huiswoud, Willy Breman, To de Ruyter, Michiel [Mike] de Ruyter, Jan Willem Schulte Nordholt, Nico Wijnen (secretary of Art Circle), Piet Cleveringa (chairman Art Circle).
Friday Sep 12	Reception Ons Suriname	Amstelkade 157, Amsterdam (home of Ons Suriname secretary Frederik M. Moll)	Frederik M. Moll, Otto and Hermie Huiswoud, Rosey Pool, two journalists of *De Waarheid,* two board members of the NGO *Vredesbeweging,* and others.
Saturday Sep 13	Trip through canals and harbors	Rokin, Amsterdam	Paul and Willy Breman, Rosey Pool, Michiel [Mike] de Ruyter
	Recording poetry reading "A Litany of Atlanta" by W.E.B. Du Bois	House Michiel [Mike] de Ruyter, Amsterdam	
Sunday Sep 14	Departure for Paris		

Table 1: Schedule of visit of W.E.B. Du Bois and Shirley Graham in the Netherlands, September 1958.

Clash of culture and expectations in The Hague

The next day W.E.B. Du Bois was interviewed on national television by John A. Thivy (1904-1959), India's ambassador to the Netherlands and prominent Malayan Indian nationalist. Afterwards there was a small dinner with the African American and Paris-based actor Gordon Heath (1918-1991) and the Dutch-Curaçaon actor Otto Sterman (1913-1997).

Paul Breman had initially planned an ambitious three-day program, with the ultimate highlight a large meeting in The Hague on Thursday with an anticipated audience of 2,500 people. However, a week before the event the Ministry of Education revoked its promised subsidy of 400 guilders. "What bastards we are in this country!" wrote Breman in frustration to the Du Boises. It is suggested that the Dutch government feared that a large event for Du Bois would be a provocation to the American government, which was building a brand-new embassy nearby.[28] Breman panicked and suggested to cancel the whole thing. "Fearing a total fiasco, Paul called in our help," Hermie Huiswoud recalled, "the day before the DuBoises arrived." There was, however, little they could do on such short notice.[29] Breman reached a compromise by holding a small meeting in The Hague at the *Haagse Kunstkring* (The Hague Art Circle). The evening consisted of an introduction by the historian Jan Willem Schulte Nordholt (1920-1995), a specialist in African American history, and a poetry recital by Rosey Pool of work by African, West Indian, and American authors.

Upon arrival Breman was "repeatedly asked for assurances that Du Bois would confine his speech to literature," his son Marc remembered, "assurances which were duly given but never reported to Du Bois."[30] Many members of the somewhat posh audience were looking forward to a nice and quiet evening on arts and literature. The notes of Du Bois's talk are to be found in his archive,[31] which are remarkably similar to how journalists quoted him.

Reportedly, Du Bois started his speech with the improvised words "Tonight, I want to speak to you about the third world war," shocking the bourgeois crowd instantly. He described the military industrial complex, connecting this with imperialism through a comparison of the exploitation of cheap labor in the American cotton industry with European colonial imperialism in the late nineteenth century.

Du Bois's bold claims, especially his comments on the USA-Soviet arms race and his comparison of the American government with Hitler, deterred his moderate sympathizers. A local newspaper thought his speech was misplaced as it contained mostly "open propaganda for Moscow."[32] The conservative paper *Het Vaderland* considered his comments "painful," and at times even "comical": "in hindsight it was rather entertaining to hear how this old man broke the sacred, admiring atmosphere that was created in his honor, through his attack on the 'super government' of the American 'big business organisations,'" they wrote. They also wanted to know whose fault it was that this evening had gotten "completely out of hand."[33] Even a social democrat newspaper concluded that his "political talk . . . greatly embarrassed both public and organizers."[34] In the end only *De Waarheid* was in favour of the talk, describing his ideas as "the truth," and the newspaper published several articles on the visit of "the leader of the American Negro population."[35]

According to Hermie Huiswoud, "there was no applause, one by one, the audience left"[36] and *Het Parool* agreed. However, both the conservative paper *Het Vaderland* and the communist *De Waarheid* refuted this notion and claim that

28 Lauri Ramey, *The Heritage Series of Black Poetry, 1962-1975: A Research Compendium* (Aldershot: Ashgate, 2008), 200-201.

29 Tamiment Library, 1.35.

30 Ramey, *The Heritage Series*, 201.

31 University of Massachusetts Amherst Libraries (UMass), Special Collections and University Archives, W.E.B. Du Bois Papers, 1803-1999 (MS 312): 81.1198: "The United States and War" (1958).

32 *Haagsch Dagblad,* 12 September 1958.

33 Arthur and Elizabeth Schlesinger Library, 15.4:41.

34 *Het Vrije Volk*, 12 September 1958.

35 *De Waarheid*, 9 September 1958.

36 Tamiment Library, 1.35.

there was a long applause after Du Bois's speech. Nonetheless, it is clear that his talk created a tense atmosphere to some people in the audience. The Art Circle's chairman, Piet Cleveringa (1917-2013), did not thank Du Bois for his talk afterwards. Instead he apologised to the audience for the political theme of the evening. "And yet," Cleveringa said, "we will still think of Dr. Dubois as a great man, because of all the things he has accomplished in his life."[37] As all of this was in Dutch, the Du Boises were somewhat isolated. Again, Hermie Huiswoud blamed Breman for all this:

> Unaware of what had taken place, the DuBoises remained in ignorance; Paul did not or could not explain to them what had happened. Otto, I, and a friend of ours from Harlem, married to a Dutchman, went forward to greet the DuBoises. Some woman member of the society thrust a bouquet that had been intended for Shirley, into my hand, saying: "Here, do something about this." So I presented the flowers to Shirley while Rosey and we, others, tried to explain what had happened. Then we all headed for the railroad station and returned to Amsterdam.[38]

Hermie Huiswoud wrote that the main problem for this estrangement was that Du Bois was "totally unaware what the mentality of his audience was."[39] However, a close inspection of the speech reveals that Du Bois cleverly addressed the audience as "intelligent Europeans," and also aimed at the more moderate visitors. He said that African Americans still believed in the "fundamental democracy and basic belief of freedom" of the USA, although "our country . . . has sorely wronged us." He concluded with a warning against corporatocracy and oligarchical tendencies, and that it was the duty of Europe "to rescue [America's] press and publishing business from the dead hand of private monopoly." His critique on America's ideal of progress probably resonated with anti-American sentiments that existed in the Netherlands, and appealed to supporters for the "other America," which were often writers and intellectuals.[40] Du Bois's reference to the arms race between the US and the Soviet Union might seem obvious to us, but to the (white) audience it was probably a reminder of Du Bois's position as a Black intellectual. The fact that the visitors were appalled by his talk was probably because of the specific historicity of Blackness during the 1950s in the western world: 'Black' was often synonymous with dangerous, 'crazy,' or – at best – radical.[41] One USIA officer at the scene reported to the FBI that Du Bois's speech in The Hague was "anti-American."[42]

---

37 *Het Vrije Volk*, 12 September 1958.

38 Tamiment Library,1.35.

39 Ibid., 1.35.

40 Hans Bak, "The Reception of American Literature in the Netherlands, 1900-1950," in *NL USA: Four Centuries of Dutch-American Relations 1609-2009*, eds. Hans Krabbendam, Cornelis A. van Minnen, and Giles Scott-Smith (Amsterdam: Boom, 2009), 468-478.

41 Tony Perucci, *Paul Robeson and the Cold War Performance Complex: Race, Madness, Activism* (Ann Arbor, MI: University of Michigan Press, 2012).

42 FBI Records: The Vault, W.E. B. Dubois: 100-99729 (part 4 of 5), Internal memo "ReBulet 9-29-58," 13 October 1958.

In transnational contact zones cultures "meet, clash, and grapple, and as this example shows this brought differences in social and cultural codes, norms, and expectations. Hermie thought the organisation was shortcoming, and blamed Breman for this. Although she described him as "[c]lever, quick to learn and ambitious," his apparent pigheadedness became a trap. She wrote that his "desire for exclusive contact with the DuBoises" excluded them from any organisational efforts. Breman, on the other hand, described the Huiswoods as "hard to get along with." He wrote to the Du Boises: "they don't like the idea of a meeting in The Hague because they would have to travel for about three quarter of an hour," possibly revealing his aversion of Amsterdam snobbery.

It appears that the young and unexperienced yet ambitious Breman was completely oblivious to the context of "highly asymmetrical relations of power," which frustrated the Huiswoods, who placed these power relations in a much more political perspective and who wanted Du Bois's ideas to resonate with the wider Suriname community in the Netherlands. On the other hand, the Huiswoods had little respect for the young Breman, who carried his responsibility as an organiser. Breman himself was not spared either: "[A] number of people have never spoken to him after that evening," his son remembered.

These frictions were, moreover, the result of the immense pressure to please these 'Pan-African royals.' Yet, the Du Boises themselves were quite tolerant and enjoyed themselves tremendously. Shirley Graham remembered their broken twin beds in Bussum "were rather eerie," but nothing more.

She later told the Huiswoods that they were just happy because it was the first invitation they had received from Europe, which they accepted "without hesitation," as it gave them the opportunity to travel and "to make use of their results of the long battle in the courts to have their passports returned."

Dissidents at Ons Suriname, Amsterdam

The next day, 'the Doctor' held a speech at Ons Suriname, Amsterdam, against Breman's advice, who thought that it would become "a miserable evening."

The communist newspaper *De Waarheid* reported that it was anything but miserable: the reception attracted many guests from the Suriname community, packed together in the private home of secretary Frederik M. Moll. Otto Huiswoud set up a radio interview with P.C.J. Radio [*Wereldomroep*] that was also broadcasted in the Caribbean and Suriname. Du Bois emphasised in an hour-long interview that the dependences of colonised countries equaled slavery, a message that must have resonated in these Dutch colonies.

Again, there was disagreement on what actually happened. According to Hermie Huiswoud Du Bois never gave a speech after his radio interview because "Shirley exercised her protective tactics." When the radio interview ended, Shirley Graham "announced that it would be too exhausting for Dr. DuBois to remain any longer. She prohibited any questions from the people gathered and Dr. DuBois, with a look of resignation, got up, bowed to the audience and flounced out of the room . . . ."

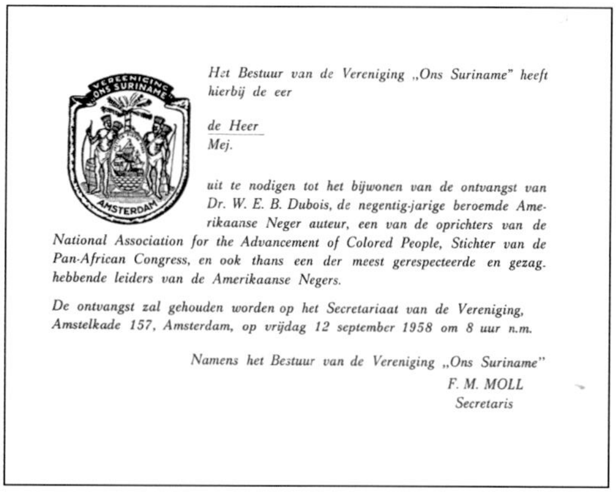

Het Bestuur van de Vereniging „Ons Suriname" heeft hierbij de eer

de Heer
Mej.

uit te nodigen tot het bijwonen van de ontvangst van Dr. W. E. B. Dubois, de negentig-jarige beroemde Amerikaanse Neger auteur, een van de oprichters van de National Association for the Advancement of Colored People, Stichter van de Pan-African Congress, en ook thans een der meest gerespecteerde en gezaghebbende leiders van de Amerikaanse Negers.

De ontvangst zal gehouden worden op het Secretariaat van de Vereniging, Amstelkade 157, Amsterdam, op vrijdag 12 september 1958 om 8 uur n.m.

Namens het Bestuur van de Vereniging „Ons Suriname"
F. M. MOLL
Secretaris

Figure 6: Invitation to reception at Ons Suriname honoring W.E.B. Du Bois, September 12, 1958. Source: W.E.B. Du Bois Papers, University of Massachusetts.

A different opinion is voiced in an intelligence report. Although the event took place at a private home and probably only 'trustworthy' people were invited, at least one informant was at the scene. This person wrote in a report to the *Binnenlandse Veiligheidsdienst* (General Intelligence and Security Service) that circa thirty people attended – all members of the Suriname community – apart from Rosey Pool, two journalists of *De Waarheid*, and two board members of the NGO *Vredesbeweging*. The informant wrote down that the visitors actually were able to ask Du Bois questions – most concerning his books. "There were more [people], who wanted to ask Du Bois questions, but he had gotten so tired that [unnamed person] closed the meeting at 11 p.m."

The visitors were probably unaware of this mole, but people were cautious. Our Suriname was monitored by the Dutch intelligence service since 1947, probably because this organisation dared to challenge nationalist frameworks and western capitalist democracy in general. At least two of its members lost their governmental jobs because they were seen as *staatsgevaarlijk* (subversive enemies of the state) because they were members of a 'communist' organisation.

It is therefore likely that the short visit of the Du Boises was quite significant as it offered visitors the opportunity to sit face-to-face with a world-famous scholar and Black leader who had been a persona non-grata for years. It is possible that the guests recognised the Du Boises, who were anti-colonial *and* observed by the FBI, as *Schicksalgenossen.* Private networks became more important than ever during the Cold War and with the Red Scare fresh in everyone's memory. Moreover, Du Bois's talk and status placed the Suriname struggle for independence in a wider imperialist and colonial framework. Although this was an era of decolonisation, anti-colonialism was still far from mainstream. In a room full of people of African descent, these cross-reference debates on colonialism and slavery and the exchange of ideas on imperialism not only turned the room into a transnational contact zone, it also cemented interracial friendships. This was a layered contact zone with personal, social, and intellectual dimensions.

The final day in the Netherlands was a day of leisure, that the DuBoises spent in the city center of Amsterdam, where they took a boat trip like other tourists. Perhaps such casual days such as these made the greatest impression upon them. Graham already wrote to a friend that they were besieged by "reporters [and]

Figure 7: The Du Boises in Amsterdam. From left to right: Rosey Pool, Shirley Graham, Willy Breman, W.E.B. Du Bois, September 1958. Source: MS 312, Identifier: mums312-b291-i234, Special Collections and University Archives, University of Massachusetts Amherst Libraries.

photographers" who "called every day." Also, on the streets of Amsterdam, the former American pariahs received a warm welcome. The "people in the street recognized" her husband, she wrote proudly, and greeted him warmly.

In the afternoon they visited radio presenter and jazz specialist Michiel de Ruyter (1926-1994), who tape-recorded Du Bois reading his poem "A Litany of Atlanta." "Of this recording, three copies are now stored at three different very safe places, as prize possessions," Shirley Graham wrote proudly. In the Netherlands they received the recognition they had been hoping for after years of isolation.

Conclusion

The visit of the Du Boises to the Netherlands in September 1958 has not yet been researched before. This is probably due to the fact that the visit was barely covered by Dutch newspapers. Together with disclosed (intelligence) files, the disclosed archives of Ons Suriname (which are about to be inventoried and digitised in the near future), and the use of archives in three different countries, it has been quite a challenge for the author to reconstruct these events. It appears that the visit made a great impression on the Du Boises, and the Schlesinger Library holds a scrapbook on the trip that Shirley Graham made. That might come as a surprise. The disagreements among the organisers, the secret agents at the scene, and especially the unwelcome environment in The Hague stood in great contrast to the welcoming ceremony they received in Moscow – there they were welcomed in the Kremlin by a smiling Nikita Khrushchev who shook their hands.

In most of the available sources the Du Boises appear as humble visitors who rarely complain. Their positive look on things was perhaps a courtesy to their hosts. But they were also among likeminded activists and some photographs even look like a get-together of old friends. The photographs are, even more than letters, evidence of an actual connection of (former) fellow travelers and 'comrades,' as they are immediate evidence of some sort of togetherness.

The disagreements in these 'contact zones' show that their battle was not yet over, and that they continued to work towards Black emancipation, civil rights, and decolonisation. Although all of the involved actors tried to transgress national borders, their actions were also firmly shaped by national frameworks. The Dutch public for example, which was overwhelmingly white, was two-sided when it came to race relations. They were generally sympathetic towards the African American struggle for civil rights, but when it came to the Dutch colonies this was a different story. When Du Bois connected imperialism with the suppression of civil rights in the US, he went beyond what was acceptable to say. At this time in the United States, but also in Western Europe, 'Black' had become synonymous with 'radical.' Government officials, but also many citizens, thought that anti-colonial and anti-imperialist statements were 'dissident' and 'un-American.'

The report of the infiltrated informer at the Ons Suriname meeting shows that these individuals were invaded in their privacy and in their private homes. The 'personal' is closely interwoven with the 'political' during these encounters. At first the criticism of Hermie Huiswoud towards Paul Breman appears to be non-relevant gossip, yet it reveals a great deal about gender and race relations. As an experienced activist who had fought against racism for over four decades, she probably tended to see the persistent ambition of Breman in a wider perspective of a western world that privileges white men.

The visualisation of networks and life lines offers the opportunity to highlight the role of women. Intelligence agencies tended to focus on 'race *men*' like W.E.B. Du Bois (followed by FBI) and Otto Huiswoud (central figure in BVD reports). Rosey Pool, Shirley Graham, and Hermie Huiswoud are barely mentioned in these reports. They were likely not considered to be a serious political threat because they were women and/or wives. Paul Breman, despite his important role, remains invisible in these reports as well – probably thanks to his whiteness. The focus of the intelligent service' focus was thus clearly gendered and racialised and shows that tailgating was racially motivated in the Netherlands.

Secondary sources

Bak, Hans. "The Reception of American Literature in the Netherlands, 1900-1950." In *NL USA: Four Centuries of Dutch-American Relations 1609-2009*, edited by Hans Krabbendam, Cornelis A. van Minnen, and Giles Scott-Smith, 468-478. Amsterdam: Boom, 2009.

Blakely, Allison. *Blacks in the Dutch World: The Evolution of Racial Imagery in a Modern Society*. Bloomington: Indiana University Press, 2000.

Bourdieu, Pierre and Loïc J. D. Wacquant. *An Invitation to Reflexive Sociology*. Chicago: University of Chicago Press, 1992.

Breman, Marc. "W.E.B. Du Bois and Shirley Graham Du Bois in the Netherlands, 1958." In *The Heritage Series of Black Poetry, 1962-1975: A Research Compendium*, edited by Lauri Ramey, 197-205. Aldershot: Ashgate, 2008.

Enckevort, Maria Gertrudis van. "The Life and Work of Otto Huiswoud: Professional Revolutionary and Internationalist (1893-1961)." PhD diss., University of the West Indies, Mona, Jamaica, 2001.

Gilmore, Glenda Elizabeth. *Defying Dixie: The Radical Roots of Civil Rights, 1919-1950.* New York: W.W. Norton & Company, 2009.

Gilroy, Paul. *The Black Atlantic: Modernity and Double-Consciousness.* Cambridge, MA: Harvard University Press, 1995.

Graham, Shane. "Black Atlantic Literature as Transnational Cultural Space." *Literature Compass* 10, no. 6 (June 2013): 508-518.

Hine, Darlene Clark, Trica Danielle Keaton, and Stephen Small, eds. *Black Europe and the African Diaspora*. Champaign, IL: University of Illinois Press, 2009.

Hondius, Dienke. *Blackness in Western Europe: Racial Patterns of Paternalism and Exclusion.* Piscataway, NJ: Transaction Publishers, 2014.

Horne, Gerald. *Race Woman: The Lives of Shirley Graham Du Bois.* New York: New York University Press, 2000.

Horne, Gerald. *W.E.B. Du Bois: A Biography.* Santa Barbara, CA: Greenwood, 2009.

Kempen, Michiel van. *Een geschiedenis van de Surinaamse literatuur: Deel 4.* Paramaribo: Okopipi, 2002.

Kennedy, James. *Nieuw Babylon in aanbouw: Nederland in de jaren zestig.* Amsterdam: Boom, 1997.

Lottman, Herbert R. *The Left Bank: Writers, Artists, and Politics from the Popular Front to the Cold War.* Boston: Houghton Mifflin, 1982.

Panter, Sarah, Johannes Paulmann, and Margit Szöllösi-Janze. "Mobility and Biography: Methodological Challenges and Perspectives." In *Jahrbuch für Europäische Geschichte/ European History Yearbook*, edited by Sarah Panter, 1-14. Berlin: De Gruyter Oldenbourg, 2015.

Perucci, Tony. *Paul Robeson and the Cold War Performance Complex: Race, Madness, Activism.* Ann Arbor, MI: University of Michigan Press, 2012.

Pratt, Mary Louise. "Arts of the Contact Zone." In *Professing in the Contact Zone: Bringing Theory and Practice Together*, edited by Janice M. Wolff, 1-20. Urbana, IL: National Council of Teachers of English, 2002.

Ramey, Lauri. *The Heritage Series of Black Poetry, 1962-1975: A Research Compendium.* Aldershot: Ashgate, 2008.

Raphael-Hernandez, Heike, ed. *Blackening Europe: The African American Presence.* London: Psychology Press, 2004.

Righart, Hans and Piet de Rooij. "In Holland staat een huis. Weerzin en vertedering over 'de jaren vijftig'." In *Een stille revolutie? Cultuur en mentaliteit in de lange jaren vijftig*, edited by Paul Luykx and Pim Slot, 11-18. Hilversum: Verloren, 1997.

Smethurst, James. "'Don't Say Goodbye to the Porkpie Hat': Langston Hughes, the Left, and the Black Arts Movement." *Callaloo* 25, no. 4 (Fall 2002): 1-14.

Vereniging Ons Suriname 18 januari 1919 – 18 januari 1989: Een aanzet tot de geschiedschrijving over zeventig jaren leven en strijd van Surinamers in Nederland. Amsterdam: Vereniging Ons Suriname, [1990].

Von Eschen, Penny M. *Race against Empire: Black Americans and Anticolonialism, 1937-1957.* Ithaca, NY: Cornell University Press, 1997.

Vries, Ellen de. *Nola: Portret van een eigenzinnig kunstenares.* Amersfoort: Klapwijk & Keijsers, 2008.

Washington, Mary. *The Other Blacklist: The African American Literary and Cultural Left of the 1950s.* New York: Columbia University Press, 2014.

Winter, Myra. "17 april 1953. Nola Hatterman vertrekt naar Suriname en ontwikkelt zich tot leermeesteres van een generatie Surinaams-Nederlandse beeldende kunstenaars. Een artistiek bemiddelaar tussen Nederland en Suriname." In *Cultuur en migratie in Nederland. Kunsten in beweging 1900-1980,* edited by Rosemarie Buikema and Maaike Meijer, 257-274. The Hague: SDU Uitgevers, 2003.

Primary sources cited in text

Arthur and Elizabeth Schlesinger Library on the History of Women in America, Radcliffe Institute for Advanced Study, Harvard University, Papers of Shirley Graham Du Bois, 1865-1998 (MC 476): 15.4: Photocopies of #15.5f [15.5f. W.E.B. Du Bois scrapbook: trip to Holland (disassembled original), 1958.]

Binnenlandse Veiligheidsdienst (BVD, currently AIVD): File *Vereniging Ons Suriname* [1947-1952]. Thanks to Ellen de Vries.

Document 71371, "Receptie Dr. DUBOIS op 12-9-1958. Amstelkade 157 hs te Amsterdam," 6 October 1958. Provided by the AIVD to the author.

Chicago Public Library, Heritage Press Archives: 6.3: Paul Breman, *The Heritage Series of Black Poetry – 1962 to 1975: A Memoir* (London, private publisher, 2006).

FBI Records: The Vault, W.E. B. Dubois: 100-99729 (part 4 of 5), Internal memo "ReBulet 9-29-58," October 13, 1958.

Tamiment Library and Robert F. Wagner Labor Archive, Hermina Dumont Huiswoud Papers and Photographs (TAM.354): 1.6: Correspondence; 1.35: Women, Biographical Essays on ("Women I Have Known Personally"), "Shirley Graham Du Bois."

University of Massachusetts Amherst Libraries (UMass), Special Collections and University Archives, W.E.B. Du Bois Papers, 1803-1999 (MS 312): 81.1198: "The United States and War" (1958).

University of Sussex Library, Rosey Pool Collection (SxMs19): SxMs19/11/1/2: Documentation *Zielen vol soul,* "Mijn zwarte ziel . . . "

Following the letters

Emile de Laveleye's transnational correspondence network

Thomas D'haeninck

In this chapter I illustrate how digital tools and techniques in general and (co-) citation analysis in particular can help scholars to widen their perspective and to 'unhinge' themselves and their research subjects from a national context of history-writing. I do so by applying particular tools and methodologies to a corpus of letters of the Belgian social reformer Emile de Laveleye (1822-1892). Social reformers originated from typically nineteenth-century forms of *sociabilité* – learned and professional societies, intellectual circles, think thanks and religious denominations – and initiated a wide variety of attempts to counter the adverse effects of industrialisation and globalisation that were emerging.

De Laveleye was a liberal minded political economist, an influential opinion maker, a professor at the university of Liège, and definitely also a social reformer. He shared a great interest in reform issues and was eager to consult ideas in countries other than his own to solve social conflicts. Emile de Laveleye embodied the nineteenth century ideal of the social reformer as a traveller and a cosmopolitan.

It is safe to say that his thoughts and activities were not bound to one nation-state but were marked by a high level of mobility. De Laveleye was also a 'networker' who corresponded with like-minded social reformers across the globe.

In the first part of this chapter Emile de Laveleye is portrayed as an important intermediary for the transnational circulation of ideas. In the second part, I show the potential to study his correspondence via a (co-)citation analysis. This structural approach enables me to analyse a selection of already well-studied contacts with internationally renowned figures by treating the letters as a representation of an evolving conversation on matters of scientific, intellectual and social reforms. This method brings to light up-till-now lost or neglected personal narratives. In the third part I will reflect on how digital tools can be applied in biographical research on transnational lives, in doing so producing new perspectives on familiar subjects.

Emile de Laveleye: Prolific writer, traveler and intermediary

Emile de Laveleye (1822-1892) was a professor of political economy at the University of Liège, specialised in bimetallism, property rights and free trade. He also published extensively on issues of agriculture, politics, international and colonial administration, women's rights and the trafficking of women, (popular) education, aesthetics, materialism, luxury and property rights. The versatility of his oeuvre reflects his view on political economy, which to him was in its essence the science of morality. According to de Laveleye, a political economist did not only study the laws of the production, distribution, trade and consumption of goods, but also the question of how moderation, good behaviour and sense of duty could be stimulated. Carmen Van Praet described him as an intellectual chameleon, and Michel Dumoulin has argued that de Laveleye did not gather much following due to the eclectic nature of his methods and work.

"Vous avez plus que tout autre à cette époque marqué la mobilité et même le caractère progressif." The Brussels sociologist Hector Denis began his letter to Emile de Laveleye in 1878 with these words, expressing his admiration for his persistent mobility and the international contacts emanating from it. De Laveleye commanded a great respect for becoming the personification of the intellectual-cosmopolitan who expanded his fields of interest and expertise by travelling. Already ten years earlier, when he was appointed to the University of Liège as professor, his colleague and friend Alphonse Le Roy mentioned in a laudation that the strongest quality of de Laveleye was his urge to travel and to encounter new experiences, interesting people and innovative ideas.

When de Laveleye died of lung congestion in 1892, his death was widely mentioned in the international press, the *Review of Reviews* for example commenting that "another great man whom the whole world knew has passed away. His versatility was remarkable. As a moral and religious reformer de Laveleye was known everywhere in Europe." De Laveleye indeed travelled all over Europe, sometimes accompanied by befriended intellectuals like Charles Potvin, Paul Frédéricq, or Nicolas Reyntjens. Most of his voyages are well documented in travel reports, letters or articles. The emergence of a 'culture' of international congresses – between 1840 and the First World War more than 2500 international congresses were organised – was a strong stimulus for de Laveleye's mobility. De Laveleye frequented many international congresses held on a wide variety of social reform questions. International congresses were – par excellence – the sites where scientists, administrators, politicians, artists and others reform-minded elites of different countries met and exchanged ideas. These international congresses can be seen as laboratories of new expert knowledge, providing a forum to exchange new experiences and innovative ideas. In the absence of international organisations, these international congresses were the most important form of 'scientific internationalisation' in the nineteenth century.

De Laveleye functioned as an intermediary actor or 'broker' for ideas between the congresses and Belgian reform-minded milieus, but also for several reformers originating from other countries. De Laveleye received letters from foreign friends and acquaintances who were prevented for various reasons from attending but who wanted to be informed of the discussions.

Emile de Laveleye met with prominent figures from London to Saint Petersburg. Olga Novikoff-Kiréeff wrote for example in her memoirs that her friend de Laveleye was one of the few "flowers of the English intellect" who tried to restore the broken contacts between the British and Russian intelligentsia. Historian Michel Dumoulin has described him as a "passeur d'idées" between France, Germany and Great Britain.

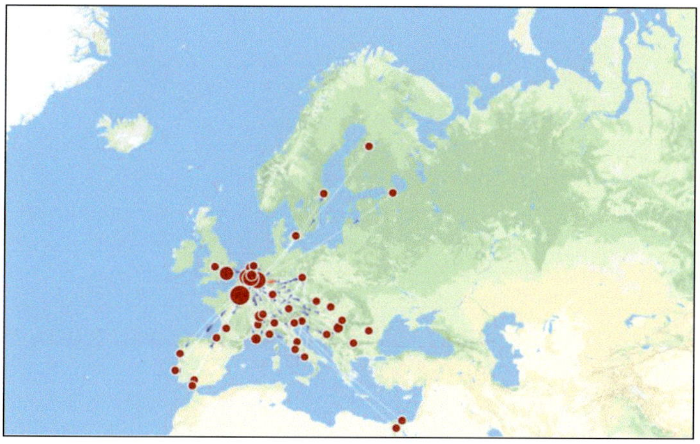

Figure 1: The mobility of Emile de Laveleye: places of residence, travels and congress visits. The size of the dots represents the relative amount of time spent there. Visualisation by the author using nodegoat.

Although de Laveleye toured all over Europe (Figure 1), he indeed predominantly travelled to Western European cities. He was probably one of the most Anglophile Belgian intellectuals of his time. According to his friend Paul Frédéricq, this was remarkable. Most Belgian politicians and theorists looked mainly to France, and Belgian scientists and academics paid in general close attention to developments at German universities.

De Laveleye's relations with the British intelligentsia were stimulated by his friendship with William Gladstone. He befriended many prominent British figures like William Stead and John Stuart Mill and was several times invited to the meetings of the Cobden Club. De Laveleye described some of these meetings to the French intellectuals Léonce De Lavergne and Charles Dupont-White, who were keen to hear of the discussions on international law, property rights, free trade and peace.

Mining Emile de Laveleye's correspondence

Besides the fact that de Laveleye was involved both on a national and international level in important debates on social, economic and political questions, his extensive correspondence (almost 3000 letters preserved) also explains the large interest he has provoked among historians. Dumoulin wrote that it is likely that de Laveleye did not reply to all incoming correspondence. Correspondence with his wife Marie-Esther Prisse tells us that he instructed her to answer letters when he was travelling. Still, de Laveleye maintained a lively correspondence with internationally renowned intellectuals (John Stuart Mill, Ernest Renan, and Pierre Kropotkine), journalists and editors (William Stead, François Buloz, and Henry Thompson), artists and writers (Elise Reclus, William Writter, Olga Novikoff-Kiréeff, and Hamilton Wright Mabie), bankers and economists (Henri Cernuschi, Marco Minghetti, and Edmond James de Rothschild) and politicians (William Gladstone, Lajos Kossuth, Jules Simon). Some of these letters have been skilfully transcribed, critically studied and published.

These publications either highlight one particular field of interest of de Laveleye, or focus on the letters he exchanged with internationally renowned figures. Until now, only a fraction of the letters have been studied thoroughly. We know that

Figure 2: residences of Emile de Laveleye's correspondents. Visualisation by the author using nodegoat.

he conducted a lively correspondence with several prominent figures and that his network of correspondents was strongly international. However, we have barely any knowledge on his network as a whole, whether his correspondents knew each other or cited the same people, publications and topics, or how the foci of interests of the discussions as expressed in the letters changed over time. Following the line of inquiry of Yves Gingras, I argue that instead of seeing each letter as a unique document, we need to look at these collected documents as a global corpus of data to be treated as a representation of the evolving conversation going on in scientific and intellectual fields in general.

I identified all correspondents and assigned to all letters a time stamp and geographic coordinates in order to collect and explore the data in *nodegoat*, a web-based database management platform with a graphical interface.

Nodegoat is first and foremost well-suited for the creation of historical data-sets and the spatial exploration of that data. This allowed me to explore the expanding correspondence network of de Laveleye over time (Figure 2). We can see that most of his correspondence network lived in Europe. However, over time his contacts gradually expanded to a global network, with links to the Americas, India and Japan. Figure 2 thus nuances the image we have of Emile de Laveleye, who has been predominantly described as a European intellectual. We can assume that several of the people who contacted de Laveleye never physically met him. Although many of the congresses de Laveleye attended claimed to be 'international' or 'universal,' most of these events were essentially (West) European. Most of his correspondents and especially those who lived far away did not go to the congresses de Laveleye attended.

I provided each letter with tags (persons, themes and publications) which allows me to map when topics were discussed. Due to the fact that I found over 250 thematically different discussions, I grouped the results into six umbrella categories: economics, political theory, religion, education, foreign policies and law.

Some of the trends we can see in Figure 3 are not that surprising. The black line indicates that a large part of the correspondence was related to economics and monetary issues and thus confirms the professional reputation of de Laveleye as an influential political economist. He regularly received letters from internationally renowned political economists like Henri Cernuschi, Marco Minghetti, and Adolph

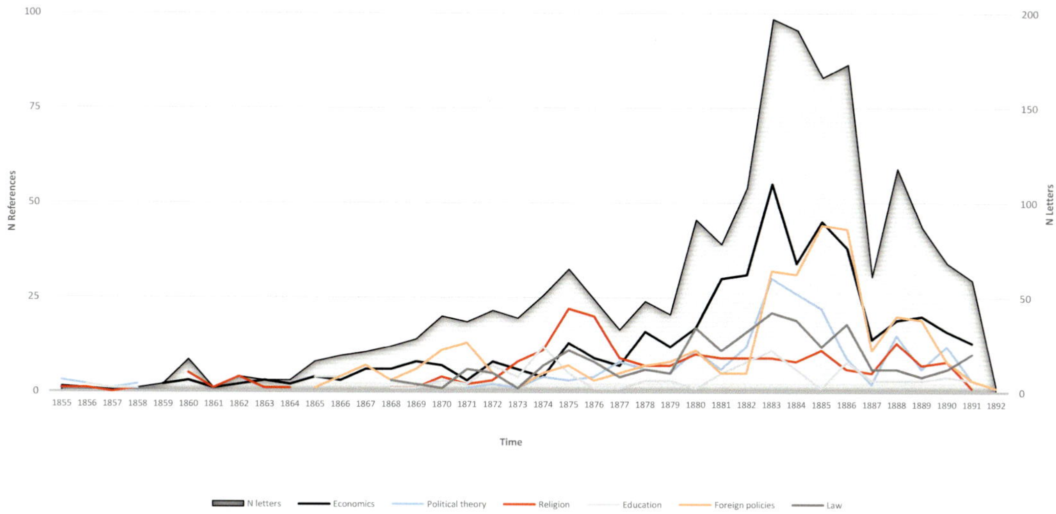

Figure 3: Citation analysis of the topics mentioned in the incoming correspondence to Emile de Laveleye.

Held. The strong peak between 1881-1883 can be explained by the fact that de Laveleye co-organised the *Conférence monétaire de Paris et le biméttalisme* in 1881.

The curve of the topic 'foreign policies' is strongly influenced by specific international events. The first peak between 1869 and 1872 can be explained by the rising international tensions between France and Prussia, which caused great apprehension amongst de Laveleye and several of his contacts. The second peak in the 1880s results from the many letters related to deprivation of the Bulgarian people and self-government for the Hungarians, Bosnians and Serbians and has already been indicated in earlier studies.

The graph also indicates two trends that have been partially neglected in earlier research. First, it is remarkable to see that the blue curve 'political theory' is fairly low until 1880, although de Laveleye is often described by historians as a Katheder Socialist. Before the mid-1870s 'socialism' is, in quantitative terms, an almost negligible topic in the corpus of letters. The peak of the curve is caused by the publication of his well-read *Le socialisme contemporain* (published in 1881).

This does of course not mean that de Laveleye was uninterested in socialism before this period. Already in the late 1840s de Laveleye frequented the meetings of the *Société Huet*, a think tank in Ghent where young progressive intellectuals met to discuss ultra-democratic and socialist ideas.

However, the peak indicates a shift in the foci of interests of de Laveleye and his correspondents as expressed in the letters. Second, the red curve grouping references to religion is consistently fairly high, with a peak between 1872 and 1876. Although de Laveleye was portrayed by some of his contemporaries as an internationally renowned religious reformer (*e.g.* in *Review of Reviews*), historians have barely focused on his religious beliefs and opinions. The analysis shows that religion and religious reform, in particular the question how dogmatic religious thinking could evolve into a modern enlightened religion which would improve the moral condition of society, was a matter that concerned both de Laveleye as well

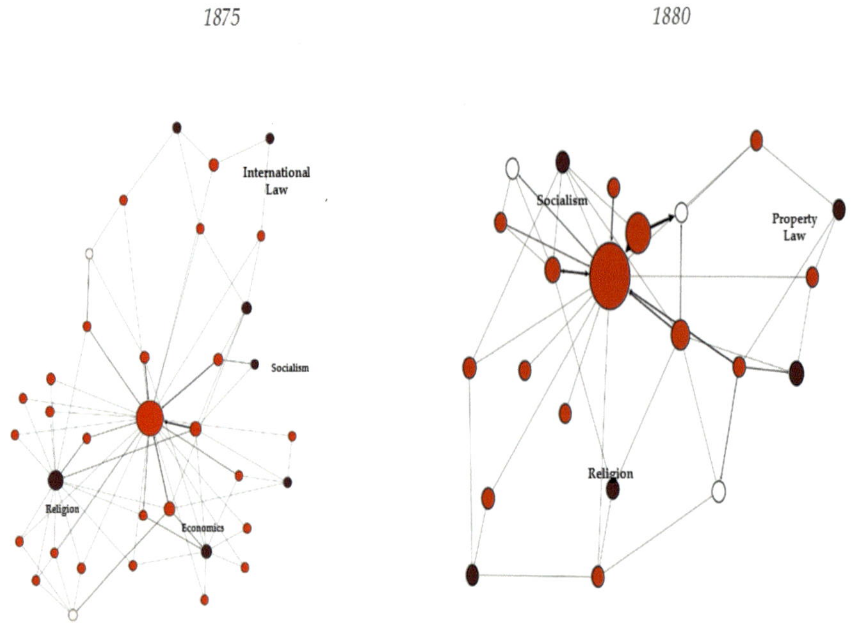

Figure 4: Co-citation analysis of people writing to Emile de Laveleye in 1875 (left) and 1880. Weighted network. Degree range > 4; red nodes: correspondents; dark nodes: topics; white nodes: references to publications. Size nodes: betweeness centrality. 1: Emile de Laveleye, Adolph Held (2), Frank Puaux (3), Luigi Luzzatti (4), Marco Minghetti (5), César De Paepe (6).

as several of his correspondents. These two trends can only partially be detected via a close reading of these letters or his oeuvre as a whole. Close reading can only point out a change of interest de Laveleye had; it indicates little, if anything, about how his conversation and interaction with others may have changed.

If we compare the curves 'religion' and 'political theory,' they look like communicating vessels: the moment he receives less letters on religion, his interest in political theory in general and socialism in particular increases. Does this indicate a shift in the foci of interests of the correspondents, or a change in who is corresponding with de Laveleye? Can we identify correspondents who wrote to de Laveleye on both matters? To answer these questions, I created two co-citation networks using *Gephi*, an open-source network analysis and visualisation software package. The data used for the citation analysis also allows me to approach his correspondence as a social network of people related to him via the letters and to each other via the topics they discussed and the references they made.

The two graphs in Figure 4 compare the co-citation networks of 1875 when the topic 'religion' peaks and 1880 when the curve of the topic 'political theory' strongly increases. Bearing in mind that de Laveleye did not answer all of his letters, the graphs only contain the highly engaged correspondents. All topics, publications and correspondents with a degree of 4 or lower are filtered out of the network.[1] The red nodes represent the correspondents, the dark nodes the topics and the white nodes refer to specific publications. The size of the nodes and edges reflects the relative numbers of letters sent and received.

The two co-citation networks confirm the shift of the discussions as expressed in the letters from religion to socialism, already indicated in the citation graph. If we look more closely at the graph of 1875, we see that the topics 'religion' and 'economics' are in the centre of the network and 'socialism' is plotted in the margin. Only one correspondent is related to both religion and socialism: the German economist and Katheder Socialist Adolph Held (2). In 1875 he wrote to de Laveleye both to discuss the question whether socialist ideology conflicted with the prevailing views on individual property rights, as well as whether a modernised form of Catholicism could stimulate popular education and social reform. The French author Frank Puaux (3) and Italian economist Luigi Luzzatti (4), who are fairly central in the network, had already earlier discussed similar matters with de Laveleye. Both de Laveleye, Puaux, Luzatti and Held can be considered as advocates for religious tolerance.[2]

The co-citation network of 1880 includes several new correspondents. The centrality of the topic 'socialism' results from de Laveleye's preparations for his *Le socialisme contemporain.*[3] Published in 1881, *Le socialisme contemporain* was a widely read reflection on the proliferation of socialist movements and ideologies in Western Europe. Although the volume was only published in 1881, the topic 'socialism' was already heavily discussed in the letters in 1880. De Laveleye used his wide network to obtain information and to discuss his thoughts and writings. Two correspondents wrote de Laveleye on both religious matters as well as socialism: the Italian economist Marco Minghetti (5) and the Belgian socialist physician César De Paepe (6). By assessing all of de Laveleye's correspondents we can see that he discussed with several internationally prominent economists (Minghetti, Cernuschi and Held) both the economic as well as the ideological and moral implications of socialism. It is more remarkable that César De Paepe is related to both topics, because most Belgian socialists saw social Darwinism as their ideological ally. De Laveleye fiercely critiqued theorists such as Herbert Spencer in *Le socialisme contemporain*: "La loi de Darwin comme parmi les espèces animales: point de règlements, point d'État, nulle entrave, liberté complète en tout et pour tous."[4] He was a strong believer in the idea that socialism and Christian religion were complementary. According to de Laveleye both the early Christians as well as contemporary socialists defended the ideas of justice, sharing, brotherhood and a sense of community. De Laveleye was convinced that socialist ideology could be spread more successfully with the support of religion. By incorporating spiritual and religious influences into socialism, this rather unfamiliar and 'dangerous'

1 The degree (or valency) of a node is the number of edges incident to the node. In weighted networks, a network where the relations between nodes have weights assigned to them (in this case depending on the number of letters sent or received), the degree of each node is determined by the number of edges and their weight incident to the node.

2 Pierre Pierrard, *Les Chrétiens et l'affaire Dreyfus* (Paris: Editions de l'Atelier, 1998) 74-82; Luigi Luzzatti, *Dio nella libertà: Studi sulle relazioni tra lo stato e le chiese* (Bologna: Zanichelli, 1926).

3 De Laveleye, *Le socialisme contemporain.*

4 Ibid., 31.

ideology would have a stronger appeal to the workers in the cities as well as in the countryside. Although César De Paepe did not agree with de Laveleye, he did respect his views and was willing to discuss several other contemporary ideas on socialism like the writings of Élisée Reclus, the mutualist thoughts of Pierre-Joseph Proudhon or the *Catéchisme révolutionnaire* of Mikhail Bakounine.[5]

Life writing and digital tools

A biography does not study a life per se, but a life with and amongst others. Transnational lives like Emile de Laveleye need to be studied via their contacts, agency and mobility instead of within a framework imposed by the researcher.[6] Bearing this in mind, I followed the line of inquiry of Yves Gingras and approached a large collection of letters sent to and written by Emile de Laveleye as one corpus which reflects an evolving conversation. Using digital humanities techniques, (co-)citation and social network analysis, I was able to explore a sizeable amount of data. In contrast to previous studies on de Laveleye, which have often overly focused on a selection of contacts with internationally renowned figures, I was able to study the network as a whole and to indicate how the foci of interests of the discussions as expressed in the letters changed over time. I have shown the importance of religion and religious reform in the correspondence, a narrative that by most scholars has been overlooked. The digital turn opens new horizons for biographers and historians.[7] The digitisation of documents, the availability of digital bibliographies, the development of biographical portals, the overwhelming amount of data available online and the possibility to exchange and link information offer exciting new prospects for historical research in general and 'life writing' in particular. Archives are swiftly digitizing their collections and biographical lemmas are more available in digital form. The open data movement has enhanced access to (biographical) information via the World Wide Web. Researchers nowadays often collect their data via collaboration and co-creation[8] and sometimes even in interaction with the (scholarly) public.[9]

The digital turn has opened new horizons, especially for historians and life writers studying so-called 'transnational lives.' These refer to individuals who cross geographical, national, cultural and social boundaries and can therefore not be understood merely in the traditional framework of national history.[10] Yet digitisation does more than provide access to relevant sources for analysing transnational lives that are often, due to their fragmented existence, scattered across different national

5 Letter from César De Paepe to Emile de Laveleye, 12 June 1880, Waver, GUCL, Ms 3640.

6 Joep Leerssen, "Bomen hebben wortels, mensen hebben benen, ideeën hebben vleugels: Een introductie," *De Negentiende Eeuw* 32 (2008): 3-14.

7 Serge ter Braake, Antske Fokkens, Ronald Sluijter, Thierry Declerck, and Eveline Wandl-Vogt, "Introduction: Biographical Data in a Digital World," *CEUR Workshop Proceedings*, vol. 1399 (2015).

8 See <http://www.tic.ugent.be/>.

9 See <http://www.iwicollectie.nl/aangespoeld.aspx>.

10 Desley Deacon, Penny Russell, and Angela Woollacott, eds., *Transnational Lives: Biographies of Global Modernity, 1700 – Present* (New York: Palgrave Macmillan, 2010), 1-13.

and local archives.[11] Digital tools allow scholars to explore much larger datasets and to search for meaningful patterns in textual corpora that are not readable via traditional close reading. Instead of (for example) focussing on one biographical lemma, researchers can query similarities and differences between numerous lemmas in several biographical dictionaries (ideas, events, contacts, people, etc.). Scholars acquainted with distant reading techniques can even investigate the bias of biographical dictionaries towards national narratives.[12] Due to user-friendly digital tools, it has for some years now become quite easy to explore, analyse and visualise complex phenomena on a larger scale.[13] The overcoming of heuristic barriers in this way has facilitated the use of geo-spatial and social network analysis, which enables scholars to study individuals via their spatial and social mobility instead of within the limited scope of a social infrastructure imposed by the researcher.

However, every coin has two sides. Scholars sometimes tend to apply digital tools and methods without fully realising their theoretical implications or without starting out from clear research questions. A life writer or a historian must critically reflect on why he relies on digital methods and which questions the chosen methodology actually will answer. The use of the tool cannot be an end in itself. Also, the high hopes that come along with the digital turn need to be tempered. It has been argued before that the use of digital tools often results in something that has to be explained instead of an explanation in itself.[14] Further research is in most cases vital. The approach described in this chapter for example did not study the nature of letters in full or lead to any explanation why certain topics were discussed or how discussions evolved. A close reading of the letters and studying the backgrounds of the correspondents was vital to come up with interpretations and explanations. However, digital humanities – combined with other approaches and methodologies – can be very useful to widen our perspective and provide a richer understanding of the actors we study, in the process assisting with unhinging the national context of history-writing.

Bibliography

D'Alviella, Eugène Goblet. *Emile de Laveleye: Sa vie et son œuvre.* Paris: Muquardt, 1895.

Basmadjian, Armand, Diana Ignatova, and Carine Van Bellingen. *Emile de Laveleye : Een andere kijk op Bulgarije.* Sofia: National Library of Bulgaria, 2001.

Bots, Marcel. *Lettres adressées à Emile De Laveleye.* Ghent: Liberaal archief, 1992.

11 Sarah Panter, Johannes Paulmann, and Margit Szöllösi-Janze, "Mobility and Biography, Methodological Challenges and Perspectives," in *Jahrbuch für Europäische Geschichte/ European History Yearbook*, ed. Sarah Panter (Berlin: De Gruyter Oldenbourg, 2015), 5.

12 See for example: Miel Groten, Serge ter Braake, Yassine Karimi, and Antske Fokkens, "Johan de Witt: De omstreden republikein," *Leidschrift* 31, no. 2 (2016): 59-73.

13 Christophe Verbruggen, Thomas D'haeninck, and Hans Blomme, "Mobility and Movements in Intellectual History: A Social Network Approach," in *The Power of Networks: Prospects of Historical Network Research,* eds. Florian Kerschbaumer, Linda Von Keyserlingk, Martin Stark, and Marten During (Abingdon: Routledge, 2020).

14 Ibid.

Ter Braake, Serge, Antske Fokkens, Ronald Sluijter, Thierry Declerck, and Eveline Wandl-Vogt," Introduction: Biographical Data in a Digital World." *CEUR Workshop Proceedings*, vol. 1399 (First Conference on Biographical Data in a Digital World 2015, CEUR WS, 2015).

Bree, Pim, and Geert van Kessels. "Nodegoat: a web-based data management, network analysis & visualisation environment." Accessed 15 June 2018. http://nodegoat.net.

Coppens, E.C. "La Societe Huet. Tussen revolutie en reactie." *Handelingen der Maatschappij voor Geschiedenis en Oudheidkunde te Gent* 26 (1972): 131-151.

D'haeninck, Thomas, Nico Randeraad, and Christophe Verbruggen. "Visualizing Longitudinal Data: Rooted Cosmopolitans in the Low Countries, 1850-1914." *CEUR Workshop Proceedings*, vol. 1399 (First Conference on Biographical Data in a Digital World 2015, CEUR WS, 2015): 116-21.

D'haeninck, Thomas. "Transnationale mobiliteit van Belgische hervormers op zoek naar een moreel reveil, 1850-1914." PhD diss., Ghent University, 2018.

Deacon, Desley, Penny Russell, and Angela Woollacott, eds. *Transnational Lives: Biographies of Global Modernity, 1700 – Present.* New York: Palgrave Macmillan, 2010.

Dumoulin, Michel. "Émile de Laveleye, passeur d'idées entre la France, l'Allemagne et l'Angleterre." In *Industries, territoires et cultures en Europe du Nord-Ouest, XIXe-XXe siècles, Mélanges en l'honneur de Jean-François Eck*, edited by Françoise Berger, Michel Rapoport, Pierre Tilly, and Béatrice Touchelay. Roubaix: Archives nationales du monde du travail, 2015.

Dumoulin, Michel. *La correspondance entre Emile de Laveleye et Marco Minghetti, 1877-1886.* Brussels: Institut historique belge de Rome, 1979.

Fuchs, Eckhardt. "Educational sciences, morality and politics: International educational congresses in the early twentieth century." *Paedagogica Historica* 40 (2004).

Fredericq, Paul. *Emile de Laveleye.* Leiden: Sijthoff, 1892.

Gingras, Yngres. "Mapping the Structure of the Intellectual Field Using Citation and Co-Citation Analysis of Correspondences." *History of European Ideas* 3 (2010): 330-339.

Groten, Miel, Serge ter Braake, Yassine Karimi, and Antske Fokkens. "Johan de Witt: De omstreden republikein." *Leidschrift* 31, no. 2 (2016): 59-73.

De Laveleye, Emile. "Les lois naturelles et l'objet de l'économie politique." *Journal des économistes* 42 (1883): 266-282.

De Laveleye, Emile. *La question monétaire en 1881: La conférence monétaire de Paris et le biméttalisme.* Brussels: Muquardt, 1881.

De Laveleye, Emile. *Le socialisme contemporain.* Brussels: Muquart, 1881.

Leerssen, Joep. "Bomen hebben wortels, mensen hebben benen, ideeën hebben vleugels: Een introductie." *De Negentiende Eeuw* 32 (2008): 3-14.

Le Roy, Alphonse. "Notice Sur Emile-Louis-Victor De Laveleye, Professeur à l'université de Liège." *Compte Rendu Des Fêtes Jubilaires de l'université de Liège.* Liège: Imprimerie de J.G. Carmanne, 1867.

Leonards, Chris, and Nico Randeraad, "Building a Transnational Network of Social Reform in the 19th Century." In *Shaping the Transnational Sphere: Experts, Networks and Issues from the 1840s to the 1930s,* edited by Davide Rodogno, Bernhard Struck, and Jakob Vogel, 111-31. Oxford/New York: Berghahn, 2014.

Leonards, Chris. "Ter bestrijding van armoede, misdaad, oorlog en immoraliteit; Europese congrescultuur in de negentiende en vroege twintigste eeuw vanuit filantropisch perspectief." In *Filantropie in Nederland. Voorbeelden uit de periode 1770-2020,* edited by Vibeke Kingma and Marco H.D. van Leeuwen, 49-62. Amsterdam: Aksant, 2007.

Luzzatti, Luigi. *Dio nella libertà: Studi sulle relazioni tra lo stato e le chiese.* Bologna: Zanichelli, 1926.

Mahaim, Ernest. *Emile de Laveleye, lettres intimes, preface de Ernest Mahaim.* Paris: La Renaissance du Livre, 1927.

Novikova, Olga Alekseevna. *Russian memories.* London: H. Jenkins, 1917.

Panter, Sarah, Johannes Paulmann, and Margit Szöllösi-Janze. "Mobility and Biography: Methodological Challenges and Perspectives." In *Jahrbuch für Europäische Geschichte/ European History Yearbook,* edited by Sarah Panter, 1-14. Berlin: De Gruyter Oldenbourg, 2015.

Pierrard, Pierre. *Les Chrétiens et l'affaire Dreyfus.* Paris: Editions de l'Atelier, 1998.

Van Praet, Carmen. "Liberale hommes-orchestres en de sociale kwestie in de negentiende eeuw. Tussen lokaal en internationaal." PhD diss., Ghent University, 2015.

Praet, Philippe. *E. de Laveleye: Bibliografie.* Ghent: Liberaal Archief, 1992.

Randeraad, Nico. "Triggers of Mobility: International Congresses (1840-1914) and their Visitors." *European History Yearbook* 16 (2015): 63-82.

Randeraad, Nico. "The International Statistical Congress (1853-1876): Knowledge Transfers and Their Limits." *European History Quarterly* 1 (January 2011): 50-65.

Tapia, Claude, and Jacques Taieb. "Conférences et congrès internationaux de 1815 à 1913." *Relations internationales* 5 (1976): 11-35.

Van Velthoven, Harry. *E. de Laveleye en de Vlaamse kwestie.* Ghent: Liberaal Archief, 1992.

Verbruggen, Christophe, Thomas D'haeninck, and Hans Blomme. "Mobility and Movements in Intellectual History: a Social Network Approach." In *The Power of Networks: Prospects of Historical Network Research,* edited by Florian Kerschbaumer, Linda Von Keyserlingk, Martin Stark and Marten During. Abingdon: Routledge, 2020.

SECTION 3

CIRCULATION

Booker T. Washington's *Up From Slavery* in the Dutch Empire, 1902-1995

Marijke Huisman

It is no secret that nationalism is woven into the historical discipline. The nation provided the basic framework for the professionalizing practice of nineteenth-century historians, from the organisation of archives to the spatial and thematic scope of research projects and the languages used to communicate the results of historical studies.[1] Historians' explicit service to nation-building projects somewhat faded in the aftermath of World War II, but 'methodological nationalism' continued to rule until at least the end of the twentieth century.[2] Demonstrating the cultural and historical work involved in nineteenth-century nation-building, historians in the 1980s and 90s denaturalised the nation but simulatenously showed the continuing power of the national framework of historical research. It is only recently that historians have gradually moved beyond the idea of nation, a shift marked by the launching of professional journals like *Journal of Global History* (2006).

Historians' move beyond the nation – referred to as the 'global turn,' 'transnational turn,' or 'cosmopolitan turn' – coincides chronologically with a 'biographical turn,' "a new preoccupation with individual lives and stories as a way of understanding both contemporary societies and the whole process of social and historical change."[3] The connection runs deeper than mere chronology, though, as is shown by many statements linking biographical approaches to post-national perspectives. For example, biographer and historian Lois W. Banner has argued in favour of 'biography as history,' because the biographical genre enables historians to transcend the national framework through historical studies of individuals who crossed national boundaries.[4] Coming from a world-historical perspective, Glenda Sluga and Julia Horne have suggested that biographical research into the lives of transnational individuals is particularly apt to study cosmopolitanism not only as a

1 Berger, Stefan and Chris Lorenz, eds., *Nationalizing the Past: Historians as Nation Builders in Modern Europe* (Houndsmill: Palgrave Macmillan, 2010).

2 Ulrich Beck, "The Cosmopolitan Condition: Why Methodological Nationalism Fails," *Theory, Culture & Society* 24, no. 7-8 (2007): 286-90.

3 Barbara Caine, *Biography and History* (New York: Palgrave Macmillan, 2010), 1; Hans Renders, Binne de Haan, and Jonne Harmsma, eds., *The Biographical Turn. Lives in History* (New York: Routledge, 2016).

4 Lois W. Banner, "AHR Roundtable Biography as History," *American Historical Review* 114, no. 3 (2009): 579-86.

normative concept or idea, but as an historical practice, a cultural form, or "a way of being in the world."[5]

In recent years, many attempts have been made to move beyond the nation through biographical studies of transnational or 'cosmobile' lives.[6] One wonders, however, to what extent a mobile historical agent is necessary in order to take such approaches to the past. Imagine, for instance, a person who never left his or her home country but wore clothes made from fabrics produced at the other end of the globe, had their dinners prepared with foreign spices, and expanded their horizons through reading international newspapers, novels, and other books that inspired the work for which he or she would be remembered. It seems perfectly possible to write about such a life from a non-national perspective, provided the biographer makes an active choice to highlight features of the subject's life that connect him or her to the world beyond their own localities. Such features do not necessarily explain why this person would be considered to be of historical importance in their national context, but is that not the price to be paid for a desire to move beyond the nation?

One might go even further and ask whether transnational life writing needs a human subject at all. Non-humans have biographies too, as the anthropologist Igor Kopytoff contended over thirty years ago in "The cultural biography of things: Commoditization as process" (1986).[7] Things, from food products to cultural goods, are grown or made, hence 'born,' and continue their 'lives' being used, exchanged, traded, and re-used until they are no longer valued as useful or otherwise important and so 'die.' Things, moreover, are at the heart of the transnational flows of exchange that characterise global capitalism and influence even people who themselves do not move. One line of research in the field of cosmopolitan studies therefore focuses on 'banal cosmopolitanism,' and investigates to what extent the consumption of global products leads to changes in national or otherwise exclusive identifications.[8] Biographies of specific things might be of use here, because, as Kopytoff has argued, they can show the process of redefinition at work in situations of cultural contact.[9] Stephen Greenblatt, more recently, made a similar point, calling for 'the patient charting of specific instances of cultural mobility' and 'microhistories' of 'displaced things and persons' in order to show cultural connections between unexpected times and places.[10]

In this essay, I will explore the biography of one thing, a book: *Up from Slavery*, written by Booker T. Washington and published in Garden City, New York, in 1901. Contrary to its author, the book of his life travelled around the world and

---

5 Glenda Sluga and Julia Horne, "Cosmopolitanism: Its Pasts and Practices," *Journal of World History* 21, no. 3 (2010): 369-73.

6 Sarah Panter, Johannes Paulmann, and Margit Szöllösi-Janze, "Mobility and Biography, Methodological Challenges and Perspectives," in *Jahrbuch für Europäische Geschichte/ European History Yearbook*, ed. Sarah Panter (Berlin: De Gruyter Oldenbourg, 2015), 5.

7 Igor Kopytoff, "The Cultural Biography of Things: Commoditization as Process," in *The Social Life of Things: Commodities in Cultural Perspective*, ed. Arjun Appadurai (Cambridge: Cambridge University Press, 1986), 64-91.

8 Jenny Germann Molz, "Cosmopolitanism and Consumption," in *The Ashgate Research Companion to Cosmopolitanism*, ed. Maria Rovisco and Magdalena Nowicka (Surrey: Ashgate, n.d.), 33-52.

9 Kopytoff, "The Cultural Biography of Things," 67.

10 Stephen Greenblatt, "Cultural Mobility: An Introduction," in *Cultural Mobility: A Manifesto*, ed. Stephen Greenblatt (Cambridge: Cambridge University Press, 2010), 16-17.

the Netherlands was one of its first destinations outside the English language zone. For this reason, as well as practical considerations, I focus my discussion on the transcultural connections between the United States and the Netherlands, including its colonies. Highlighting the biography of this particular book-thing I argue that studies into transnational life writing do not necessarily need a 'cosmobile' human agent as its subject. But before I zoom into the micro-history of *Up from Slavery* in the Dutch empire, I will introduce Booker T. Washington and his autobiography in order to problematize too sharp a distinction between things and people.

On things: Slaves, books, and slave narratives

Booker T. Washington (1856-1915) started his life as a thing; he was born in bondage on a plantation in Franklin County, Virginia.[11] Nine years later, he and and millions of other American slaves were emancipated and legally transformed into human beings who were recognised as rights-bearing citizens by the American constitution. Justified by the motto 'separate but equal', these rights were effectively withdrawn towards the end of the nineteenth century, but Washington was able nonetheless to compose an optimistic life narrative. *Up from Slavery* (1901) is the story of a self-made man who became a teacher and founder-director of the Tuskegee Institute in Alabama, one of the largest schools for black students in the United States.

Up from Slavery was meant to raise funds for the necessitous Tuskegee Institute. Washington therefore rewrote his first autobiography, *The Story of My Life and Work* (1901), for an audience of white readers and potential donors. The result was a narrative in which Washington used his own life and work to emphasize the importance of education and economic independence for the future of black emancipation. Building on a famous speech he delivered at the Cotton States Exhibition (Atlanta, 1895), Washington argued that the era of black striving for social and political rights was over. He therefore asked his audience to make use of the black labour force. This did not require social equality: "In all things that are purely social we can be as separate as the fingers, yet one as the hand in all things essential to mutual progress."[12] Because of this statement, competing black leaders scorned him as a materialist selling out black people's political and social rights, but by the turn of the century Booker T. Washington was at the top of his game. In 1901, President Roosevelt invited Washington to the White House to have dinner with his family and discuss race relations in the United States.

In "Europe," the penultimate chapter of his autobiography, Washington described how in 1899 he and his wife spent a three-month holiday in Belgium, the Netherlands, France, and the United Kingdom. Eleven years later, in 1910, Washington returned once more to Europe to study the living conditions of the poor and working class.[13] Washington, however, lived the bulk of his life in the country in which he was born: the United States. Thus, it is difficult to see him as a transnational subject in the sense of this volume. *Up from Slavery*, on the

11 Robert J. Norrell, *Up from History: The Life of Booker T. Washington* (Cambridge/London: The Belknap Press, 2009).

12 Booker T. Washington, *Up from Slavery* (New York: New American Library, 2010), 154.

13 Booker T. Washington, *The Man Farthest Down: A Record of Observation and Study in Europe* (Garden City: Doubleday, Page & Co, 1912).

other hand, did travel the globe. British editions were published in 1901 and 1902, and the book was translated into many languages – from Dutch (1902), German (1902), French (1903), and Swedish (1904) to Japanese (1920), Chinese (1922), and Turkish (1951), to Marathi (1913), Sinhi (1918), and Urdu (1936) for readers in Pakistan and India, and Sotho (1947) and Xhosa (1951) for readers in South-Africa. It is this mobility that inspired me to focus not on the human agent Washington, but on the life of his book instead.

Shifting the perspective from man to book raises the question what kind of thing a book-shaped life narrative of a former slave actually is. On the one hand, such a book is a commodity like any other book: a thing that can be bought for money. From this perspective, there is not much difference between a book, a slave, or a car. On the other hand, books were never just commodities. Historian Robert Darnton pointed out that the phenomenon of the material book has long served as a "basic metaphor of making sense of life," as is shown from the use of expressions like 'the book of nature' or 'turn over a new leaf.'[14] This metaphorical understanding of life as a book morphed into a new cultural praxis in the modern era, when ever more people were writing and/or publishing accounts of their lives. Whereas this autobiographical book production has traditionally been appreciated as the signal of a rising individual self-consciousness or even of modern man himself, recent critics have interpreted the act of autobiographical writing in more ethical terms, as an author's claim for recognition as human being – with a face, a voice, and a history; in short: a book of life.[15]

It is the fusion of man, life, and book that is relevant for slave narratives, the genre that *Up from Slavery* belongs to.[16] Booker T. Washington continued a tradition that started in the late eighteenth century, when anti-slavery activists in the United Kingdom and the United States would publish life stories of former and fugitive slaves to combat the very idea that underpinned the slave trade and the slavery system: that black people were not human beings, but animals or things. The medium was part of this message: the book-shape of slave narratives proved the humanity of its subjects, in particular when they wrote their narratives themselves. Building on these contemporary ideas, later critics would successfully

---

14 Robert Darnton, "History of Reading," in *New Perspectives on Historical Writing*, ed. Peter Burke, 2nd ed. (Cambridge: Polity Press, 2001), 177.

15 Georges Gusdorf, "Conditions and Limits of Autobiography," in *Autobiography. Essays Theoretical and Critical*, ed. James Olney (Princeton: Princeton University Press, 1980), 28-48; Karl Joachim Weintraub, *The Value of the Individual: Self and Circumstance in Autobiography* (Chicago: Chicago University Press, 1978); Michael Mascuch, *Origins of the Individualist Self: Autobiography and Self-Identity in England, 1591-1791* (Oxford: Polity Press, 1997); Paul John Eakin, "Breaking Rules: The Consequences of Self-Narration," *Biography* 24, no. 1 (2001): 113-27; Kay Schaffer and Sidonie Smith, *Human Rights and Narrated Lives: The Ethics of Recognition* (New York: Palgrave Macmillan, 2004); Gillian Whitlock, *Soft Weapons: Autobiography in Transit* (Chicago: Chicago University Press, 2007); Meg Jensen and Margaretta Jolly, *We Shall Bear Witness: Life Narratives and Human Rights* (Madison: University of Wisconsin Press, 2014).

16 William L. Andrews, *To Tell a Free Story: The First Century of Afro-American Autobiography, 1760-1865* (Urbana/Champaign: University of Illinois Press, 1986); Philip Gould, "The Rise, Development, and Circulation of the Slave Narrative," in *The Cambridge Companion to the African American Slave Narrative*, ed. Audrey Fisch (Cambridge: Cambridge University Press, 2007), 11-27; Leon Jackson, "The Talking Book and the Talking Book Historian," *Book History* 13 (2010): 251-308; William L. Andrews, ed., *Slave Narratives After Slavery* (New York: New York University Press, 2011).

promote the historical and literary significance of slave narratives. Henry Louis Gates jr. in particular repeatedly stressed the link between books, literacy, and freedom, because, "Reading and writing was no mean thing in the life of the slave. Learning to read and write meant that this person of African descent took one giant step up in the Great Chain of Being: the 'thing' became a human being."[17]

Following this argument, a book-shaped life narrative of a former slave is not easy to locate in a scheme that imagines things and people as opposites. This is one reason to think that transnational life writing could be about things too. Book-things, moreover, have the interesting quality that they travel by means of the mechanisms of a trade that has been transnational or global since the invention of the printing press. Using Latin as lingua franca, the book trade moved books throughout the literate world to members of what came to be known as the Republic of Letters.[18] In the modern era the book business became nationalised in terms of language, but the supply of books was never exclusively home-grown.[19] Foreign books were, and are, very present on national book markets, either in their original language or in translation – as the global distribution of *Up from Slavery* suggests. The question is what happens to things called books when they end up in another context.

Focusing on the Netherlands and its overseas empire, I will highlight fragments from the life of Booker T. Washington's *Up from Slavery*. The following analysis makes clear that it is next to impossible to separate the material book from its author, his name, his fame, and the story of his life, but there are still important methodological advantages to taking the book as basis for research. The life of the book makes it possible to track transnational encounters beyond the limits of space and time that defined the life of Booker T. Washington as human agent and following the book's movements allows us to see how the ambiguous mix of man-life-book was (re)framed and (re)valued in the Netherlands during the twentieth century.

In order to get a grip on *Up from Slavery*'s life in the Dutch empire, I checked WorldCat and Picarta, the collective library catalogue of Dutch libraries, studied the text and paratext of the one Dutch edition that is still available, and searched for mentions of the book in newspapers and magazines. To this end, I used the lists of book reviews in the Dutch book trade's professional journal, *Nieuwsblad voor den Boekhandel*, and searched the book and its author in Delpher, a full-text digital collection of newspapers and magzines from the Netherlands – including its colonies (the Dutch Indies, Suriname, the Antilles) and the Dutch communities in the United States – that covers the period 1618-1995. The result is a partial view because, at the time of my research, Delpher contained only 15 percent of the total

17 Henry Louis Gates jr., "The Language of Slavery," in *The Slave's Narrative*, ed. Charles T. Davis and Henry Louis Gates Jr. (Oxford/New York: Oxford University Press, 1985), xxix.

18 Pascale Casanova, *The World Republic of Letters* (Cambridge: Harvard University Press, 2004); Asa Briggs and Peter Burke, *A Social History of the Media: From Gutenberg to the Internet*, 2nd ed. (Cambridge: Polity Press, 2005).

19 Marijke Huisman, "Translation Politics: Foreign Autobiographies on the Nineteenth-Century Dutch Book Market," in *Life Writing Matters in Europe*, ed. Marijke Huisman et al. (Heidelberg: Winter Verlag, 2012), 57-74.

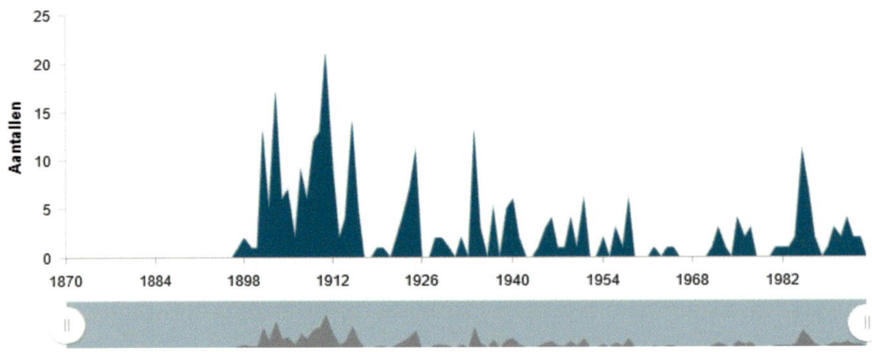

Figure 1: Distribution of 306 mentions of Booker T. Washington and/or Up from Slavery (in English and Dutch) in database Delpher (accessed December 8, 2017).

number of pages that have ever been published in Dutch.[20] Still, this partial view shows immediately that Booker T. Washington and his book have been alive in the Netherlands from the late 1890s until 1995 (Figure 1). To see what that life looked like, I will contextualize the peaks in the figure, starting with the publication of the Dutch translation of *Up from Slavery* in 1902.

Uit Slavernij in Vrijheid: Birth of the Dutch edition

In 1899, when Booker T. Washington and his wife spent a few days in the Netherlands as part of their trip through Europe, he was as of yet unknown among the Dutch. Before the turn of the century, his name is only mentioned in newspapers of Dutch Reformed communities in the United States. In November 1901, however, several newspapers in the Netherlands and its colonies reported on Washington's visit to the White House.[21] One year later, in late 1902, *Uit Slavernij in Vrijheid: Autobiographie van Booker T. Washington* [From Slavery to Freedom: Booker T. Washington's Autobiography] was presented to the Dutch audience and generated many articles about the book and its author.

The book was translated by Lodewijk Pierson and published by Pieter Marinus Wink. This was a surprising pairing, as the two had very different worldviews and lived in separate segments of Dutch society. Wink was a former teacher who was involved with the socialist and anarchist movements, lost his job because of his ideological viewpoints and started a new career as a publisher.[22] Pierson, on the other hand, was a Dutch Reformed minister who was active in the movement that argued for government funding of Orthodox Protestant schools. These so-called 'Schools with the Bible' were meant to strengthen the Reformed identity of the

20 Database Delpher was expanded with another million newspaper pages in mid-December 2018, just after my research in November and early December 2018.

21 "Een Klein Schandaal," *De Locomotief: Samarangsch Handels- En Advertentieblad*, 20 November 1901; "Een Klein Schandaal," *Het Nieuws van Den Dag Voor Nederlandsch-Indië*, 21 November 1901; "Een Klein Schandaal," *De Sumatra-Post*, 23 November 1901; "Buitenlandsch Overzicht," *Leeuwarder Courant*, 4 November 1901.

22 Bert Altena, "Pieter Marinus Wink," in *Biografisch Woordenboek van Het Socialisme en de Arbeidersbeweging in Nederland*, vol. 1, 1986, 153-55.

Dutch nation in a period when the liberal governments granted more rights to the Catholic minority.[23] Pierson had read about Washington in a French magazine, and started to translate *Up from Slavery* into Dutch. Looking for a publisher of his own choice, he found out that Wink possessed the translation rights but did not yet have a translator. The two decided to work together, but Pierson used the preface to state that he did not share Wink's political opinions and that the reasons for their collaboration were purely practical.[24]

In the same preface, Pierson introduced Booker T. Washington to Dutch readers. He did this first by framing the book as a sequel to Harriet Beecher Stowe's famous novel *Uncle Tom's Cabin* (1852). In a second move, Pierson compared Washington to George Washington, the American hero who "led his people from political slavery, installed by arrogant England, to full freedom and independence," and then to a Dutch hero: Prince William of Orange, "to us, Dutch, the symbol of freedom."[25] The 'us' in this quote refers not to Wink and Pierson together, but to people like Pierson: the Reformed part of the Dutch population. In its take on Dutch history and identity, the Dutch revolt against the Catholic king of Spain, between 1568 and 1648, was understood through analogies with the Biblical story of the Jews' exodus from slavery in Egypt – which made William of Orange into a second Moses.[26] Pierson regarded Booker T. Washington as yet another Moses, who led his people–"the despised Negro race"–"to a future in which the old will have passed and everything will have become new."[27]

Wink, in his book advertisements and flyers, never referred to Pierson's Protestant rhetoric. He connected education and emancipation in socialist terms, relating Washington's pedagogy to European ideas about the integration of vocational training and liberal education to further the emancipation of the working class.[28] Precisely because of their different perspectives, publisher and translator managed to disseminate the book into different corners of Dutch society. Pierson steered it into the Protestant world of newspapers and magazines like *Pniël: Weekblad voor het Christelijk Huisgezin* [Pniel: Weekly for the Christian Family], whilst Wink distributed Washington's book through socialist newspapers and placed it next to works by the Dutch anarchist Ferdinand Domela Nieuwenhuis and the *Memoirs* of the Russian anarchist Peter Kropotkin.[29] Both parties, however, shared a striking lack of interest in the emancipation of the people whom Washington's book was about: former slaves.

---

23 J.C. Van der Does, *Biografisch Woordenboek van Het Protestants-Christelijk Onderwijs* (Zeist: Dijkstra, 1949); Annemarie Houkes, *Christelijke Vaderlanders: Godsdienst, Burgerschap en de Nederlandse Natie, 1850-1900* (Amsterdam: Wereldbibliotheek, 2009), 185-230.

24 J.L. Pierson, "Voorwoord," in *Uit Slavernij in Vrijheid: Autobiographie van Booker T. Washington* (Gorinchem: P.M. Wink, 1902), iii-vii.

25 Pierson, "Voorwoord," vi-vii.

26 Simon Schama, *Overvloed en Onbehagen: De Nederlandse Cultuur in de Gouden Eeuw* (Amsterdam: Contact, 1989), 114; G.J. Schutte, *Het Calvinistisch Nederland: Mythe en Werkelijkheid* (Hilversum: Verloren, 2000), 90.

27 Pierson, "Voorwoord," vi-vii.

28 P.M. Wink, "Flyer," c 1902, KVB-PPA 545:12, Library University of Amsterdam, Special Collections (Bijzondere Collecties).

29 "[Book Advertisement P.M. Wink]," *De Toekomst: Socialistisch Weekblad Voor Zeeland en Westelijk Brabant*, 25 April 1904.

Up from Slavery in Suriname

On 1 July 1863 slavery was abolished in the Dutch colonies of Suriname and the Antilles, but emancipated slaves in Suriname had to submit to a period of State Surveillance.[30] During these ten years, children were obliged to attend schools and adults had to continue their work on sugar plantations as wage laborers. This measure was instrumental to the survival of the plantation economy, but it was framed as a learning period in which former slaves could transform themselves into hard-working individuals ready for citizenship. The process did not develop as planned, not least due to a lack of government funding for schools and teachers.[31] Colonial officials, however, found the main obstacle to lie in the work ethic of the Creole people, who were considered lazy. Installing the right work ethic therefore was, and remained, in Suriname the main target of colonial policies.

In this context, Washington's autobiography came to the attention of Meier Salomon Bromet.[32] Born in 1839 as a Jew in the Suriname capital, Paramaribo, he converted to Christianity, worked for the Scottish Mission in Amsterdam in the 1870s, and returned to Paramaribo in the 1880s to stimulate religious life through the founding of a Vrije Evangelische Gemeente (Free Evangelical Community), Sunday schools, choirs, and youth clubs for boys and girls. On 7 September 1904, Bromet gave a lecture about Booker T. Washington's life and work, which was published as *De Neger-Kwestie. Een lezing over Booker T. Washington* [The Negro Question: A Lecture on Booker T. Washington] (1905).

Bromet's central message was that each race had a place in the social order designed by God, with the white descendants of Noah's sons Sem and Japhet at the top and those of the cursed Ham at the bottom. In 1905, Bromet considered this God-given order to be in danger because emancipated slaves showed dissatisfaction with their designated place and increasingly looked down on agricultural and manual labour. Washington, in *Up from Slavery*, had observed the same problem among African Americans, explaining it as one of the devastating effects of slavery. In Bromet's mediation of Washington's book, it was emancipation that had caused the alleged weak work ethic of Surinamese ex-slaves. In his view, the abolition of slavery had liberated slaves only in a "physical and material sense," leaving them enslaved to "other, invisible, cruel and tyrannical masters," such as "evil passions, the natural and cultivated vices and flaws that are part of sinful human nature."[33]

To conquer these vices, and thus to complete the 'partial' emancipation of 1863, Bromet argued for black character-formation through education. This was hardly a new idea; the colonial government had been working on that since the abolition of slavery. In 1905, however, Bromet found a solution in Booker T.

---

30 Kwame Nimako and Glenn Willemsen, *The Dutch Atlantic: Slavery, Abolition and Emancipation* (London: Pluto Press, 2011), 87-122; Ellen Klinkers, "The Transformation and Downfall of Plantation Culture in Suriname," in *Migration, Trade, and Slavery in an Expanding World*, ed. Wim Kloosterman (Leiden/Boston: Brill, 2009), 289-304.

31 Lila Gobardhan-Rambocus, *Onderwijs Als Sleutel Voor Maatschappelijke Vooruitgang: Een Taal- en Onderwijsgeschiedenis van Suriname, 1651-1975* (Zutphen: Walburg Pers, 2001).

32 "M.S. Bromet," *Suriname: Koloniaal Nieuws- En Advertentieblad*, 18 May 1905; John H. Bye, *Historische Schetsen uit het Surinaamse Jodendom* (Schoorl: Conserve, 2002), 210-212.

33 M.S. Bromet, *De Neger-Kwestie: Een Lezing over Booker T. Washington* (Paramaribo: De Vrije Evangelische Gemeente, 1905), 3.

Washington's book of life, which showed him that it was indeed possible to educate and elevate black people – if only the Surinamese would copy his zeal, ambition, and dedication. Bromet thus emphasised that Washington had taken charge of his own life:

> Booker Washington was not complaining or exclaiming, "There is a lion on the street," "It does not matter," or similar jeremiads of pessimists and lazy people. During hard and difficult labor he had certainly felt and believed as David–"With my God I jump over a wall, and I go through a mob" (Psalms 18: 30-33), and "It is God who girds me with power, and He has made my way perfect"; or experienced with Paul: "I can do all things through Christ who gives me power" (Philippians IV: 1).[34] (my translation, MH)

Self-help is indeed a major part of the message in *Up from Slavery*, but Washington did not use the Bible to make his point. These were additions of Bromet's. His hand is also visible in a passage on the joys of agricultural work. Using more references to the Bible, Bromet maintained that agricultural work was not to be looked down upon: "Art thou greater than the Christ who commands us in one of his parables: 'Go, work in my vineyard'?"[35] In order to interest former slaves and their descendants in agricultural labour, Bromet finally took a special interest in the combination of book learning, manual labour, job training, and general character-formation including personal hygiene that Washington employed at the Tuskegee Institute. Such an educational mix would be very beneficial in Suriname too, according to Bromet, who argued for "well-furnished and well-supported agricultural schools next to our small craft school."[36]

Bromet's voice stopped when he died in May 1905, but his message was heard for decades to come. Washington, his pedagogical ideas and methods, and the Tuskegee Institute continued to inspire colonial officials in Suriname. Still, as late as 1950, a colonial newspaper referred to *Up from Slavery*, and more specifically to the earlier mentioned text of Washington's 1895 Atlanta speech, to remind the black people of Suriname of their place in the colonial order by publishing this quote: "No race acquires wealth before it realises that there is as much dignity in labouring the field as in the writing of a poem."[37] In 1958, the same newspaper transformed Washington's life narrative into a comic, once more in order to point out that even the great Booker T. Washington had not shied away from manual labour.[38]

Up from Slavery after Booker T. Washington's death

In the Netherlands, *Up from Slavery* was never presented in relation to the legacy of slavery in the Dutch colonies. But the book and its author remained alive. Following the publication of *Uit slavernij in vrijheid* in 1902, all sorts of special incidents in the life of its author were reported. In 1903, for instance, Dutch newspapers in both the United States and the Netherlands broke the news that a

---

34 Bromet, *De Neger-Kwestie*, 21.
35 Bromet, *De Neger-Kwestie*, 33.
36 Bromet, *De Neger-Kwestie*, 47.
37 "De Uitstalkast," *Het Nieuws: Algemeen Dagblad*, 3 June 1950.
38 "Ware Verhalen: Booker T. Washington," *Het Nieuws: Algemeen Dagblad*, 19 February 1958.

white maid in Indianapolis had refused to make Washington's hotel bed.[39] Later reports refer to more instances of discrimination, but also to speeches that he delivered, or big donations to the Tuskegee Institute.[40] This large range of small news messages, visible in Figure 1, suggests that Washington had become a household name in the Netherlands and its colonies. This could also explain the many reports of his death, on 15 November 1915. Even local and provincial Dutch newspapers commemorated Washington in obituaries.[41]

In the United States, Washington's star faded quickly in the interwar period, when the New Negro Movement disqualified him as an 'Old Negro.'[42] In the Netherlands, Washington's name and fame survived the test of time – even though his book was mentioned less and less. The mid-1920s peak shown in Figure 1, for instance, refers to reports in newspapers from Suriname and the Rotterdam region about a ship named the *Booker T. Washington*, which was part of Marcus Garvey's Black Cruise Line used to 'return' African Americans to Africa.[43] In 1934, Surinamese newspapers enthusiastically anticipated the arrival of the *Booker T. Washington* airplane and its crew of black pilots.[44] In 1940, newspapers in the Dutch Indies and the Netherlands announced that the U.S. Post Office Department had launched a new, collectible series of post stamps, which ranked Booker T. Washington among its 'Famous Americans.'[45] Between the world wars, moreover, Dutch newspaper articles on racial tensions in the United States often referred to Washington as a wise, cool-headed leader who had always stressed the importance of racial reconciliation and harmony.[46]

This benevolent image of Booker T. Washington was reproduced in the mid-1950s, when Jan Willem Schulte Nordholt published *Het volk dat in duisternis wandelt: De geschiedenis van de Negers in Amerika* [The People Who Walk in Darkness: The History of the Negroes in America] (1956). In this best-selling book, the Protestant historian and poet narrates the historical background of the Civil Rights Movement as *pars pro toto* for a universal struggle of man towards a future of 'equality and freedom and peace.'[47] Schulte Nordholt's hopes for that future

39 "Mejuffrouw Was Er Te Fijn Voor," *De Grondwet*, 19 March 1903; "Ze Kreeg 2500: 't Kan Altoos Nog Gekker," *De Grondwet*, 26 May 1903; "Een Negergeschiedenis," *Het Volk: Dagblad Voor de Arbeiderspartij*, 19 July 1903.

40 "Negerhaters: Rebellie Onder de Studenten," *De Grondwet*, 24 October 1905; "Het Negervraagstuk," *Algemeen Handelsblad*, 21 January 1908; "Vriendelijke Zeden," *Preanger-Bode*, 11 November 1908; "Blanken En Negers," *Nieuws van Den Dag Voor Nederlandsch-Indië*, 16 March 1909; "Millioenen-Studiën," *Nieuws van Den Dag Voor Nederlandsch-Indië*, 7 December 1909; "De Ontwikkeling van Het Neger-Ras," *Algemeen Handelsblad*, 8 October 1910; "Het Negervraagstuk," *Algemeen Handelsblad*, 25 April 1911.

41 "Booker T. Washington," *Provinciale Geldersche en Nijmeegsche Courant*, 18 November 1915.

42 Norrell, *Up from History*, 421-42.

43 "5000 Garvey Folks Pay to See Ship," *Suriname: Koloniaal Nieuws- en Advertentieblad*, 19 September 1924; "De Zwarte Kruislijn," *De Maasbode*, 20 February 1925.

44 "Bezoek van Kleurling Vliegers," *De West: Nieuwsblad Uit en Voor Suriname*, 2 November 1934; "Bezoek van Kleurlingen Vliegeniers," *Suriname: Koloniaal Nieuws- en Advertentieblad*, 20 November 1934.

45 "Famous Americans: De Beroemde Amerikanen Zijn in Aantocht," *De Maasbode*, 17 February 1940; "Famous Americans: Philatelistisch Allerlei," *De Sumatra-Post*, 9 March 1940.

46 "Kleurlingenhaat in Amerika," *Rotterdamsch Nieuwsblad*, 27 December 1924; "De Nieuwe Emancipatie Der Kleurlingen," *De Tijd*, 17 December 1939.

47 Jan Willem Schulte Nordholt, *Het Volk Dat in Duisternis Wandelt: De Geschiedenis van de Negers in Amerika* (Arnhem: Van Loghum Slaterus, 1956), 260.

paradise of light were set on Martin Luther King, Jr., in whom he observed the post-war rise of a new, social Christianity. The one and only biographical chapter of the book, however, was devoted to Booker T. Washington, the 'predecessor' of King, and the greatest black leader ever.[48]

By that time the Dutch edition of *Up from Slavery* was over half a century old and out of print. The book was not yet dead, though, as is shown by mentions in newspaper articles on 'Negro literature' from 1940 and 1951.[49] In the 1960s and 1970s, Booker T. Washington and his book almost disappeared from the landscape of Dutch media, as Figure 1 suggests, but in the mid-1980s his book-based life story resurfaced in another genre, a film. On 15 October 1985, the American youth-oriented movie *Booker* was aired on television by the Nederlandse Christelijke Radio Vereniging (NCRV)[Dutch Christian Radio Service].[50] Following in the footsteps of Pierson, Bromet, and Schulte Nordholt, the airing of the film by this Protestant broadcasting company suggests once again that Dutch Reformed mediators were crucial for continuing the life of Booker T. Washington and his book in the Netherlands. But the influence of the Dutch Reformed waned in the 1980s, as secularisation gave rise to a more general 'public theology of engagement with the world and humanity'[51] and the Dutch engaged en masse with causes like women's liberation, the 'Third World', and the anti-Apartheid movement in South Africa.

In the new context of the late twentieth century, 'world culture' became fashionable and publishers flooded the market with books written by 'non-western' authors.[52] Booker T. Washington's autobiography became part of this market. In 1985, for instance, an English edition of *Up from Slavery* was offered by the Koöperatieve Uitgeverij van Schrijvers en Kunstenaars SoMa [Cooperative Publishing House of Writers and Artists SoMa]. In an ad in the Communist newspaper *De Waarheid* [The Truth], this group announced a number of books on 'the women's struggle and women's participation in the struggles in the Netherlands, Spain, Belgium, the US, Germany, and China.' *Up from Slavery* was described as a book in which Washington paid special attention to his mother, and advertised in between books on women and peace, the history of female labourers, children's rights, the Holocaust, and the Civil War in Spain.[53] One year later, an English edition of *Up from Slavery* was sold in Dutch venues that staged a play by the African American actor Charles Dumas on the life and work of Booker T. Washington.[54] These venues were activist theatres like Rasa in Utrecht, De Evenaar in Rotterdam, and Soeterijn in Amsterdam, which strongly engaged with the Third World Movement.

48 Schulte Nordholt, *Het Volk Dat in Duisternis Wandelt*, 183.

49 Eliza Hess-Binger, "Amerikaansche Neger-Poëzie," *Algemeen Handelsblad*, 7 April 1940; "Bijdrage van de Neger in Amerika's Muziek, Letteren en Wetenschap," *Het Nieuws: Algemeen Dagblad*, 3 November 1951.

50 "Morgen Op Tv," *Leeuwarder Courant*, 14 October 1985.

51 James Kennedy, *Bezielende Verbanden: Gedachten over Religie, Politiek en Maatschappij in het Moderne Nederland* (Amsterdam: Bert Bakker, 2010), 109.

52 Graham Huggan, *The Postcolonial Exotic: Marketing the Margins* (London/New York: Routledge, 2001); Sandra Ponzanesi, *The Postcolonial Cultural Industry: Icons, Markets, Mythologies* (Houndmills/Basingstoke: Palgrave Macmillan, 2014).

53 "Koöperatieve Uitgeverij van Schrijvers en Kunstenaars SoMa in Den Bosch Presenteert," *De Waarheid*, 1 March 1985.

54 "Educatief Portret van een Zwarte Idealist," *NRC Handelsblad*, 6 November 1986.

The Third World Movement was mostly a white movement, in which white people did the activist work and non-white 'others' served as world cultural decoration during protest meetings or festivals.[55] In the 1990s, however, post-colonial migrants from the Caribbean became more visible and vocal in Dutch society. In that process of black emancipation in a multiculturalizing society, Booker T. Washington and his book continued to play a role. In 1990, for instance, Surinamese-Dutch Patrick 'Rudeboy' Tilon, leading man in the rock/hip-hop group Urban Dance Squad, mentioned Washington in a lecture on "150 years of black consciousness." Commemorating the 25th anniversary of Malcolm X's murder at the pop venue De Melkweg (Amsterdam), Tilon placed Washington on an equal footing with Nat Turner, Marcus Garvey, and Malcolm X.[56] However, when a white journalist described Malcolm X and Booker T. Washington as equals, in a review of Spike Lee's movie *Malcolm X* (1992), a woman named Edith Faber took a stance. She sent a letter to the newspaper arguing that Washington had led African Americans into submission to the white establishment. He could, in other words, not be mentioned in the same terms as 'a radical' like Malcolm X.[57] In 1993, on the other hand, Surinamese-Dutch boxer Regilio Tuur found in Washington's works and words the fighting spirit he needed while preparing a match to defend his title as European champion: "I shall allow no man to belittle my soul by making me hate him, but I will destroy all who try to rob me from what is mine."[58]

Conclusion

In an attempt to practice transnational life writing, I have argued that biographies of things are at least as interesting as those of people. While some people in the modern era lived their lives crossing national borders, many more were affected by the global flows of capitalism that brought foreign *things* into their lives – such as books. In reconstructing the wanderings of one book-thing, Booker T. Washington's autobiographical *Up from Slavery*, through the Netherlands in the twentieth century, it has become clear that this particular book had a life in the Dutch empire, that this life continued long after the death of its author, and that the book served many different audiences and purposes. While the translator, Pierson, appropriated it for his cause of Dutch Reformed emancipation through Dutch Reformed education in 1902, the book's publisher, Wink, exemplifies a reading that is geared towards emancipation of the working-class.

Over time, the Dutch Reformed dominated the book's life in the Netherlands: from the evangelist Bromet, who used it to help maintain the traditional colonial order in Suriname in 1905, to the historian Schulte Nordholt, who emphasised racial harmony in man's common struggle for social and moral progress in the

55 Jos van Beurden and Chris Huinder, *De Vinger op de Zere Plek: Solidariteit met Zuidelijk Afrika, 1961-1996* (Amsterdam: Singel, 1996), 154-155.

56 Eddy Determeyer, "Malcolm X na 25 Jaar Weer Springlevend," *Nieuwsblad van het Noorden*, 24 February 1990.

57 Edith Faber, "Booker T. Washington," *NRC Handelsblad*, 11 December 1992; Maarten Huygen, "Ken U Zelf, Verdedig U Zelf: Malcolm X, Filmheld voor Zwart en Blank," *NRC Handelsblad*, 20 November 1992.

58 Luuk Blijboom, "Tuur Mist Ontzag voor La Fratta," *De Telegraaf*, 23 March 1993.

mid-1950s, to the NCRV, which broadcast a movie adaptation of the book in the mid-1980s. In the 1980s and 1990s, however, the book was appropriated for new causes too: the emancipation of people in the so-called Third World and of black people in Dutch society. Overviewing this trajectory, one could conclude that the book was finally read 'right' in the 1990s. But such an understanding would miss the point of this micro-history of the book's life, which ultimately shows the unpredictable, suprising effects of transcultural contacts and the complex links between a man, the book of his life, and readers in places and times beyond the scope of that man's life.

Bibliography

"5000 Garvey Folks Pay to See Ship." *Suriname: Koloniaal Nieuws- en Advertentieblad*, 19 September 1924.

Altena, Bert. "Pieter Marinus Wink." In *Biografisch Woordenboek van het Socialisme en de Arbeidersbeweging in Nederland*, 1:153-55, 1986.

Andrews, William L., ed. *Slave Narratives after Slavery*. New York: New York University Press, 2011.

——. *To Tell a Free Story: The First Century of Afro-American Autobiography, 1760-1865*. Urbana/Champaign: University of Illinois Press, 1986.

Banner, Lois W. "AHR Roundtable Biography as History." *American Historical Review* 114, no. 3 (2009): 579-86.

Beck, Ulrich. "The Cosmopolitan Condition: Why Methodological Nationalism Fails." *Theory, Culture & Society* 24, no. 7-8 (2007): 286-90.

Berger, Stefan, and Chris Lorenz, eds. *Nationalizing the Past: Historians as Nation Builders in Modern Europe*. Houndsmill: Palgrave Macmillan, 2010.

Beurden, Jos van, and Chris Huinder. *De Vinger Op de Zere Plek: Solidariteit met Zuidelijk Afrika, 1961-1996*. Amsterdam: Singel, 1996.

"Bezoek van Kleurling Vliegers." *De West: Nieuwsblad uit en voor Suriname*, 2 November 1934.

"Bezoek van Kleurlingen Vliegeniers." *Suriname: Koloniaal Nieuws- en Advertentieblad*, 20 November 1934.

"Bijdrage van de Neger in Amerika's Muziek, Letteren en Wetenschap." *Het Nieuws: Algemeen Dagblad*, 3 November 1951.

"Blanken en Negers." *Nieuws van den Dag voor Nederlandsch-Indië*, 16 March 1909.

Blijboom, Luuk. "Tuur Mist Ontzag voor La Fratta." *De Telegraaf*, 23 March 1993.

"[Book Advertisement P.M. Wink] ." *De Toekomst: Socialistisch Weekblad voor Zeeland en Westelijk Brabant*, 25 April 1904.

"Booker T. Washington." *Provinciale Geldersche en Nijmeegsche Courant*, 18 November 1915.

Briggs, Asa, and Peter Burke. *A Social History of the Media: From Gutenberg to the Internet*. 2nd ed. Cambridge: Polity Press, 2005.

Bromet, M.S. *De Neger-Kwestie: Een Lezing over Booker T. Washington*. Paramaribo: De Vrije Evangelische Gemeente, 1905.

"Buitenlandsch Overzicht." *Leeuwarder Courant*, 4 November 1901.

Bye, John H. *Historische Schetsen uit het Surinaamse Jodendom*. Schoorl: Conserve, 2002.

Caine, Barbara. *Biography and History*. New York: Palgrave Macmillan, 2010.

Casanova, Pascale. *The World Republic of Letters*. Cambridge: Harvard University Press, 2004.

Darnton, Robert. "History of Reading." In *New Perspectives on Historical Writing*, edited by Peter Burke, Second edition, 157-86. Cambridge: Polity Press, 2001.

"De Nieuwe Emancipatie der Kleurlingen." *De Tijd*, 17 December 1939.

"De Ontwikkeling van het Neger-Ras." *Algemeen Handelsblad*, 8 October 1910.

"De Uitstalkast." *Het Nieuws: Algemeen Dagblad*, 3 June 1950.

"De Zwarte Kruislijn." *De Maasbode*, 20 February 1925.

Determeyer, Eddy. "Malcolm X na 25 Jaar Weer Springlevend." *Nieuwsblad van Het Noorden*, 24 February 1990.

Does, J.C. van der. *Biografisch Woordenboek van Het Protestants-Christelijk Onderwijs*. Zeist: Dijkstra, 1949.

Eakin, Paul John. "Breaking Rules: The Consequences of Self-Narration." *Biography* 24, no. 1 (2001): 113-27.

"Educatief Portret van een Zwarte Idealist." *NRC Handelsblad*, 6 November 1986.

"Een Klein Schandaal." *De Locomotief: Samarangsch Handels- en Advertentieblad*, 20 November 1901.

"Een Klein Schandaal." *Het Nieuws van den Dag voor Nederlandsch-Indië*, 21 November 1901.

"Een Klein Schandaal." *De Sumatra-Post*, 23 November 1901.

"Een Negergeschiedenis." *Het Volk: Dagblad voor de Arbeiderspartij*, 19 July 1903.

Faber, Edith. "Booker T. Washington." *NRC Handelsblad*, 11 December 1992.

"Famous Americans: De Beroemde Amerikanen Zijn in Aantocht." *De Maasbode*, 17 February 1940.

"Famous Americans: Philatelistisch Allerlei." *De Sumatra-Post*, 9 March 1940.

Gates Jr., Henry Louis. "The Language of Slavery." In *The Slave's Narrative*, edited by Charles T. Davis and Henry Louis Gates Jr., xi-xxxiv. Oxford/New York: Oxford University Press, 1985.

Gobardhan-Rambocus, Lila. *Onderwijs Als Sleutel voor Maatschappelijke Vooruitgang: Een Taal- en Onderwijsgeschiedenis van Suriname, 1651-1975*. Zutphen: Walburg Pers, 2001.

Gould, Philip. "The Rise, Development, and Circulation of the Slave Narrative." In *The Cambridge Companion to the African American Slave Narrative*, edited by Audrey Fisch, 11-27. Cambridge: Cambridge University Press, 2007.

Greenblatt, Stephen. "Cultural Mobility: An Introduction." In *Cultural Mobility: A Manifesto*, edited by Stephen Greenblatt, 1-23. Cambridge: Cambridge University Press, 2010.

Gusdorf, Georges. "Conditions and Limits of Autobiography." In *Autobiography: Essays Theoretical and Critical*, edited by James Olney, 28-48. Princeton: Princeton University Press, 1980.

Hess-Binger, Eliza. "Amerikaansche Neger-Poëzie." *Algemeen Handelsblad*, 7 April 1940.

"Het Negervraagstuk." *Algemeen Handelsblad*, 21 January 1908.

"Het Negervraagstuk." *Algemeen Handelsblad*, 25 April 1911.

Houkes, Annemarie. *Christelijke Vaderlanders: Godsdienst, Burgerschap en de Nederlandse Natie, 1850-1900*. Amsterdam: Wereldbibliotheek, 2009.

Huggan, Graham. *The Postcolonial Exotic: Marketing the Margins*. London/New York: Routledge, 2001.

Huisman, Marijke. Translation Politics: Foreign Autobiographies on the Nineteenth-Century Dutch Book Market," in *Life Writing Matters in Europe*, ed. Marijke Huisman et al. Heidelberg: Winter Verlag, 2012.

Huygen, Maarten. "Ken u zelf, verdedig u zelf: Malcolm X, filmheld voor zwart en blank." *NRC Handelsblad*, 20 November 1992.

Jackson, Leon. "The Talking Book and the Talking Book Historian." *Book History* 13 (2010): 251-308.

Jensen, Meg, and Margaretta Jolly. *We Shall Bear Witness: Life Narratives and Human Rights*. Madison: University of Wisconsin Press, 2014.

Kennedy, James. *Bezielende Verbanden: Gedachten over Religie, Politiek en Maatschappij in Het Moderne Nederland*. Amsterdam: Bert Bakker, 2010.

"Kleurlingenhaat in Amerika." *Rotterdamsch Nieuwsblad*, 27 December 1924.

Klinkers, Ellen. "The Transformation and Downfall of Plantation Culture in Suriname." In *Migration, Trade, and Slavery in an Expanding World*, edited by Wim Kloosterman, 289-304. Leiden/Boston: Brill, 2009.

"Koöperatieve Uitgeverij van Schrijvers en Kunstenaars SoMa in Den Bosch Presenteert." *De Waarheid*, 1 March 1985.

Kopytoff, Igor. "The Cultural Biography of Things: Commoditization as Process." In *The Social Life of Things: Commodities in Cultural Perspective*, edited by Arjun Appadurai, 64-91. Cambridge: Cambridge University Press, 1986.

Mascuch, Michael. *Origins of the Individualist Self: Autobiography and Self-Identity in England, 1591-1791*. Oxford: Polity Press, 1997.

"Mejuffrouw Was Er Te Fijn Voor." *De Grondwet*, 19 March 1903.

"Millioenen-Studiën." *Nieuws van den Dag voor Nederlandsch-Indië*, 7 December 1909.

Molz, Jenny Germann. "Cosmopolitanism and Consumption." In *The Ashgate Research Companion to Cosmopolitanism*, edited by Maria Rovisco and Magdalena Nowicka, 33-52. Surrey: Ashgate, n.d.

"Morgen Op Tv." *Leeuwarder Courant*, 14 October 1985.

"M.S. Bromet." *Suriname: Koloniaal Nieuws- en Advertentieblad*, 18 May 1905.

"Negerhaters: Rebellie Onder de Studenten." *De Grondwet*, 24 October 1905.

Nimako, Kwame, and Glenn Willemsen. *The Dutch Atlantic: Slavery, Abolition and Emancipation*. London: Pluto Press, 2011.

Norrell, Robert J. *Up from History: The Life of Booker T. Washington*. Cambridge/London: The Belknap Press, 2009.

Panter, Sarah, Johannes Paulmann, and Margit Szöllösi-Janze. "Mobility and Biography: Methodological Challenges and Perspectives." In *Jahrbuch für Europäische Geschichte/ European History Yearbook*, edited by Sarah Panter, 1-14. Berlin: De Gruyter Oldenbourg, 2015.

Pierson, J.L. "Voorwoord." In *Uit Slavernij in Vrijheid: Autobiographie van Booker T. Washington*, iii-vii. Gorinchem: P.M. Wink, 1902.

Ponzanesi, Sandra. *The Postcolonial Cultural Industry: Icons, Markets, Mythologies*. Houndmills, Basingstoke: Palgrave Macmillan, 2014.

Renders, Hans, Binne de Haan, and Jonne Harmsma, eds. *The Biographical Turn: Lives in History*. New York: Routledge, 2016.

Schaffer, Kay, and Sidonie Smith. *Human Rights and Narrated Lives: The Ethics of Recognition*. New York: Palgrave Macmillan, 2004.

Schama, Simon. *Overvloed en Onbehagen: De Nederlandse Cultuur in de Gouden Eeuw*. Amsterdam: Contact, 1989.

Schulte Nordholt, Jan Willem. *Het Volk Dat in Duisternis Wandelt: De Geschiedenis van de Negers in Amerika*. Arnhem: Van Loghum Slaterus, 1956.

Schutte, G.J. *Het Calvinistisch Nederland: Mythe en Werkelijkheid*. Hilversum: Verloren, 2000.

Sluga, Glenda, and Julia Horne. "Cosmopolitanism: Its Pasts and Practices." *Journal of World History* 21, no. 3 (2010): 369-73.

"Vriendelijke Zeden." *Preanger-Bode*, 11 November 1908.

"Ware Verhalen. Booker T. Washington." *Het Nieuws: Algemeen Dagblad*, 19 February 1958.

Washington, Booker T. *The Man Farthest Down: A Record of Observation and Study in Europe*. Garden City: Doubleday, Page & Co, 1912.

——. *Up from Slavery*. New York: New American Library, 2010.

Weintraub, Karl Joachim. *The Value of the Individual. Self and Circumstance in Autobiography*. Chicago: Chicago University Press, 1978.

Whitlock, Gillian. *Soft Weapons: Autobiography in Transit*. Chicago: Chicago University Press, 2007.

Wink, P.M. "Flyer." c 1902. KVB-PPA 545:12. Library University of Amsterdam, Special Collections (Bijzondere Collecties).

"Ze Kreeg 2500: 't Kan Altoos Nog Gekker." *De Grondwet*, 26 May 1903.

The production and contestation of biography: New approaches from South Africa

Ciraj Rassool

The methodological objective of much of my biographic and life writing research has involved the search for a theory of discursive practice rather than a theory of the knowing subject. In this paradigm, the subject is not abolished or abandoned, but, acquires a decentred or displaced position. This approach makes it possible to create a framework that transcends a dualist understanding of the relationship between the individual and social processes, to open up ways of understanding life histories as productions.

This has meant going beyond conventional approaches to life history as chronological narrative, where the major research challenges have been understood as archival and empirical, to open up questions about narration and self-narration, gender and biography's relationship with autobiography. Only then might it be possible to develop more complex understandings in the field of life writing about "the lives people live and the way they tell them."[1] This emphasis on narration is also concerned with the multiple genres, locations and formats through which lives have been presented and represented, through oral narrative, academic text and public historical production, and it is interested in the ways biography and life writing can transcend the boundaries and terms of the nation.

It also seeks to understand such productions and contestations of lives and life narratives in transnational settings and across national boundaries, especially when these have occurred under conditions of political repression and forced exile. These productions of lives were also often built on genealogies of prior narrations and, as we shall see, came to be the subject of intense contestation and dispute. This saw a transition from biographic disavowal and an emphasis on the collective to the embrace of biography as part of a politics of presidentialism. While biographic disavowal and reticence began at home, with the idea of collective leadership as the chosen means of political mobilisation, the presidential frame emerged as the main mode of political expression in exile.

---

1 Vincent Crapanzano, '"Self"-Centering Narratives,' in *Natural Histories of Discourse*, eds. Michael Silverstein and Greg Urban (Chicago: University of Chicago Press, 1996), 106.

Auto/biography and production

A central feature of conventional biography, marked as it was by "a biographical illusion,"[2] was that it presumed that there was a 'real person' who lived a life, who was born, perhaps died, and who may have influenced others. Mary Evans has gone further to argue that the pattern of the conventional biography was also a masculinist one, with life, consisting of work in the public world, perceived as a career, constructed as a path of progress and achievement and the production of 'works' and 'products.' Male biography and life writing tended to construct lives of "supposedly rational, adult human beings," and was "frightened by affectivity" and "terrified of considering the impact of the irrational." The 'personal' was perceived as a separate space, with very little of this work sensitive to the personal lives of their subjects. This compartmentalising mode rejected analytical consideration of intimacy and "the impact, and indeed the relationship, of the emotional to the rational world."[3]

In contrast, social historians have worked with biographic approaches to the individual life narrative as a unit of social forms, and as a prism of collective experience of structural economic and social conditions, in which the individual remains an expression of the social.[4] I want to suggest that there is another element in the equation between 'individual subject' and 'society' that can enable the approach to biography as 'prism' for social processes, collectivities and representativeness to be transcended. This entails an approach to life writing that locates individual lives within human relationships. Viewed in this way, the notion of a life history as a 'laboratory of identity,' as developed by literary scholar and biographer Steven Clingman,[5] can really come into its own.

Human beings enter into relations of many different kinds with others, through which they construct meanings and narratives and fashion their identities. It becomes possible for biography to emerge as the study of *reciprocal constructions* and the ways in which people narrate each other in relationships. While these relations may be ongoing, regular and formative, they may not always entail equal access to the tools of reconstruction. Nevertheless, it is in these 'biographical relations' that individual-society relations are mediated discursively. This is also where identities are constituted through representation within specific institutional sites, and through particular enunciative strategies. Through this perspective, it also becomes possible to breach the divide between the public and the private, the

---

2 Pierre Bourdieu, "The Biographical Illusion," *Working Papers and Proceedings of the Center for Psychosocial Studies*, no. 14, trans. Yves Winkin and Wendy Leeds-Hurwitz (Chicago, Center for Psychosocial Studies, 1987): 1-7.

3 Mary Evans, "Masculine and Feminine Biography," in *Imitating Art: Essays in Biography*, ed. David Ellis (London: Pluto Press, 1993), 109-115.

4 For examples of this approach, see Franco Ferrarotti, "On the Autonomy of the Biographical Method," in *Biography and Society: The Life History Approach in the Social Sciences*, ed. Daniel Bertaux (Beverley Hills: Sage, 1981), 19-27, and Paul Thompson, "Life Histories and the Analysis of Social Change," in the same volume, 289-306.

5 Stephen Clingman, "Biography and Representation: Some Analogies from Fiction," History Workshop Conference, University of the Witwatersrand, February 1987.

political and the personal, and to reflect on the individual in a more complex way in processes of life writing.[6]

It is tempting merely to distinguish between lives as lived and experienced, and lives as told or produced. However, from Richard Ochberg we learn that lives do not simply become narrativised after the fact, once people have lived or experienced their lives. Instead, people live out their lives in a storied manner in ways that are deeply embedded in narrative. Individuals conduct their life episodes in patterns similar to the plots of stories. In other words, the 'storied life' should become much more of a focus in the ways in which people think about life writing and biography.[7]

And as Hannah Arendt has noted, we are part of narratives right from birth and these make us both subject and object. We become greatly aware of the narrative connections and attached meanings to certain life actions and these direct the choices made, relations entered into and courses decided upon.[8] In this way, life becomes lived almost like a kind of argument in which one construction of experience is privileged over some other one. In this argument about the potential complexities of approaching life writing, the choices made and the directions decided upon become the narratives of life as it is lived and debated.

As much as people create themselves, they also recreate themselves and refashion their identities, drawing from encounters with a range of ready-made identities. It is language and narrative, which make it possible to think about these identities and to shape new ones.[9] Modernity gave rise to lives that can be seen as "biographically ordered." People live their lives biographically and construct their reality on the basis of biography. Indeed, as Birgitta Svensson has suggested, modern existence can be seen as "ordered as an autobiographical presentation."[10] The narrated life is characterised by a "struggle between concordance and discordance," the aim of which is to discover narrative identity. Through narrative identity, one is able to develop a sense of one's self as a subject.[11]

Conventionally, a distinction is made between *the life as lived*, supposedly in an unmediated way, and *the life as told* through a subsequent process of narration. However, according to Paul Ricoeur, the process of selection and narration begins "in life itself, with attention and planned activity." Life is experienced in a temporal way. For Ricoeur, temporality and narrativity are mutually imbricated. Literature and history have in common the human experience of time, of human "within-timeness." Life, for Ricoeur, "*prefigures*" narrative. There is a "relation of dynamic

---

6 In her work on 'complex agency' Corinne A. Kratz begins to talk of 'collective individuals.' See Corinne A. Kratz, "Forging Unions and Negotiating Ambivalence: Personhood and Complex Agency in Okiek Marriage Arrangement," in *African Philosophy as Cultural Inquiry*, eds. Ivan Karp and D.A. Masolo (Bloomington: Indiana University Press, 2000), 136-172.

7 Richard L. Ochberg, "Life Stories and Storied Lives," in *Exploring Identity and Gender: The Narrative Study of Lives: Volume 2*, eds. Amia Lieblich and Ruthellen Josselson (London: Sage, 1994), 113.

8 Birgitta Svensson, "The Power of Biography: Criminal Policy, Prison Life, and the Formation of Criminal Identities in the Swedish Welfare State," in *Autoethnography: Rewriting the Self and the Social*, ed. Deborah Reed-Danahay (Washington: Berg Publishers, 1997), 72.

9 Kwame Anthony Appiah, "Cosmopolitan Patriots," *Critical Inquiry* 23 (Spring 1997), 625.

10 Birgitta Svensson, "Lifetimes – Life History and Life Story: Biographies of Modern Swedish Intellectuals," *Ethnologia Scandinavica* 25 (1995), 26.

11 David Wood, "Introduction: Interpreting Narrative," in *On Paul Ricoeur: Narrative and Interpretation*, ed. David Wood (London: Routledge, 1991), 11.

circularity" between life and narrative. People are born into a world of narratives, and life is lived "in quest of narrative."[12]

We refer to a life-story as the interval between birth and death. However, knowledge over the past few decades, for the most part, has tended to distance narrative from lived experience and to confine it to fiction. It is not only history that has a direct relation with life. Ricoeur argues that fiction contributes to making life. He distinguishes between first order narrative, in which "emplotment constitutes the creative centre" and narratology, which is a second order "rational reconstruction of the rules." This second order is "always preceded by a narrative understanding stemming from the creative imagination." "There is," he argues, "a *life* of narrative activity." With this, Ricoeur bridges the gap and revises the paradox between stories which are seen as recounted and lives which are seen as lived.[13]

It has been suggested by Laura Marcus that attempts to persist in defining autobiography conceptually away from biography are inadequate and unhelpful. According to Marcus, "far more exciting conjunctures occur, showing how autobiography and biography function together." She suggests two forms of interaction: that recounting one's own life "almost inevitably entails writing the life of an other" and that the writing of another's life "must surely entail the biographer's identifications with his or her subject, whether these are made explicit or not."[14] Indeed, Marcus' use of the category 'auto/biography' is directed at challenging a conceptual division in life writing between autobiography and biography.

My research on South African political movements, leadership and life history suggests that there is a third, perhaps more important interaction between biography and autobiography. This is that the writing of another's life almost inevitably means that one enters into the existence of autobiographical texts, of narrations of self on the part of the subject. This includes narratives lived out in life itself, and biographical texts that the subject had a hand in creating and establishing. In the process of life writing, the act of biography necessarily entails such encounters with auto-narrations and autobiography.

These storied lives are also lived out inside the narrative world of institutions, where people are immersed in the biographical ordering that occurs through their structures, procedures and discourses. Birgitta Svensson has examined the operation of power in the coercive institutional edifice of the prison, and the mania of the welfare state for recording and cataloguing individuals. Their administrative and bureaucratic procedures of documentation reflect the power of the biographical project of the prison system and penal policy in constituting specific criminal identities and biographies.[15] These, in turn, have a profound effect on shaping autobiographic narrations and understandings.

---

12 Wood, "Introduction," 16-17.

13 Paul Ricoeur, "Life in Quest of Narrative," in *On Paul Ricoeur: Narrative and Interpretation*, ed. David Wood (London: Routledge, 1991), 24.

14 Laura Marcus, *Auto/biographical Discourses: Theory, Criticism, Practice* (Manchester: Manchester University Press, 1994), 272-273.

15 Svensson, "The Power of Biography," 71-104.

Other bureaucratic institutions of the national state that register persons as citizens and subjects, and regulate their settlement and movement through deep documentation, are not only expressions of a biometric state,[16] but can also be understood to be immersed in a biographic order. At times this biographic bureaucracy extends beyond the state and the nation to the domain of international migration and the regulation of international movement of colonial subjects.[17] But beyond the central institutions of state regulation, and the coercive biographies of the prison, Svensson's arguments can be extended to understanding the biographic character of other institutions of assembly, social order and regulation such as schools and political movements. These institutions are also characterised by rules and codes, and the lives of their members become a subject for registration, regulation, evaluation, classification and record-keeping. What emerges is a documentary record, that talks to the history of these institutions, and to their discursive frames, which shape the life narratives of the individuals who constitute them. The resultant archive stands as testimony, not merely to the existence of these institutions, their members and their decisions, but to the capacity of these institutions to constitute subjectivities and biographic possibilities (and constraints), as a key element of the social knowledge that they produce.

There will always be a dialogue between the biographical process and autobiographical narrative traces, even where no autobiography as such exists. These life narrations are to be found in archival collections, interviews, diaries, and other forms of life writing and self-production. They are also to be found in the 'storied life' of the subject, just as they may have been forged in the mutually constitutive settings of biographical relations and in the documentary imperatives, plots and patterns of biographical institutions. Indeed, they constitute genealogies of biographical production, which shape and influence the contours of contemporary productions through their narrative selections, silences and transactions.

This perspective suggests ways in which it is possible to view biography through the methodological lens of *the production of history*, in which history is understood as "the processing of the past in societies and historical settings . . . and the struggles for control of voices and texts in innumerable settings which animate this processing of the past." As a "field of practice" *the production of history* encompasses, inter alia, "the organising sociologies" of historicising projects, commemorative events, "the structuring of frames of record-keeping" as well as "the contentions and struggles which evoke and produce texts and which also produce historical literatures."[18] This broader approach to the production of historical knowledge is also concerned to understand the practices and genres of history making outside the academy, as well as how these relate to the peculiar routines and rituals of

16 Keith Breckenridge, *Biometric State: The Global Politics of Identification and Surveillance in South Africa, 1850 to the Present* (*New York*: *Cambridge* University Press, 2014).

17 Uma Dhupelia-Mesthrie, "The Form, the Permit and the Photograph: An Archive of Mobility between South Africa and India," *Journal of African and Asian Studies* 46, no. 6 (September 2011): 650-662.

18 David William Cohen, *The Combing of History* (Chicago: University of Chicago Press, 1994), 244-245; see also David William Cohen, "Further Thoughts on the Production of History," in *Between History and Histories: The Making of Silences and Commemorations*, eds. Gerald Sider and Gavin Smith (Toronto: University of Toronto Press, 1997), 300-310.

academic practice. With these questions and methods, it may indeed be possible to speak of *the production of auto/biography*.

As part of understanding the process of producing biography and life writing, it is necessary to question the claim that some historians may make to be uncovering 'the truth.' What is being created, instead, is a subject in a text that is written. There is no 'real' person behind the text. The language of biography in fact cannot be taken as a window "into the 'real' world of 'real' interacting subjects." Rather, persons are created in texts. Any approach to life writing that perpetuates a distinction between 'factual history,' containing non-fictional scholarship as truth, and 'fiction,' taken to consist of imagined facts and facticities, is unhelpful in enabling a stronger theoretical grasp of the narration of lives. Indeed, for Norman Denzin, all writing about lives is fictional.[19]

Likewise, for Raymond Williams, the dichotomy between fiction and fact, described very negatively as 'myth' as against 'fact'–what did happen – is crippling. Biography and autobiography, for Williams, should be seen as test cases, suggesting an overlap between fact and fiction.[20] Biographies, according to Denzin, are always "*incomplete* literary productions." Conventionally, they use narrative devices, which conform to the presumption that lives have beginnings and the "cultural myth that lives have endings." These devices convey the idea that complete stories about lives can be told. Indeed, according to Denzin, lives are not 'real.' They are constructions, "constrained by the cultural writing practices of the time."[21] For Laura Marcus, the distinction between auto/biography and fiction needs to be effaced, by asserting the fictionality of all discourse. In auto/biography, the 'life' and 'the subject' are constructed in writing. Indeed, "[the] self does not pre-exist the text but is constructed by it."[22]

Seeking an approach to life writing that overcomes the chronological narrative procedures of traditional biography does not mean rejecting narrative altogether. Indeed, this study suggests that narrative should be taken more seriously in the construction of lives and in the production of local, national and transnational histories. Merely to impose a narrative structure on events in the reconstruction of the past, as a chronological 'history of events' or as a life history, in realist mode, placed in a 'historical context,' is not sufficient. Furthermore, we need to be attuned to the ways these histories often contradict the framework of the nation through the complexities of the local and the intimate, and the recurrence of transnational narratives.

We should therefore recognise the existence of multiple narrations intersecting and crosscutting each other, paralleling and contradicting each other as they compete for the creation of historical meaning. These narratives and representations constitute historicising projects differing between past and present, subject and historian, personal and political, the local, national and transnational and transcending

19 Norman K. Denzin, *Interpretive Biography* (Newbury Park, CA: Sage, 1989), 22-24.

20 Raymond Williams, *Marxism and Literature* (Oxford: Oxford University Press, 1977), 146-149.

21 Denzin, *Interpretive Biography*, 24-26.

22 Marcus, *Auto/biographical Discourses*, 180. Marcus's writing is a direct challenge to the much-cited work on autobiography by James Olney. Olney had argued for the concept of a unified human nature pre-existing textual expression and stood by a fact-fiction dichotomy. See James Olney, *Metaphors of Self: The Meaning of Autobiography* (Princeton: Princeton University Press, 1972).

the distinction between fact and fiction. Moving beyond conventional narrative means taking account of these various historicising projects and understanding the politics, sociologies and genealogies of their production. It means questioning the presumption of national frames, and requires the recognition that the academic historian's narrative is "one 'voice' among others."[23]

Here I suggest that it is possible to transcend documentary methods by becoming more attuned to questions about the culture of politics.[24] Political and intellectual history can become open to cultural questions about the repertoires of resistance, the rituals of spoken words and speech genres in public gatherings, and the written transcripts and rhetorical strategies of the printed word.[25] With their focus on texts mainly as sources of evidence for narrativised histories of politics or social life, documentary and social historians have missed out on some of the more intriguing questions about language and verbal performances, which have their own narrative structures and strategies.

Rethinking South African political biography

What could this mean for rethinking political biography in South Africa? In the last 10 years or so, new approaches to life writing have begun to emerge that pay attention to institutions and their rules and codes, that open up issues of the political and the personal, and which reflect an experimental engagement between biographer and subject.[26] In the case of my research on the life history of Unity Movement leader Isaac Bangani Tabata (1909-1990), I utilised the above insights about biographic production to develop an understanding of the production and contestation of biographic narration. Indeed, what started off as an account of political history became a study of the cultural history of politics as well as the politics of historical production. What began as a biography of Tabata became a much broader encounter with the cultural politics of biography in the academy and the public domain, drawing where possible on those theoretical insights which might produce a much more nuanced study of biographic formation and contestation.[27]

---

23 Peter Burke, "History of Events and the Revival of Narrative," in *New Perspectives on Historical Writing*, ed. Peter Burke (Cambridge: Polity Press, 1991), 283-300.

24 See Lynn Hunt, *Politics, Culture and Class in the French Revolution* (Berkeley: University of California Press, 1984). For Southern African history, see Clifton Crais, *The Politics of Evil: Magic, State Power, and the Political Imagination in South Africa* (Cambridge: Cambridge University Press, 2002).

25 See Roger Chartier, *Cultural History: Between Practices and Representations*, trans. Lydia G. Cochrane (Oxford: Polity Press, 1988) for a discussion of these matters. See also Robert Darnton, "Intellectual and Cultural History," in *The Past Before Us: Contemporary Historical Writing in the United States*, ed. Michael Kammen (Ithaca: Cornell University Press, 1980), 327-354.

26 See, for example, Pregs Govender, *Love and Courage: A Story of Insubordination* (Johannesburg: Jacana 2007); Padraig O'Malley, *Shades of Difference: Mac Maharaj and the Struggle for South Africa* (New York: Viking, 2007); Raymond Suttner, *Inside Apartheid's Prison* (Johannesburg: Jacana, 2017). The latter was first published in 2001, and was republished under very different political conditions in 2017 with a new introduction and "contemporary reflections on life outside the ANC."

27 For a discussion of these issues, see Ciraj Rassool, "'Taking the Nation to School': I.B. Tabata and the Politics of Knowledge," in *Out of History: Re-imagining South African Pasts*, eds. Jung Ran Forte, Paolo Israel, and Leslie Witz (Pretoria: HSRC Press, 2017), 170-189.

From this vantage point, Tabata's life trajectory can be understood as having undergone a transition from biographic disavowal and a stress on collective leadership, to biographic narration under conditions of repression. This process culminated in the embrace of biography as an element of a politics of presidentialism, with Tabata's biography at the apex of a liberation movement constituted as a biographic order. In this transition, Tabata's biography became a means of projecting the movement in exile. While this transition from collectivity and reticence to individuation and biography was evident in photographic images,[28] it was Tabata's work of writing and authorship, characterised by a process of individuation, that constituted a biographic threshold. The most significant relationship through which Tabata became a writer and author was that with activist, author and literary critic Dora Taylor.[29]

This was also the relationship through which Tabata acquired a biography. Indeed, it can be argued that it was Dora Taylor who was the primary author of Tabata's biographic narrative. Tabata's complex relationship with Dora Taylor for 40 years, characterised by mutuality, devotion and desire, was one that unfolded in a borderland between the public and the private domains. This was a relationship that included assistance with political agitation through writing and epistolary engagement with and support of local activists, especially in the Eastern Cape. It also incorporated mutual cultural interests and the development and intensification of a love relationship. In return, Tabata supported Taylor's efforts at literary and historical writing, and assisted in attempts to have these published, although without success in the 1960s.[30]

What began as a working relationship of underground party members grew into a vital intellectual and emotional partnership that went through different phases in South Africa and overseas, and lasted until Taylor's death in England in 1976. As comrades and lovers, theirs was a relationship across South Africa's colour line, and between a black male political leader and a white female comrade, characteristics that marked multiple vectors of inequality. Yet in their interconnected comradeship and love relationship, their commitment to equality and mutuality also masked an unevenness in which public political commitments were the priority, and which relied upon a sense of duty and selflessness on Taylor's part. And it was through her devotion to the political cause and to Tabata himself that she produced the narrations of his biography. These biographic narrations were incorporated into the politics of presidentialism that came to mark the Unity Movement's struggle for national liberation in South Africa, conducted as it was from its exiled locations in Zambia, Tanzania, Botswana and Britain.

---

28 See Ciraj Rassool, "The Individual, Auto/biography and History in South Africa" (Ph.D diss., University of the Western Cape, 2004), 340-353.

29 Ciraj Rassool, "Writing, Authorship and I.B. Tabata's Biography: From Collective Leadership to Presidentialism," *Kronos* 34, no. 1 (November 2008), 181-214.

30 Ciraj Rassool, "Mutuality, Desire and Biographical Relations in a South African Liberation Movement," Fellow's Lecture presented at Morphomata Center for Advanced Studies in the Humanities, University of Cologne, 2 November 2015. Due largely to the efforts of her daughter, Sheila Belshaw, many of Dora Taylor's literary writings began to be published in the 2000s. See the following by Dora Taylor: *Kathie: A Novel* (Johannesburg: Penguin, 2008); *Rage of Life* (Johannesburg: Penguin, 2009); *Don't Tread on My Dreams: A Collection of Short Stories* (Johannesburg: Penguin, 2008).

Over the years, in South Africa and in exile, the records of all the agitation, mobilisation, organising, petitioning and fund raising were carefully managed by Taylor. As an archival collection, these records that entered the University of Cape Town from exile from 1989 came to constitute perhaps the most significant biographical tribute to Tabata that Taylor constructed. Largely the product of Taylor's sense of duty and service to the cause of the movement and to Tabata, these records came to constitute the foremost biographic ordering of Tabata's life. More than merely a chronological assemblage of the traces of Tabata's political career, this collection has borne the traces of a range of interventions, mediations and processes of production. And the primary form of mediation (and even authorship) that left its mark on almost every feature of this collection was the efforts of Dora Taylor. Subsequent interventions by other Unity Movement activists in Britain after her death in 1976 were not able to wipe away the primary mark of Dora Taylor, nor the extent to which the archival collection stands as a biography of Tabata and Taylor's relationship of intensity that unfolded and developed across national borders.[31]

The rise of presidentialism in the Unity Movement in the 1960s needs to be understood in the context of relations of paternalism and patronage that characterised the movement, notwithstanding the assertion of collective leadership. The movement, as it emerged in the 1940s and developed in the 1950s, was in some ways marked by a family structure, but in a more significant way took on the features of a school. While schools have been enabling institutions, they have also been institutions of discipline and constraint. This certainly was the case with the Unity Movement, whose forums of knowledge formation were also structures of person formation. In this educational structure characterised by gendered relationships of paternalism and patronage, Tabata's biography of male leadership of a national liberation movement was narrated as historical lesson, and deployed as a model to be followed in the development of the disciplined, male cadre.[32]

Yet, the contests and challenges over I.B. Tabata's leadership that erupted in the movement in South Africa in the 1950s and in Lusaka in the 1960s emerged out of the ambiguities and contradictions of paternalism and patronage. Internal dissent gave rise to contests over Tabata's biography, which had become a form of authority, and turned into lessons of leadership. This biographic order was challenged for the modes of authoritarianism and deception it represented. At Tabata's funeral, secular eulogies of his life were made to accommodate Christian narrations, as a severely weakened political movement was unable to contain the narrative boundaries of Tabata's biography.

This biographic contestation occurred within an exiled liberation movement that was initially critical of the terms of nationalist mobilisation, as expressed through its original disavowal of biography. Under conditions of exile and in the transnational setting of Lusaka, temporary home to southern African liberation movements, where the Unity Movement needed to vouch for itself as a representative

31 Idem.

32 Ciraj Rassool, "National Longing, Political Belonging and the Politics of Affect in a South African Liberation Movement," Paper presented to the Love and Revolution III Conference, Nehru Memorial Museum and Library, New Delhi, India, 20-22 January 2012.

political structure of the nation, the organisational model that was presented was marked by a politics of presidentialism. In this model, a presidential biography of I.B. Tabata, as constructed through Dora Taylor's life writing efforts, was propagated and deployed within the movement itself. However, this presidential biography was also challenged by younger members of the movement as evidence of bureaucratic authority and nationalist deviation.[33]

A perspective on biography as production, mobilisation and contestation enables us to understand how biographic politics were incorporated into imaginaries of the nation and the person, with the liberation movement constituted as a biographic order. With this approach, life writing can become more complex with a perspective that is simultaneously attuned to the transnational as well as relations of intimacy. And with the attainment of democracy, and the transformation of the formerly exiled liberation movement into the governing party, in the case of the African National Congress, it has also been possible to understand how resistance lives of repression, imprisonment and exile across borders became narrated into extended national stories of reconciliation and triumph. Such national narratives also saw masculinist life writing about leadership and greatness incorporated into a new national memorial complex, where the transnational became incorporated into the grand narrative of the nation.[34] Yet, beyond epic accounts of the 'long walk to freedom,'[35] the framework of biographic production and contestation has also revealed how it might be possible to rethink biography itself beyond the gendered frames of nationalist narration and triumphal celebration.

Biography and rehumanisation

Another domain of biographic contestation has involved the assertion of personhood and the construction of a biographic narrative, when these had been denied through deep, long-term processes of dehumanisation and genericisation. Here, biographic narration was marshalled as a decolonial strategy in the case of Khoesan persons whose corpses and skeletons had been illegally disinterred from their graves and thereafter, traded to museums and scientists. The stolen dead had been incorporated into the collections of natural history and anthropology museums as objects of race, and as examples of living fossils. This was biography as epistemic intervention in reversing long-term processes of typology, depersonalisation, and colonial objectification through physical anthropology and racial science.

This biographic work seeks to tell the story of Klaas and Trooi Pienaar whose bodies had been disinterred from their graves at Pienaarsputs near Gamopedi in the Kuruman district of the Northern Cape in 1908. The Pienaars had lived lives of dispersal, migrancy and agricultural labour in the Trans-/Garieb transfrontier landscape between German South West Africa and the northern Cape, amidst the upheavals of colonial violence and social disruption around the turn of the

33 Idem.

34 Ciraj Rassool, "Human Remains, the Disciplines of the Dead, and the South African Memorial Complex," in *The Politics of Heritage in Africa: Economies, Histories,and Infrastructures*, eds. Derek R. Peterson, Kodzo Gavua, and Ciraj Rassool (New York: Cambridge University Press, 2015), 133-156.

35 Nelson Mandela, *Long Walk to Freedom: The Autobiography of Nelson Mandela* (Boston/London: Little Brown, 1994).

20th century. Their dead bodies were transferred across national and continental boundaries to scientific collecting institutions in Vienna, where they were turned into museum objects, the subject of anatomical research into racial and gendered difference. Their corpses were eventually macerated five decades later after they were deemed to have deteriorated.

In the early 2010s, more than a century after their journeys across transnational and transcontinental locations, the Pienaars' remains became the subject of restitution and repatriation negotiations between the governments of South Africa and Austria. These negotiations occurred at the start of a decade during which museums, colonial history and the provenance of collections began to be rethought, as well as the future of the racialised body in museum collections.[36] These processes were increasingly connected to efforts to consider what it might mean for museums to be decolonised. The bodies of Klaas and Trooi Pienaar eventually took their final transnational journey and were repatriated to South Africa as the remains of persons, not objects. Klaas and Trooi Pienaar were reburied at Kuruman as persons, a status denied to them in life and at the time of their death, as well as in the Austrian museum lives of their dead bodies. In addition, the Pienaars were accorded the status of post-apartheid citizens, and deployed as agents of national social cohesion.[37]

This biographical research has also proceeded from the ways biography has been extended to understanding the lives of objects, such as museum and archival collections,[38] except that the remains of the Pienaars experienced processes of genericisation, typology and depersonalisation. Denied the status of rights-bearing persons in life, and having lived labouring and racialised lives that dehumanised them, this dehumanisation was perpetuated after their deaths and burial, when their dead bodies acquired the status of museum objects, the remains of supposed racial and gender difference. It was not until research on their illegal disinterment generated knowledge of their lives, that it was possible to make the argument for the return of their remains to take place through a heretofore unchartered method. The South African claimants demanded that the return of the remains of Klaas and Trooi Pienaar be framed not only as one of 'repatriation' but also as one of 'rehumanisation' notwithstanding initial unwillingness of the Austrian authorities, who asserted that this would not be possible under European law. In the end, this method of return that necessitated funereal ceremonies, mourning events and the use of caskets succeeded because of research on their original dates and places of

---

36 Viv Golding and Wayne Modest, eds., *Museums and Communities: Curators, Collections and Collaboration* (London: Bloomsbury, 2013); Larissa Förster, Iris Edenheiser, Sarah Fründt, and Heike Hartmann, eds., *Provenienzforschung zu Ethnologischen Sammlungen der Kolonialzeit: Positionen in der Aktuellen Debatte.* E-book, published on the e-doc-server of Humboldt-Universität zu Berlin (https://edoc.hu-berlin.de/handle/18452/19769).

37 Martin Legassick and Ciraj Rassool, *Skeletons in the Cupboard: South African Museums and the Trade in Human Remains, 1907-1917* (Cape Town: Iziko Museums of South Africa, 2015 [2000]); Ciraj Rassool, "Re-storing the Skeletons of Empire: Return, Reburial and Rehumanisation in Southern Africa," *Journal of Southern African Studies* 41, no. 3 (June 2015): 653-670.

38 John Randolph, "On the Biography of the Bakunin Family Archive," in *Archive Stories: Facts, Fictions, and the Writing of History*, ed. Antoinette Burton (Durham, N.C: Duke University Press, 2005), 209-231.

death, resulting in a landmark method of repatriation and reburial close to the original site of death and burial.[39]

It was the record of a 1909 police enquiry that took place into these illegal collecting activities that generated knowledge about the names, working lives, and deaths of Klaas and Trooi Pienaar, about their burials and the illegal disinterment of their bodies. The policing of this export trade in Khoesan corpses and skeletons occurred as part of the assertion by the newly emerging white South African settler nation of its own scientific capacity, a process described as the 'South Africanisation of science.'[40] These were the circumstances that led to the passing of the Bushman Relics Act in 1911, South Africa's first law on heritage, that sought to prohibit the export of rock art as well as Khoesan human remains. South African museums competed with scientists in Europe for access to the bushman body as museumised object of racial research. Notwithstanding the categorisation of the remains of the Pienaars as racialised objects and fossils, the archival evidence of the Pienaars' lives contained in the police enquiry was able to generate elements of a biographical narrative of their lives. The repatriation process was able to effect a transformation from racialised museum objects that had been illegally exported to named persons.

This biographic research was interested in how it might be possible to think about personhood and biography amid long histories of subjection, objectification and racial research and the depersonalising, genericising and typologising forms of representation that museum processes gave rise to. It has also needed to consider these matters outside the paradigms of preservation, salvation and cultural rescue, which remain the main tropes of Khoesan studies in Southern Africa, that tend to perpetuate discourses of extinction and disappearance and the concept of living fossils, renamed as first people.[41] In addition to colonial histories, there are also whole literatures on the 'political lives of dead bodies' and the emotive materiality and affective presence of bones that need to be considered.[42]

Research on the life narratives of Klaas and Trooi Pienaar and the lives of their dead bodies has entailed necessary consultation processes with local communities in the Northern Cape on how they had been remembered across generations, and on the social effects of grave robbery more than a century ago. It has also canvassed discussions and debates about how to give effect to 'rehumanisation' through ritual and ceremony. This research involved the search for the original site of burial of the Pienaars as well as considerations on the appropriate site for their reburial. In being present at the official funeral and reburial of the Pienaars,

39 Rassool, "Re-storing the Skeletons of Empire," 653-670.

40 Saul Dubow, "Human Origins, Race Typology and the other Raymond Dart," *African Studies* 55, no. 1 (1996): 1-30; Ciraj Rassool and Patricia Hayes, "Science and the Spectacle: /Khanako's South Africa 1936-1937," in *Deep Histories: Gender and Colonialism in Southern Africa*, eds. Wendy Woodward, Patricia Hayes, and Gary Minkley (Amsterdam: Rodopi, 2002), 117-161.

41 Ciraj Rassool, "Ethnography and Indigeneity in Post-apartheid South Africa: Continuities and Contestations of Culture," in *Popular Snapshots and Tracks to the Past: Cape Town, Nairobi, Lubumbashi*, eds. Danielle de Lame and Ciraj Rassool (Tervuren: Royal Museum of Central Africa, 2010), 261-276; Ciraj Rassool, "Biography and the Dead of Anthropology," Fellow's Lecture presented at Morphomata Center for Advanced Studies in the Humanities, University of Cologne, 25 April 2016.

42 Katherine Verdery, *Political Lives of Dead Bodies: Reburial and Postsocialist Change* (New York: Columbia University Press, 1999).

it was important to think about the relationship between their dead bodies and the modern memorial complex in South Africa. While a major feature of this complex has been biographic, with the inscription of life narratives of the heroic leaders into centralised public memorials, a key element has entailed the recognition of the 'missing person' as an important vector of social reconstruction. And many of the cases of missing persons tended to fall outside the discursive terms of heroic nationalist narration.[43]

As racialised subjects of physical anthropology in life, excluded even from emerging forms of native administration, their existence as subjects across multiple colonialisms in a transfrontier region had placed them outside the bounds of the nation through a denial of coevalness. While the Pienaars had been missing and missed for more than a century, the entire process of their repatriation, from research, identification, negotiations, return and reburial ensured that they were inscribed with personhood and accorded the dignity of biographic narration. The terms of these narratives of life exceeded the boundaries of the nation, in their transfrontier southern African lives, in their colonial exclusion from personhood and citizenship, and in the transnational and trans-continental lives of their stolen dead bodies. The restitution and repatriation of Klaas and Trooi Pienaar also turned them into important figures in the growing transnational field of repatriation and the decolonisation of museums. On their return, the belated inclusion of Klaas and Trooi Pienaar into the national citizenry more than a century after their deaths represented not merely a point of closure for a transfrontier and transnational history, but also a reconceptualisation of the meaning of citizenship and perhaps even the idea of the nation itself.

Bibliography

Appiah, Kwame Anthony. "Cosmopolitan Patriots." *Critical Inquiry* 23 (Spring 1997).

Bourdieu, Pierre. "The Biographical Illusion." *Working Papers and Proceedings of the Center for Psychosocial Studies*, no. 14, 1-7. Translated by Yves Winkin and Wendy Leeds-Hurwitz. Chicago, Center for Psychosocial Studies, 1987.

Breckenridge, Keith. *Biometric State: The Global Politics of Identification and Surveillance in South Africa, 1850 to the Present.* New York: Cambridge University Press, 2014.

Burke, Peter. "History of Events and the Revival of Narrative." In *New Perspectives on Historical Writing*, edited by Peter Burke, 283-300. Cambridge: Polity Press, 1991.

Chartier, Roger. *Cultural History: Between Practices and Representations.* Translated by Lydia G. Cochrane. Oxford: Polity Press, 1988.

Clingman, Stephen. "Biography and Representation: Some Analogies from Fiction." History Workshop Conference, University of the Witwatersrand, February 1987.

Cohen, David William. *The Combing of History.* Chicago: University of Chicago Press, 1994.

43 Nicky Rousseau, "Identification, Politics, Disciplines: Missing Persons and Colonial Skeletons in South Africa," in *Human Remains and Identification: Mass Violence, Genocide, and the 'Forensic Turn,'* eds. Élisabeth Anstett and Jean-Marc Dreyfus (Manchester: Manchester University Press, 2015), 175-202.

Cohen, David William. "Further Thoughts on the Production of History." In *Between History and Histories: The Making of Silences and Commemorations*, edited by Gerald Sider and Gavin Smith, 300-310. Toronto: University of Toronto Press, 1997.

Crais, Clifton. *The Politics of Evil: Magic, State Power, and the Political Imagination in South Africa*. Cambridge: Cambridge University Press, 2002.

Crapanzano, Vincent. "'Self'-Centering Narratives." In *Natural Histories of Discourse*, edited by Michael Silverstein and Greg Urban, 106-127. Chicago, University of Chicago Press, 1996.

Darnton, Robert. "Intellectual and Cultural History." In *The Past Before Us: Contemporary Historical Writing in the United States*, edited by Michael Kammen, 327-354. Ithaca: Cornell University Press, 1980.

Denzin, Norman K. *Interpretive Biography*. Newbury Park, CA: Sage, 1989.

Dhupelia-Mesthrie, Uma. "The Form, the Permit and the Photograph: An Archive of Mobility between South Africa and India." *Journal of African and Asian Studies* 46, no. 6 (September 2011): 650-662.

Dubow, Saul. "Human Origins, Race Typology and the other Raymond Dart." *African Studies* 55, no. 1 (1996): 1-30.

Evans, Mary. "Masculine and Feminine Biography." In *Imitating Art: Essays in Biography*, edited by David Ellis, 109-115. London: Pluto Press, 1993.

Ferrarotti, Franco. "On the Autonomy of the Biographical Method." In *Biography and Society: The Life History Approach in the Social Sciences*, edited by Daniel Bertaux, 19-27. Beverley Hills: Sage, 1981.

Förster, Larissa, Iris Edenheiser, Sarah Fründt, and Heike Hartmann, eds. *Provenienzforschung zu ethnologischen Sammlungen der Kolonialzeit: Positionen in der aktuellen Debatte.* E-book, published on the e-doc-server of Humboldt-Universität zu Berlin (https://edoc.hu-berlin.de/handle/18452/19769).

Golding, Viv, and Wayne Modest, eds. *Museums and Communities: Curators, Collections and Collaboration*. London: Bloomsbury, 2013.

Govender, Pregs. *Love and Courage: A Story of Insubordination*. Johannesburg: Jacana 2007.

Hunt, Lynn. *Politics, Culture and Class in the French Revolution*. Berkeley: University of California Press, 1984.

Kratz, Corinne A. "Forging Unions and Negotiating Ambivalence: Personhood and Complex Agency in Okiek Marriage Arrangement." In *African Philosophy as Cultural Inquiry*, edited by Ivan Karp and D.A. Masolo, 136-172. Bloomington: Indiana University Press, 2000.

Legassick, Martin, and Ciraj Rassool. *Skeletons in the Cupboard: South African Museums and the Trade in Human Remains, 1907-1917*. Cape Town: Iziko Museums of South Africa, 2015 [2000].

Mandela, Nelson. *Long Walk to Freedom: The Autobiography of Nelson Mandela*. Boston/London: Little Brown, 1994.

Marcus, Laura. *Auto/biographical Discourses: Theory, Criticism, Practice*. Manchester: Manchester University Press, 1994.

Ochberg, Richard L. "Life Stories and Storied Lives." In *Exploring Identity and Gender: The Narrative Study of Lives: Volume 2*, edited by Amia Lieblich and Ruthellen Josselson, 113-144. London: Sage, 1994.

Olney, James. *Metaphors of Self: The Meaning of Autobiography*. Princeton: Princeton University Press, 1972.

O'Malley, Padraig. *Shades of Difference: Mac Maharaj and the Struggle for South Africa*. New York: Viking, 2007.

Randolph, John. "On the Biography of the Bakunin Family Archive." In *Archive Stories: Facts, Fictions and the Writing of History*, edited by Antoinette Burton, 209-231. Durham, N.C: Duke University Press, 2005.

Rassool, Ciraj. "Biography and the Dead of Anthropology." Fellow's Lecture presented at Morphomata Center for Advanced Studies in the Humanities. University of Cologne, 25 April 2016.

Rassool, Ciraj. "Ethnography and Indigeneity in Post-apartheid South Africa: Continuities and Contestations of Culture." In *Popular Snapshots and Tracks to the Past: Cape Town, Nairobi, Lubumbashi*, edited by Danielle de Lame and Ciraj Rassool, 261-276. Tervuren: Royal Museum of Central Africa, 2010.

Rassool, Ciraj. "Human Remains, the Disciplines of the Dead, and the South African Memorial Complex." In *The Politics of Heritage in Africa: Economies, Histories, and Infrastructures*, edited by Derek Peterson, Kodzo Gavua and Ciraj Rassool, 133-156. New York: Cambridge University Press, 2015.

Rassool, Ciraj. "Mutuality, Desire and Biographical Relations in a South African Liberation Movement." Fellow's Lecture presented at Morphomata Center for Advanced Studies in the Humanities, University of Cologne, 2 November 2015.

Rassool, Ciraj. "National Longing, Political Belonging and the Politics of Affect in a South African Liberation Movement." Paper presented to the Love and Revolution III Conference, Nehru Memorial Museum and Library, New Delhi, India, 20-22 January 2012.

Rassool, Ciraj. "Re-storing the Skeletons of Empire: Return, Reburial and Rehumanisation in Southern Africa." *Journal of Southern African Studies* 41, no. 3 (June 2015): 653-670.

Rassool, Ciraj. "'Taking the Nation to School': I.B. Tabata and the Politics of Knowledge." In *Out of History: Re-imagining South African Pasts*, edited by Jung Ran Forte, Paolo Israel, and Leslie Witz, 170-189. Pretoria: HSRC Press, 2017.

Rassool, Ciraj. "The Individual, Auto/biography and History in South Africa." PhD diss., University of the Western Cape, 2004.

Rassool, Ciraj. "Writing, Authorship and I.B. Tabata's Biography: From Collective Leadership to Presidentialism." *Kronos* 34 (November 2008): 181-214.

Rassool, Ciraj, and Patricia Hayes. "Science and the Spectacle: /Khanako's South Africa 1936-1937." In *Deep Histories: Gender and Colonialism in Southern Africa*, edited by Wendy Woodward, Patricia Hayes and Gary Minkley, 117-161. Amsterdam: Rodopi, 2002.

Ricoeur, Paul. "Life in Quest of Narrative." In *On Paul Ricoeur: Narrative and Interpretation*, edited by David Wood, 20-33. London: Routledge, 1991.

Rousseau, Nicky. "Identification, Politics, Disciplines: Missing Persons and Colonial Skeletons in South Africa." In *Human Remains and Identification: Mass Violence, Genocide, and the 'Forensic Turn,'* edited by Élisabeth Anstett and Jean-Marc Dreyfus, 133-156. Manchester: Manchester University Press, 2015.

Suttner, Raymond. *Inside Apartheid's Prison*. Johannesburg: Jacana, 2017.

Svensson, Birgitta. "Lifetimes – Life History and Life Story: Biographies of Modern Swedish Intellectuals." *Ethnologia Scandinavica* 25 (1995): 25-42.

Svensson, Birgitta. "The Power of Biography: Criminal Policy, Prison Life, and the Formation of Criminal Identities in the Swedish Welfare State." In *Autoethnography: Rewriting the Self and the Social*, edited Deborah Reed-Danahay, 71-106. Washington: Berg Publishers, 1997.

Taylor, Dora. *Kathie: A Novel*. Johannesburg: Penguin, 2008.

Taylor, Dora. *Rage of Life*. Johannesburg: Penguin, 2009.

Taylor, Dora. *Don't Tread on My Dreams: A Collection of Short Stories*. Johannesburg: Penguin, 2008.

Thompson, Paul. "Life Histories and the Analysis of Social Change." In *Biography and Society: The Life History Approach in the Social Sciences*, edited by Daniel Bertaux, 289-306. Beverly Hills, CA: Sage, 1981.

Verdery, Katherine. *Political Lives of Dead Bodies: Reburial and Postsocialist Change*. New York: Columbia University Press, 1999.

Williams, Raymond. *Marxism and Literature*. Oxford: Oxford University Press, 1977.

Wood, David. "Introduction: Interpreting Narrative." In *On Paul Ricoeur: Narrative and Interpretation*, edited by David Wood. London: Routledge, 1991.

Ordinary lives: teaching history with life narratives in transnational perspective

Nancy Mykoff

Introduction

It is the beginning of a new semester and the first day of the *History of Women and Gender* class.[1] I teach the course at an international College in the Netherlands, with Susan Ware's *Modern American Women: A Documentary History,*[2] and supplement the text with studies of women's lives and constructions of gender globally. They include Gwyn Kirk and Margo Okazawa-Rey's, *Women's Lives: Multicultural Perspectives* and Rhacel Salazar Parrenas, *Servants of Globalization: Women, Migration and Domestic Work.*[3] The approach invites my primarily Dutch students to think about the United States and the world (i.e., its relationships with different cultures); and the United States in the world (i.e., as a participant in global trends and developments). As the students enter the classroom, I write four questions on the board. What is your name? Where are you from? What are your interests? Why are you taking this course? When they settle in I explain that during the next few hours they will introduce each other to the class. I ask them to turn to their neighbour and address the questions written on the board, listen closely, dig deeply, take notes, and reflect on the narrative they record. The exercise sets the stage for the semester.[4]

The following chapter draws from my approach to the course. It argues that teaching American history with primary materials, like contemporary literature, first person narratives, photographs and film, renders the past rich, recognizable and relevant. The sources include visual autobiographies of gender refugees that record local and global experiences of people fleeing persecution because of their sexual identification. Hailing from different nation-states, their experiences are

---

1 My deep gratitude to Dario Fazzi, Saverio Giovacchini, and Faren Siminoff for their essential insights.

2 History of Women and Gender (hereafter, HOWAG), American History, University College Roosevelt of Utrecht University, 2017. The course is part of the American Studies Minor. Susan Ware, ed., *Modern American Women: A Documentary History*, 2nd ed. (New York: McGraw Hill, 2002).

3 Rhacel Salazar Parrenas, *Servants of Globalization: Women, Migration and Domestic Work* (Stanford: Stanford University Press, 2001); Gwyn Kirk and Margo Okazawa-Rey, *Women's Lives: Multicultural Perspectives* 4th edition (New York: McGraw-Hill, 2007).

4 My class, like the college itself, is international. Most have not studied American history. If they have, the education focused narrowly on a few 'important' dates.

nevertheless strikingly similar. For example, stories of desperate crossings told by gay, lesbian, bisexual, transgender and other nonconforming people, often begin with forced exile at home. Crossing borders requires masking identity. [5] Our study of their moving narratives, along with the memoirs, letters, fiction and photographs at the heart of the class and this chapter, assumes ordinary citizens as, "relevant historical actors in their own right."

Seminal works in transnational history help us understand what we read, hear, and witness. Examples are Akira Iriye's, *Global and Transnational History: The Past, Present and Future* and Emily Rosenberg's *Transnational Currents in a Shrinking World (1870-1945)*. The transnational approach looks at routes as well as roots, by charting the flow of ideas, goods and people. It also calls for a comparative framework that explores shared humanity between narrator and reader across nations and generations.[6] The result is a transcultural vantage point particularly relevant given the cross-cultural encounters that define my students' daily lives. Many are members of diasporic student communities. All are members of 'networked publics,' such as Facebook and Twitter, that shape politics and culture, as well as moral and ethical landscapes. Each engages with transnational flows of information that pave the way for global resistance to, and participation in, the democratic process.[7] Regardless of engagement, they bear witnesses to world-wide developments unbound by political states, like climate change, a global pandemic and gender based violence. These experiences deeply affect their sense of self, ideas about the 'other,' interpersonal and communal relationships, and mutual (mis) understanding.

A transnational approach to the past fosters awareness of living within a global present. It also challenges the fixed nation-state frame that often defines the study of North American history which, as historian Ian Tyrrell notes, has always been, "deeply connected to the world, its peoples and its traditions," and is itself transnational.[8] The chapter that follows shows, for instance, how a primary source based, transnational perspective gainfully questions the national focus often used in teaching the immigrant experience. Rather than focusing on the immigrant's impact on the sending and receiving national societies, it focuses on the border-crossing itself and investigates, among others, the hopes and fears, dreams and concerns, shared by the different people crossing national borders at the point of departure, during the journey, and after arrival.[9]

Our critical analyses of their stories of life draw from seminal works in the field of life writing. These include Miriam Fuchs and Craig Howes, *Teaching Life Writing Texts* and Sidonie Smith and Julia Watson's *Life Writing in the Long Run:*

---

5 Andreas Hackl, "Key Figure of Mobility," *The Exile Journal of Anthropology* 25 no.1 (February 2017), 56-68; Carlos Motta, *Crossings* (Amsterdam: Stedelijk Museum, 16 September – 21 January 2018).

6 "AHR Conversation: On Transnational History, with C.A.Bayley, Sven Beckert, Matthew Connely, Isabel Hofmeyer, Wendy Kozol, and Patricia Seed," *American Historical Review* 111, no.5 (2006): 1450.

7 Examples are 'fake news' on the one hand and the Woman's March on the other. Andrew Chadwick, "Donald Trump, the 2016 Presidential Campaign and the Intensification of the Hybrid Media Systems," Keynote for the Association of Internet Researchers (University of Tartu, Estonia: 18-21 October 2017), retrieved from http://www.uttv.ee/naita?id=26302#.

8 Ian Tyrrell, *Transnational Nation: United States History in Global Perspective Since 1789* (Basingstoke: Palgrave Macmillan, 2007), 1.

9 Seed, "AHR Conversation," 1443.

Autobiography Studies Reader. Challenging students' assumption that first person narratives represent "what really happened," these works raise questions about the ways authors often craft stories to serve political and social agendas.[10] Amongst them are: how does the author's present shape his or her interpretations, and thus our understanding, of the past? How does the intended audience inform the text itself? What gets changed in translation from one language to another and why? How, in the case of visual narratives, do colour, hue and point of view, present the illusion of 'life as lived' to support the writer's goals?[11]

Whilst the questioning hones critical thinking skills, the first-person narratives develop understanding of individuals beyond, as well as within, the North American landscape. They do this, in part, by closing gaps between 'self' and 'other' that renders historical actors 'similar' if not 'same.' This makes it possible for international students to imagine the women, men and children that lived in the distant past and close to the present, within a variety of national and social contexts.

The class interprets *and* crafts narratives throughout the term. Students conduct open interviews of ordinary people across the globe;[12] write reflections on readings and research; and compose weekly journals that explore the ways course themes and topics play out in their daily lives. The act of reflecting helps them identify with people that practiced similar forms of life writing. It also provides a space to formulate thoughts, clarify ideas, raise questions, and explore historical significance. "I find it intriguing," writes a student about Civil Rights, "how a seemingly insignificant act such as saying no when someone asks you to give up your seat in a bus, can have such a big impact." The personal, he concludes, *is* political.[13]

Our study of the ways that political developments shape personal lives begins in 19th century North America, with the forging of a nation in the aftermath of civil war. Notions of crime, punishment and citizenship were carved out of racialised systems of justice and entitlement that, in turn, were linked to gender, ethnicity and religion. They were expressed in state, federal, and supreme court legislation, like the notorious Black Codes that controlled and brutalised black lives; the 1882 Chinese exclusion Act, banning an entire class of immigrants on the basis of their race and national origin; and Plessy v. Ferguson (1896), enshrining the doctrine of separate but equal that divided the nation for half of a century. These judgements laid the foundation for the 20th century. The course examines their significance from the perspective of ordinary people and within a transnational perspective. On the

10 Miriam Fuchs and Craig Howes, eds., *Teaching Life Writing Texts* (New York: The Modern Language Association of America, 2008); Sidonie Smith and Julia Watson, eds., *Women, Autobiography, Theory: A Reader* (Wisconsin: University of Wisconsin Press, 1998); Sidonie Smith and Julia Watson, eds., *Life Writing in the Long Run: A Smith & Watson Autobiography Studies Reader* (Michigan: Michigan Publishing, 2016); Julie Rak, *Boom! Manufacturing Memoir for the Popular Market* (Ontario, Canada: Wilfrid Laurier University Press, 2013).

11 Philippe Lejeune, "The Autobiographical Pact," in *The Routledge Auto/Biography Studies Reader*, eds. Ricia Anne Chansky and Emily Hipchen (New York: Routledge, 2016), 34-48; Rak, *Boom!*; Carolyn Kay Steedman, "Stories," in *Women, Autobiography, Theory*, eds. Smith and Watson, 243-254; Roger J. Porter, "Introduction to World Narrative," in *Teaching Life Writing Texts*, eds. Fuchs and Howes, 23-29.

12 International interviews take place via Skype.

13 My approach to learning through writing is informed by John Bean's *Engaging Ideas: The Professor's Guide to Integrating Writing, Critical Thinking and Active Learning in the Classroom*, 2nd ed. (San Francisco: Jossey-Bass, 2011). In-class reflection, HOWAG (30 October 2017).

one hand, the approach reveals human histories from 'the bottom up,' instead of the more common 'top down' perspective that focuses on famous leaders. On the other hand, students see connections with post-civil war nation-states across the globe.

Testimony

Our starting point is 1865. The context is the violent freedom that followed the end of slavery. The focus is on racism and misogyny. Readings include primary documents, like constitutional amendments and ex-slave narratives, on the many meanings of freedom. The Thirteenth Amendment to the United States Constitution is an example of the former. It "abolished slavery and involuntary servitude, except as punishment for a crime."[14] Students are generally 'ok' with the second clause because they connect crime with punishment and do not question the historical construction of either.

The questioning begins when they read about the wide range of behaviours defined 'criminal' by the black codes, a series of discriminatory state laws enacted in 1865 and 1866. Amongst them was not having a job. This was called 'vagrancy.' Another was quitting work. The reasons varied. Severe consequences for these criminal acts, like forced labor and imprisonment, are read in concurrence with unpunished acts of crime like rape, torture and murder, suffered by former slaves.[15]

Testimony made by Rhode Ann Childs to the Freedmen's Bureau in Griffin Georgia, dated 25 September 1866, provides a sense of the suffering. Childs describes how she "was more dead than alive" after a brutal beating and rape by eight members of the Ku Klux Klan. "One of the men stood upon my breast," testified Childs, "while two others took hold of my feet and stretched my limbs as far apart as they could, while the man Standing upon my breast applied the Strap to my private parts until fatigued into stopping . . . ." When they were finished with Rhode Ann, they "seized [her] two daughters and beat them." The violence, according to a report made by a congressional committee on, "the Condition of Affairs in the Late Insurrectionary States," was not unique.[16]

Referred to as 'resistance literature' by literary scholar Caren Kaplan, testimonials like Rhode Ann Childs' foster empathy and a sense of solidarity between speaker and reader. They forge the connections by rendering historical scenes vivid.[17] The vividness reflects in journal entries stating that students, "felt like they were there," and were "shocked" by what they had read. They share their collective confusion about the testimonies of abuse during the class discussion. Most had believed that a state of peace defined the end of war. Some wonder if freedom was worse than slavery because there was no master to "protect" black lives. The class passionately debates

---

14 13th Amendment of the U.S. Constitution: Abolition of Slavery (1865), accessed 18 December 2017, https://www.ourdocuments.gov/doc.php?flash=false&doc=40.

15 Tera W. Hunter, "Reconstruction and the Meanings of Freedom," cited in Linda K. Kerber and Jane Sherron De Hart, eds., *Women's America: Refocusing the Past* 6th edition (Oxford: Oxford University Press, 2003), 235-236; 239.

16 Rhode Ann Childs, "I was more dead than alive," excerpted from *Freedom: A Documentary History of Emancipation, 1861-1876*, eds. Ira Berlin, Joseph P. Reidy, and Leslie S. Rowland (Cambridge, MA: Cambridge University Press, 1882), 807; cited in Kerber and De Hart, eds., *Women's America*, 234-235.

17 Caren Kaplan, "Resisting Autobiography: Out-Law Genres and Transnational Feminist Subjects," in *Women, Autobiography, Theory*, eds. Smith and Watson, 210.

the question. The lesson that follows heightens awareness of the ways that conflict defines peace in post war societies, throughout history and across the globe.

Non-Western testimonials, in the form of graphic memoir, support the conclusion. Our critical read of the genre helps the students also develop visual and verbal interpretative skills that promote cross cultural dialogue and understanding.[18] Commenting on the genre itself, cultural historian John Lamothe argues that graphic narratives, "speak truths that could otherwise not be spoken," and relate experience in an immediate way.[19] Illustrations convey painful moments. Silences, images without text, promote reader reflection. Both render the foreign familiar. Both foster a sense of 'being there.' Marjane Satrapi's *Complete Persepolis* illustrates how. On the one hand, the memoir spotlights violence between civilians and the state. On the other hand, it brings foreign life within the context of revolutionary change close to home. *Persepolis* engages readers with text and illustration that simplify and amplify a young girl's life in revolutionary Iran. For instance, the reader bears witness to the fate of audiences in a local cinema featuring Western films. The movie house was set on fire. Satrapi writes that, "the doors had been locked from the outside [and] the police stood guard. They forbade people [from rescuing] those locked in the theater."[20] The simple drawings accompanying the short text picture soldiers blocking entry into the burning building, people trying desperately to help, and 400 souls as they drift out of their bodies. The images haunt.[21]

While the violence and suffering shock, Satrapi's coming of age story resonates. Students identify with the protagonist as she grows from a child into a teenager; and from a teenager into a woman. They recall their younger selves in scenes of parental defiance. They contrast their 'easy' lives with the suffering that defines Marjane's teenaged years. They recognise her struggles with sexuality, friendship and love, and empathize with her sense of 'statelessness' *and* allegiance that takes root whilst living in Austria, blossoms after returning to Iran, and results in a questioning of citizenship and 'home.' On the one hand, movement across national borders defines Satrapi's young life and supports the consensus among scholars that motion is at the heart of transnationalism. On the other hand, experiences of physical and emotional rootedness within the different nations, and at the heart of her struggles with citizenship, support Ellen Fleischmann's compelling argument that transnationalism is also about bonds.[22] More than a sense of obligations and rights tied to a state, citizenship is a complex and central part of identity that evolves over and with time.[23]

---

18 Gillian Whitlock, "Autographics: The Seeing 'I' of the Comics," *Modern Fiction Studies* 52, no. 4 (2006): 965-979; Rak, *Boom!*, 157-206. See also Julia Watson, "Parsua Bashi's *Nylon Road*: The Visual Dialogics of Witnessing in Iranian Women's Graphic Memoir (Watson 2016)," in *Life Writing in the Long Run*, eds. Smith and Watson, 679-730.

19 Lamothe referencing Edward Said in John Lamothe, "Speaking Silently: Comics' 'Silent Narratives' as Immersive Experience," *Studies in Popular Culture* (Spring 2019), 69-93.

20 Marjane Satrapi, *The Complete Persepolis: A Story of Childhood* (New York: Pantheon Books Inc., 2004), 14-15.

21 Wendy Kozol addresses this lack of belonging in "AHR Conversation: On Transnational History," 1441-1464.

22 Ellen Fleischmann, "'I Only Wish I had a Home on This Globe': Transnational Biography and Dr. Mary Eddy," *Journal of Women's History* 21, no.3 (2009): 108-130.

23 Rak, *Boom!*, 155.

In the final pages of the graphic memoir, Marjane Satrapi returns to Europe in pursuit of national belonging. Whilst her journey underscores the identity struggles that define transnational life, it also offers the promise of a new beginning. The hopeful conclusion appeals to European and American sensibilities. The title, cover and stories that unfold within do the same. The subtitle of the American edition is: *A Story of Childhood.* The cover pictures a child sitting on a couch in the center of her family. Throughout the memoir they share love and suffer loss. Writing from a post-911 traumatic present, positioning *Persepolis* as a story of childhood and detailing shared humanity, serve Marjane Satrapi's political agenda. It effectively counters perceptions of the 'evil Islamic other,' with ordinary human beings that are 'just like (an American) us.'[24]

Photography, letters, fiction

The class returns to turn-of-the-century North America, and continues its exploration of migration, by focusing on immigrant women and girls. Themes of continuity and change, and conflict and citizenship, repeat. Most had memorised seminal legislation in earlier history classes, like the 1882 Chinese Exclusion Act, and the 1924 Immigration Act that restricted Southern and Eastern European immigration. According to their journals, however, they had not envisioned the migrants as individual people.[25]

Many see them for the first time through the eyes of Jacob Riis in photographs like "In the home of an Italian rag-picker, Jersey Street, 1894"[26] taken in the dark of night. All are struck by the woman's expression. They read despair and hopelessness in her gaze into nothingness. They are taken aback by the bare room called home, more an outdoor place of storage than an indoor space to dwell.

The discussion that ensues questions photographs as evidence of history, and explores them as historical in and of themselves. Topics include the ways that technological developments, like the flash, helped photo journalists, like Louis Hines and Jacob Riis, spotlight suffering and vulnerability to rally support for social change.[27] The class reflects on the 'muckraking' goals, and questions the photograph's authenticity. Did Riis capture the moment in, and with, a flash? Did he stage the woman in the dwelling to elicit empathy from his viewers, positioned on the outside looking in? We debate the questions and conclude that fiction and fact inform our understanding of the past. This is a new perspective for students accustomed to history defined by 'important' dates and the deeds of men. The realisation is pivotal.

---

24 On biographers crafting their narratives to serve political agendas, see Hannes Schweiger, "Global Subjects: The Transnationalisation of Biography," *Life Writing* 9, no.3 (2012), 249-258.

25 Journal entries, HOWAG (11 September 2017). This was repeated in in-class reflections.

26 Jacob Riis, *How the Other Half Lives* (New York: Dover Publications, 1971), 35; Riis, "In the Home of an Italian Rag-Picker," accessed 15 November 2017, https://commons.wikimedia.org/wiki/File:In_the_Home_of_an_Italian_Rag-Picker,_Jersey_Street.jpg.

27 John Tagg, "Evidence, Truth and Order: Photographic Records and the Growth of the State," in *The Photography Reader*, ed. Liz Wells (New York: Routledge, 2003), 257-361.

The female suffering, central to Jacob Riis's photographs, repeats in contemporary works of fiction, like Alice Nelson Dunbar's *Tony's Wife*.[28] The short story is about an Italian immigrant and his German wife in turn of the century New Orleans. He is called Tony. She remains nameless. Tony beats his wife throughout the text and abandons her in the end. He dies. She is left penniless. This is because he denies their marriage and transfers his wealth to his brother. "Why," the class asks, "didn't she get help?" "What," they wonder, "was her identity?" We discuss how a woman's identity depended on her provable link to a man. First her father and then a husband. These were recorded in legal documents, like birth and marriage certificates. Without the proof, a woman was a shadow in the margins of society. This is the plight of Tony's wife.

This focus on ordinary individuals allows students to narrow historical analysis down to personal identities. Letters written to the *Jewish Daily Forward* provide a window through which we glimpse both. Amongst them is a 'Shop Girl' living in Vineland [sic] New Jersey who, in 1907, took pen in hand and composed a letter to the editor seeking advice. "Dear Editor," she wrote, "I am one of those unfortunate girls thrown by fate into a dark and dismal shop, and I need your counsel. . . . Though my few hard-earned dollars mean a lot to my family of eight souls, I didn't . . . accept the foreman's vulgar advances . . . I am left without a job."[29] Like the editor of the press, class members empathize with the shop girl's struggles and admire her courage. Referencing the modern day 'confessions' of sexual coercion in the world-wide #MeToo campaign, they comment on the deeply personal ways that patriarchy shapes ordinary lives throughout time globally.[30]

They are equally struck by the editor's replies "encourage[ing] the letter writers to not endure passively, but to act and, "reach beyond their troubles."[31] An example is the reply to a letter written by a 'Faithful Reader' in 1914 asking for guidance. The correspondence invites us to experience the 1911 Triangle Shirtwaist Factory fire as people did "at that time," rather than as a decisive moment in urban history that we recognise from hindsight. The life writing achieves this by painting clear and compelling images that bridge time and space. Students witness the fire; experience the shock of those trapped in the flames; and hope for closure for those that survive. The letter to the editor describes a survivor's sorrow over the death of her "beloved bridegroom and rescuer," who died after rescuing her from the fire and whilst attempting to rescue "other girls" burning alive. Fearing that, "everything can only be alright for [her] only in the grave," and convinced that, "she could never love another man," she writes that a young man wants to marry her. The 'Worthy Editor' tells the 'Faithfull Reader' that "she has suffered enough in . . . life . . . and is advised to take herself in hand and begin her life anew."[32]

---

28 Alice Dunbar-Nelson, "Tony's Wife (1899)," accessed 25 May 2020, https://americanliterature.com/author/alice-dunbar-nelson/short-story/tonys-wife.

29 Isaac Metzker, ed., *A Bintel Brief: Sixty Years of Letters from the Lower East Side to the Jewish Daily Forward*, cited in Susan Ware, *Modern American Women*, 63; Margaretta Jolly and Liz Stanley, "Letters As/Not a Genre," in *The Routledge Auto|Biography Studies Reader*, eds. Ricia Ann Chansky and Emily Hipchen (New York: Routledge, 2015), 193-202.

30 Bayley et al., "AHR Conversation: On Transnational History."

31 In-class reflections, HOWAG (11 September 2017).

32 Metzker, *A Bintel Brief*, 62-65; Jolly and Stanley, "Letters As/Not a Genre," 193-201.

Suffering and strength are also central themes in fictional accounts of immigrant life. Anzia Yezierska's novel *Bread Givers,* published in 1924, tells the story of a Jewish daughter named Sarah Smolensky, living in New York City's Lower East Side in the1920's.[33] Sarah's struggles with the 'old world' and the new are placed in sharp relief within the context of her family. She is expected to marry a man of her father's choice and financially support her parents. She, however, expects to wed a person she loves and pursue an education. Her father's insistence and mother's acquiescence compel her to leave 'home' to pursue her dreams. The pain, conflict and conviction that define the young girl's life, help students see the tension between cultures *and* generations quintessential to historical and contemporary migration.

The quilt titled Tumbling Blocks also casts clear light on the pathos and promise that texture the fabric of immigrant life. According to its owner, it was woven by Jewish women living in New York City the early 20th century.[34] I bring the quilt into the classroom so that students can analyse the design. The goal of the exercise is twofold. First, to convey the historical significance of material culture. Second, to learn about perspective and bias by experiencing the ways that the former informs the latter, and vice versa. At first glance, class members see blocks tumbling. Familiar with the images of tenement life pictured by Jacob Riis in *How the Other Half Lives*, and stories of immigrant women's struggles and sorrows told by themselves and novelist Anzia Yezierska, they interpret the pattern as representing the heaviness of life. "Their lives are falling apart," states a student. The class echoes her claim. I push them to take a step back and look further. To 'let go' of the blocks and search for other symbols. Some recognise the Jewish Stars that seem to rise through the fabric. They think that this must symbolize hope.

Poetry, prose and oral histories

Hopelessness, in contrast, is their impression of the Chinese women detained in San Francisco's Angel Island Immigration Station between 1910 and 1940. The sorrows and suffering of life in transit are etched into the walls of the detention cells.[35] One woman writes, "grief and bitterness entwined are heaven sent. The sad person sits alone, leaning by a window." Another professes that, "America has power, but no Justice. In prison, we were victimized as if we were guilty. Given no opportunity to explain, it was really brutal. I bow my head in reflection but there is nothing I can do."[36] The poetic reflections of lives interrupted touch class

33 Anzia Yezierska, *Bread Givers* (New York: Persea Books, 2003 [1925]).

34 The author would like to thank Mrs Beverley Reich for the beautiful quilt and story. Beverley Reich, Interview by Nancy Mykoff, Conn.: 18 May 1999.

35 Hofmeyr, "AHR Conversation: On Transnational History," 144.

36 Ying Diao, "Echoes of History: Chinese Poetry at the Angel Island Immigration Station," *Smithsonian Folk Life Festival Blog*, accessed 3 May 2017: https://festival.si.edu/blog/echoes-of-history-chinese-poetry-and-the-angel-island-immigration-station; Christine Talcott, "If these Walls Could Talk: Angel Island's Chinese Immigration Tales," *Washington Post*, 11 October 2009. http://www.washingtonpost.com/wp-dyn/content/article/2009/10/09/AR2009100902438.htm; Judy Yung, *Unbound Voices: A Documentary History of Chinese Women in San Francisco* (Berkeley: University of California Press, 1999); Him Mark Lai, Genny Lim, and Judy Yung, *Island: Poetry and History of Chinese Immigrants on Angel Island, 1910-1940* (Seattle: University of Washington Press, 1991); "Angel Island Immigration Station Poetry: 1910-1949," *Ancestors in the Americas* http://www.cetel.org/angel_poetry.html accessed 20 December 2018.

members. "I was struck by the poems," writes a student. "I couldn't speak. I never thought of immigration like this. I knew about the Chinese Exclusion Act, but never thought about the excluded people."[37] They also wonder about the place of the Chinese women's history. To which country does 'it' belong? China or America? Perhaps, like the women themselves, their histories belong to neither? The question unhinges the national framework.

Inclusion and exclusion are the leitmotivs of the poetry and prose centered on transnational life *within* the North American continent as well. Native American Tribes, referred to by the U.S. Constitution as domestic dependent nations, are both a part of and apart from the United States of America.[38] Their histories are part of the larger transnational context of indigenous studies. Spiritual and social ties to community, land and kin define Native life. Contrary to the Euro-Western tradition of privileging the individual, unique social and cultural contexts account for indigenous life writing that is as much about the People as about the individual.[39] Like Sherman Alexie's *Absolutely True Diary of a Part Time Indian*, Native narratives provide sites of decolonisation and resistance, by humanizing the Indian other and revealing the community's continued oppression. They also spotlight the 'inbetweenness' of people living transnational lives.

The 'self-in-community' at the heart of Sherman Alexie's *Diary*, is an adolescent boy on and of the Spokane Indian Reservation. The poor education, alcoholism, diabetes, poverty and despair that speak to the lingering and transnational impact of settler colonialism, define the nation he deeply loves and struggles to leave. Journeying daily to attend a 'white' school in the bordering state, he describes himself as an "immigrant in an immigrant nation," and likens his story to the, "millions of other Americans who left their birthplaces in search of a dream."[40] The likeness weaves the foreign (Indian other) into a familiar national narrative.

Called Junior in the red world and by his Christian name Arnold in the white, the two names represent the 'twoness' of living in two nations, that defines the migrant's experience historically and globally, and is pictured as a person divided literally in half.[41] Characteristics of the white and right side of his body include, "a bright future," "positive role models," and "hope." Characteristics of the red and left side are, "a vanishing past," "a family history of diabetes and cancer," and "bone crushing reality."[42] The 'part-time Indian' expresses this division with words as well as illustrations. "I felt like two different people inside of one body," he writes. "No, I felt like a magician slicing myself in half, with Junior living on the north side of the Spokane River and Arnold living on the south." [43]

---

37 Student reflection, HOWAG (11 September 2017).

38 "Indian Reservations as Sovereign Nations," *Native Heritage Project* (19 March 2012) https://nativeheritageproject.com/2012/03/19/indian-reservations-as-sovereign-nations/; "The State of the Native Nations: Conditions under U.S. Policies of Self-Determination," Harvard Project on American Indian Economic Development (Boston: Oxford University Press, 2007).

39 Daniel Heath Justice, "No Indian Is an Island: On the Ethics of Teaching Indigenous Life Writing Texts," *Teaching Life Writing Texts*, eds. Fuchs and Howes, 255.

40 Sherman Alexie, *The Absolutely True Diary of a Part-Time Indian* (New York: Little, Brown and Co., 2007), 217.

41 Red and Christian are Alexie's terms.

42 Ibid., 57.

43 Ibid., 61.

Conflict and change define life on both sides of the border. The reader witnesses and experiences both. A sign post guides Junior to and from the off reservation 'white' school. Right is the direction of "Hope and the Unknown." Left is the direction of the "Rez and Home."[44] The journey is inward as well as outward. As he walks with and towards hope and uncertainty, he takes his culture with him. He takes on another, literally and figuratively, when he crosses over. "I woke up on the reservation as an Indian," Junior writes. "And somewhere on the road to [the white school] Reardan, I became something less than Indian. And once I arrived at Reardan, I became something less than less than less than Indian."[45] At Reardan, fellow class-mates refer to him as Sitting Bull, Tonto, Red-Skin, Squaw Boy, and Chief.[46] He is also the butt of cruel jokes. "Hey Chief," one asks, "did you know that Indians are living proof that niggers fuck buffalo?" Arnold punches the boy in the face. The violent defense stemmed from his deep solidarity,"I wasn't just defending myself," he writes, "I was defending black people, Indians *and* buffalo."[47]

Oral histories collected by student interviews speak less to the liminality of daily life and more to the violent consequences of transnational phenomena. They tell the stories, for instance, of non-native men crossing national borders onto 'Indian Country,' to mine the land (i.e., fracking) or lay pipes to transport oil. The workers live in all male camps and demand women for sex. The consequences for the receiving communities speak to an impact of transnational migration. Aubrey Skye of the Hunkpapa nation narrated the effects that male migrant workers have on the Standing Rock Reservation in North Dakota, in an open interview via Skype given in November 2017. His account focused on the 'women gone missing' since oil was discovered on the Standing Rock Reservation. The discovery, he stated, changed the reservation's physical and social landscapes. On the one hand, Native peoples sold land to the oil industry for a profit. As a result, oil rigs dot the landscape. On the other hand, a concurrent influx of male laborers and lack of affordable housing resulted in 'man camps' demanding sex. [48]

The demand was and is met by the abduction and trafficking of young girls and women. They are referred to collectively as 'stolen sisters.' A report to the United States Department of Justice Office on Violence Against Women notes the growth of the crime. It states that the, "rapid development for oil production in the Bakken region has brought a massive influx of itinerant workers and a sharp increase in . . . human trafficking"[49] The reservation press reveals that abducted women and children remain missing or are discovered dead. An article titled, "Standing Rock Sends crew to join search for Olivia Lone Bear," features on the front page of the 6 December edition of the *Teton Times*. The article traces, "the

---

44 Ibid., 43.

45 Ibid., 83.

46 Ibid., 63.

47 Ibid., 65.

48 Mr. Aubrey Skye, Skype interview by students, Middelburg, the Netherlands, November 2017.

49 "Missing mother of five," *Teton Times*, 6-13 December 2017, 2. Federal legislation works against the prosecution of traffickers. The 1978 Supreme Court decision in Oliphant v. Suquamish, for instance, states that tribes do not have criminal jurisdiction over non-Natives and thus cannot prosecute non-Native sex traffickers in tribal courts. Gabrielle Mandeville, "Sex Trafficking on Indian Reservations," *Tulsa Law Review* 51, no.1 (Summer 2015): 187.

Lone Bear family's weeks long search for their missing daughter [and mother of five] in the Bakken oil fields." The missing girl's father states that, "with the recent loss of Savanna Lafontaine-Greywind, another Native sister lost in the epidemic of marginalization and invisibility to non-Native, North American community members, we want to bring Olivia home before she become another Missing and Murdered Indigenous Woman statistic."[50] The gender-based violence experienced by indigenous peoples across national borders speaks to the ways that international capitalism gives rise to violent exploitation that often leads to death. Commerce yields culture that takes life transnationally.[51]

Literary memoir and activist art

Our exploration of the intersectionality of race, age and gender in the twentieth century continues with a shift in attention to the 'memories of black girlhood' in the 1950's, recorded by bell hooks in her memoir *Bone Black*.[52] Hooks' recollections of the rhythms and rituals of a segregated life speak to the many ways that separate was very unequal.[53] An example is the school she attended that was far less-than-equal to its white counterparts, and far distances from black children's homes. They journeyed to the "little white wood-frame [school] where all the country kids [went] . . . from miles and miles away . . . because they [were] black."[54] Also recalled were the myriad ways that race and class intersected and divided. The anger of the light-skinned woman that lived in the beautiful 'storybook house' is one illustration. hooks explains the anger by explaining that the folks that look white, ". . . hate white folks for having what they want . . . and dark black folks for reminding the world that they are colored and thus keeping them from really getting what they want."[55]

Hooks' memories of girlhood, a confluence of what she refers to as "myth, dream and reality," fuel self-reflection and historical understanding.[56] They do both by raising awareness of the cultural privileging of white over black. What black people

---

50 Ibid.

51 *Sexual Exploitation and Trafficking of Aboriginal Women and Girls: Literature Review and Key Informant Interviews* (Native Women's Association of Canada: March 2014). https://www.canadianwomen.org/wp-content/uploads/2017/09/NWAC-Sex-Trafficking-Literature Review_2.pdf *Teton Times*, 6-13 December 2017, 2. Children are also abducted. "Senate Bill expands AMBER Alert System in Indian Country," *Teton Times*, 6-13 December 2017, 6. According to Reuters reporter Ellen Wulfhorst, sex trafficking in Indian country is rooted in the 20th century. It was not addressed, however, because "it had no name." Ellen Wulfhorst, "Sex Trafficking on American Indian Reservations -Old Problem, New Name," *World News* (18 May 2016https://www.reuters.com/article/us-trafficking-nativeamericans-awareness/sex-trafficking-on-american-indian-reservations-old-problem-new-name-idUSKCN0Y91H1). https://uk.reuters.com/article/us-trafficking-nativeamericans-awareness/sex-trafficking-on-american-indian-reservations-old-problem-new-name-idUSKCN0Y91H1https://www.reuters.com/article/us-trafficking-nativeamericans-awareness/sex-trafficking-on-american-indian-reservations-old-problem-new-name-idUSKCN0Y91H1.

52 bell hooks, *Bone Black: Memories of Girlhood* (New York: Henry Hold and Co., 1996).

53 The notion that separate facilities for black and white people were legal as long as they were 'equal' was confirmed in the *Plessy vs. Ferguson* Supreme Court decision of 1896 allowing for state-sponsored segregation.

54 hooks, *Bone Black*, 4-5.

55 Ibid., 73.

56 bell hooks, "Writing Autobiography," in *Women, Autobiography, Theory*, eds. Smith and Watson, 430.

"really wanted," bell hooks writes, was "to see reflections of the world [they] live in, not someone else's world." Student journals refer to a 'click' of understanding after reading this passage. They 'finally' grasped the significance of white privilege.[57]

Like the privileging of whiteness, homophobia is unbound by nation or state and permeates and misshapes history and life. A concurrent reading of *Boys Beware*, a social guidance film broadcast on television in 1961; and video interviews of lesbian, gay, bisexual, transgender, queer and intersex (LGBTQI) refugees from the Middle East living in the Netherlands, collected and exhibited by activist artist Carlos Motto in 2017, speaks to the cross-cultural existence and persistence of the fear of sexual nonconformity. The televised film explains that homosexuality is a criminal offense, and urges young boys to avoid homosexual men. Not just because they are criminal, but because, according to the narrator, they suffer from, "a sickness . . . not visible like small pox, but no less dangerous and contagious" and deadly.[58] Laughter at the narrative is silenced with comment on contemporary resonance.

Stigmatisation and persecution of homosexual people echo in Motto's videoed memoirs, like the one narrated by Faysal. He fled his home to save his life. He kissed his boyfriend. The kiss was witnessed. His boyfriend's family, "didn't want a gay son." So, "they killed him in the name of honor." The "rule that both (lovers) must die," compelled Faysal to flee to the Netherlands. His family helped him. His father paid the price. He "was killed to keep the family honor."[59] The death broadens understanding of the impact transnationalism has on families left behind. The common focus on family disruption resulting from transnational migration, is on the struggles that result when the breadwinner or primary caregiver migrates. Another topic is the psychological trauma of separation between parents and children. The story of Faysal questions the heteronormativity of transnational avenues of inquiry. It does this by spotlighting the power and reach of homophobia, its role in motivating and shaping migration, and the devastation it reaps on families remaining in the country of origin.

Other portraits featured in Motto's exhibit reveal the physical and psychological abuse suffered by LGBTQ refugees at the hands of their compatriots. The continuous and often deadly confrontations, whilst in flight and after arrival in detention centers, place them at odds with their ethnicity. According to student reflections, the intimate portraits elicit a visceral response. "The way the exhibition gave a face to . . . refugees was amazing," writes a student. "It is so different from just hearing theoretical examples. [A] face with a story creates much more empathy.[60] Another states that she "learnt [sic] to consider more concretely so many things I had known only abstractly."[61] Still another reflects that she had,

---

57 George Lipsitz, *The Possessive Investment in Whiteness* (Philadelphia: Temple University Press, 2009).

58 *Boys Beware* (Sid Davis Productions, 1961), accessed 15 October 2017: https://archive.org/details/boys_beware https://archive.org/details/boys_beware. Interestingly, independence and trust in men is the threat to young girls. The price is abuse and death. *Girls Beware* (1961)https://archive.org/details/0840_Girls_Beware_12_42_58_00.

59 Carlos Motta, "Video Portrait: Faysal – Peshawar Pakistan. Gay," *Crossings* (Amsterdam: Stedelijk Museum, 16 September – 21 January 2018). I would like to thank Margriet Schavemaker for hosting my class at the Stedelijk Museum.

60 Student reflection, Stedelijk Museum (October 2017).

61 Ibid.

"heard of the terrible stories of refugees drowning and dying on the news," but the exhibition turned numbers and groups into regular people like, "yourself, your friends, your family." This, she argues, "makes the prejudice and hate and shame [and] injustice intolerable." Another simply states, "I could not move."[62]

The media's tendency to lump refugees into ethnic categories of homogeneous groups fleeing war, and split them into male/female binary camps, overlooks tensions within migrant groups and the very unique migration experiences.[63] Students had viewed, read, and thought about the stories of women, men, children and families crossing borders. [64] Most, however, did not know that some fled persecution because of their sexual orientation. They had never thought about gender refugees.

Motto's *Crossings* inspired critical thinking about the act of migration by those gendered 'other.' Giving voice and visibility to the historically silenced and unseen, the visual narratives deepen awareness and understanding of intersectionality, by representing the gendered, sexual, racial and religious identities that mediate citizenship. They also unhinge the national context of genderism, by revealing bodies figured foreign 'at home' and abroad. Stories of abuse unfold throughout the migration process, from punishment with solitary confinement within the family home, to the denial of health care in the refugee nation. Described as "beautiful, poignant, moving and haunting," the rich and revealing profiles made it "hard to speak," "difficult to move," and "urgent to act."[65] Ideas about action coalesce. One suggests transnational cooperation between private insurance companies to meet the medical needs of transgender migrants. Another suggests transnational policies crafted between nation-states.

Viewing persecution through a transnational lens focuses attention on global gender and racial inequality. Like Carlos Motto, visual activist and photographer Zanele Muholi showcases oppression. Her recent installation of Sonmyama Ngonyama (Hail the Dark Lioness!), at the Stedelijk Museum in Amsterdam, train our eyes on the hate crimes targeting members of the LGBTI communities in post-Apartheid South Africa.[66] Students articulate the impact in their exhibition reviews. "At the end of the [exhibition] hall," writes one, "there is a wall with the names of victims of anti-LGBTI

---

62 Sarah Brophy and Janice Haldki, *Embodied Politics of Visual Autobiography* (Toronto: University of Toronto Press, 2015), 5; Student Reflections, Stedelijk Museum (4 October 2017).

63 See, for instance, Donna R. Gabaccia, "'Is Everywhere Nowhere?' Nomads, Nations, and the Immigrant Paradigm of US History," *Journal of American History* 86, no.3 (December 1999): 1115-1134.

64 Images that had 'gone viral' were the basis of their picture of 'the' refugee. See, for instance, Charles Homans, "The Boy on the Beach," *The New York Times Magazine*, 3 September 2015. https://www.nytimes.com/2015/09/03/magazine/the-boy-on-the-beach.html; and Oliver Laurent, "What the Image of AlyanKurdi Says about the Power of Photography," *Time*, 4 September 2015 http://time.com/4022765/aylan-kurdi-photo/. See also "All the words and TV reporting of the refugee crisis in a single photo Humbled by @DanielEtterFoto, Twitter @paraicobrien. Accessed 5 December 2017, https://twitter.com/paraicobrien/status/633935385882697728/photo/1?ref_src=twsrc%5Etfw&ref_url=http%3A%2F%2Fwww.thejournal.ie%2Fdaniel-etto-syria-family-2281164-Aug2015%2F

65 Student journal, HOWAG (2 October 2017).

66 Zanele Muholi and Sonmyama Ngonyama, *Hail the Dark Lioness* (Amsterdam: Stedelijk Museum, 19 July-15 October 2017); Martha Rosier, "In, Around, and Afterthoughts (On Documentary Photography)" in *The Photography Reader*, ed. Wells, 261-274.

violence [that] hits almost as hard, as the brick wall it was painted on."[67] Others tie the art works into class readings. They wonder, for instance, how sexual orientation and rigid social norms (mis)shaped the lives of transnational migrants to the United States in the 19th and 20th centuries. They ask if there are letters or diaries or artistic accounts that provide insight into this aspect of immigration history.

Conclusion

At the end of the term the class evaluates the course by addressing a series of questions. Amongst them are what have you learned? What will you take with you? What did you like most about the course? For many, it was the life histories they had written. "Throughout the semester," a student writes, "this journal has helped me to step back from gender norms and analyze them. It made me pay attention to things I wouldn't ordinarily see."[68]

Open interviews spoke to the clear connections between past and present. Reiterated by all was the ways literary, poetic and artistic expressions, of ordinary men, women and nonconforming genders, educated, resonated, and inspired. Some wrote about how life writing conveyed clear and often visceral impressions of people fleeing civil war or coping with its aftermath. Others were taken with the plight of individuals crossing national borders because of gender oppression. Striking was the shared conviction that reading the past through narrations of life from a transnational perspective deepened their understanding of the past and helped them to imagine future possibilities for studying history and addressing current social, economic, environmental, political, and personal challenges.

Life writing narratives teach history through story telling. The stories told in the *History of Women and Gender* class are about people and developments in the past living within, and crossing into, different nation-states. Transgressing the borders that define and divide the state, illustrations, testimonies, letters, diaries, oral histories, portrait photographs and biographical film weave rich and detailed narratives that render the foreign familiar. The histories touch and move my students. They feel anger. They develop empathy. They gain insight into the present. Inviting us to experience historical developments as people did 'at that time,' within 'foreign' countries internationally, life writing dares us to reimagine notions of other and self, question dominant historical narratives, and appreciate shared humanity transnationally.

Bibliography

"AHR Conversation: On Transnational History, with C.A.Bayley, Sven Beckert, Matthew Connely, Isabel Hofmeyer, Wendy Kozol, and Patricia Seed," *American Historical Review* 111, no.5 (2006): 1450.

Bean, John. *Engaging Ideas: The Professor's Guide to Integrating writing, Critical Thinking and Active Learning in the Classroom*. 2nd ed. San Francisco: Jossey-Bass, 2011.

67 Student reflection, Stedelijk Museum (4 October 2017).
68 Journal entries (8 December 2017).

Brophy, Sarah, and Janice Haldki. *Embodied Politics of Visual Autobiography*. Toronto: University of Toronto Press, 2015.

Childs, Roda Ann. "I was more dead than alive." In *Freedom: A Documentary History of Emancipation, 1861-1876*, Series 2, edited by Ira Berlin, Joseph P. Reidy, and Leslie S. Rowland, 807. Cambridge, MA: Cambridge University Press, 1982.

Diao, Ying. "Echoes of History: Chinese Poetry at the Angel Island Immigration Station." *Smithsonian Folk Life Festival Blog*, accessed 3 May 2017. https://festival.si.edu/blog/echoes-of-history-chinese-poetry-and-the-angel-islandimmigration-station.

Dunbar-Nelson, Alice. "Tony's Wife (1899)." Accessed 25 May 2020, https://americanliterature.com/author/alice-dunbar-nelson/short-story/tonys-wife.

Fleischmann, Ellen. "'I Only Wish I had a Home on This Globe': Transnational Biography and Dr. Mary Eddy." *Journal of Women's History* 21, no.3 (2009): 108-130.

Fuchs, Miriam, and Craig Howes, *Teaching Life Writing Texts*. New York: The Modern Language Association of America, 2008.

Hackl, Andreas. "Key Figure of Mobility." *The Exile Journal of Anthropology* 25, no.1 (February 2017): 56-68.

Justice, Daniel Heath. "No Indian Is an Island: On the Ethics of Teaching Indigenous Life Writing Texts." In *Teaching Life Writing Texts*, edited by Miriam Fuchs and Craig Howes, 252-260. New York: The Modern Language Association of America, 2008.

hooks, bell. *Bone Black: Memories of Girlhood*. New York: Henry Hold and Co., 1996.

hooks, bell. "Writing Autobiography." In *Women, Autobiography, Theory,* edited by Sidonie Smith and Julia Watson, 429-433. Madison Wisconsin: The University of Wisconsin Press, 1998.

Hunter, Tera W. "Reconstruction and the Meanings of Freedom." In *Women's America: Refocusing the Past*, edited by Linda K. Kerber and Jane Sherron De Hart, 235-244. 6th ed. Oxford: Oxford University Press, 2003.

"Indian Reservations as Sovereign Nations" (Posted 19 March 2012). *Native Heritage Project*. https://nativeheritageproject.com/2012/03/19/indian-reservations-as-sovereign nations/.

Jolly, Margaretta and Liz Stanley. "Letters As/Not a Genre." In *The Routledge Auto|Biography Studies Reader,* edited by Ricia Ann Chansky and Emily Hipchen, 193-202. New York: Routledge, 2015.

Kaplan, Caren. "Resisting Autobiography: Out-Law Genres and Transnational Feminist Subjects." In *De/Colonizing the Subject: The Politics of Gender in Women's Autobiography*, edited by Sidonie Smith and Julia Watson, 115-138. Minneapolis: The University of Minnesota Press, 1992.

Kerber, Linda K. , and Jane Sherron De Hart, eds. *Women's America: Refocusing the Past* 6th edition. Oxford: Oxford University Press, 2003.

Kirk, Gwyn, and Margo Okazawa-Rey, eds. *Women's Lives: Multicultural Perspectives*. 4th ed. New York: McGraw-Hill, 2007.

Lai, Him Mark, Genny Lim, and Judy Yung, eds. *Island: Poetry and History of Chinese Immigrants on Angel Island, 1910-1940*. Seattle: University of Washington Press, 1991.

Lamothe, John. "Speaking Silently: Comics' 'Silent Narratives' as Immersive Experience." *Studies in Popular Culture* (Spring 2019): 69-93.

Lejeune, Philippe. "The Autobiographical Pact." In *The Routledge Auto/Biography Studies Reader*, edited by Ricia Anne Chansky and Emily Hipchen, 34-28. New York: Routledge, 2016.

Lipsitz, George. *The Possessive Investment in Whiteness*. Philadelphia: Temple University Press, 2009.

Mandeville, Gabrielle. "Sex Trafficking on Indian Reservations," *Tulsa Law Review* 51, no. 1 (Summer 2015): 181-207.

Porter, Roger J. "Introduction to World Narrative." In *Teaching Life Writing Texts*, edited by Miriam Fuchs and Craig Howes, 23-32. New York: The Modern Language Association of America, 2008.

Rak, Julie. *Boom! Manufacturing Memoir for the Popular Market*. Ontario, Canada: Wilfrid Laurier University Press, 2013.

Riis, Jacob. *How the Other Half Lives*. New York: Dover Publications, 1971.

Rosier, Martha. "In, Around, and Afterthoughts (On Documentary Photography)." In *The Photography Reader*, edited by Liz Wells, 261-274. New York: Routledge, 2002.

Parrenas, Rhacel Salazar. *Servants of Globalization: Women, Migration and Domestic Work.* Stanford: Stanford University Press, 2001.

Satrapi, Marjane. *The Complete Persepolis: A Story of Childhood.* New York: Pantheon Books Inc., 2004.

Sexual Exploitation and Trafficking of Aboriginal Women and Girls: Literature Review and Key Informant Interviews. Native Women's Association of Canada: March 2014.

Schweiger, Hannes. "Global Subjects: The Transnationalisation of Biography." *Life Writing* 9, no.3 (August 2012): 249-258.

Sherman, Alexie. *The Absolutely True Diary of a Part-Time Indian*. New York: Little, Brown and Co., 2007.

Smith, Sidonie, and Julia Watson, eds. *Women, Autobiography, Theory: A Reader*. Wisconsin: University of Wisconsin Press, 1998.

Smith, Sidonie, and Julia Watson. *Life Writing in the Long Run: A Smith & Watson Autobiography Studies Reader.* Michigan: Michigan Publishing, 2016.

Steedman, Carolyn Kay. "Stories." In *Women, Autobiography, Theory: A Reader*, edited by Sidonie Smith and Julia Watson, 243-254. Wisconsin: University of Wisconsin Press, 1998.

Tagg, John, "Evidence, Truth and Order: Photographic Records and the Growth of the State." In *The Photography Reader*, edited by Liz Wells, 257-361. New York: Routledge, 2003.

Talcott, Christine. "If These Walls Could Talk: Angel Island's Chinese Immigration Tales," *Washington Post*, 11 October 2009. http://www.washingtonpost.com/wpdyn/content/article/2009/10/09/AR2009100902438.htm.

"The State of the Native Nations: Conditions under U.S. Policies of Self-Determination." Harvard Project on American Indian Economic Development. Boston: Oxford University Press, 2007.

Tyrrell, Ian. *Transnational Nation: United States History in Global Perspective Since 1789.* Basingstoke: Palgrave Macmillan, 2007.

Ware, Susan, ed. *Modern American Women: A Documentary History.* 2nd ed. New York: McGraw Hill, 2002.

Watson, Julia. "Parsua Bashi's *Nylon Road*: The Visual Dialogics of Witnessing in Iranian Women's Graphic Memoir." In *Life Writing in the Long Run: A Smith & Watson Autobiography Studies Reader*, edited by Sidonie Smith and Julia Watson, 679-730. Michigan: Michigan Publishing, 2016.

Whitlock, Gillian. "Autographics: The Seeing 'I' of the Comics." *Modern Fiction Studies* 52, no. 4 (2006): 965-979.

Wulfhorst, Ellen. "Sex Trafficking on American Indian Reservations – Old Problem, New Name." *World News*, 18 May 2016https://www.reuters.com/article/us-trafficking-nativeamericans-awareness/sex-trafficking-on-american-indian-reservations-old-problem-new-name-idUSKCN0Y91H1. https://uk.reuters.com/article/us-trafficking-nativeamericans-awareness/sex-trafficking-on-american-indian-reservations-old-problem-new-name-idUSKCN0Y91H1.

Yezierska, Anzia. *Bread Givers.* New York: Persea Books, 1925 [2003].

Yung, Judy. *Unbound Voices: A Documentary History of Chinese Women in San Francisco.* Berkeley: University of California Press, 1999.

Starring Morgenland!

The life and work of Jan Johannes Theodorus Boon (1911-1974)

Edy Seriese

For a while now the Indisch Wetenschappelijk Instituut (IWI) has been preparing to reprint "Piekerans van een straatslijper" (Musings of a Gadabout), a weekly column published between 1951 and 1956 in Jakarta, Indonesia, in the Dutch daily *Nieuwsgier.*[1] It was written by Jan Johannes Theodorus Boon under his pseudonym Tjalie Robinson.[2] Jan Boon is the most important author to write in the Dutch language about Indonesia from Indonesia since Multatuli, yet the "Piekerans" and other columns he published between 1946-1956 are hardly known in the Netherlands.[3] His many writings brought him lasting fame not only with the inhabitants of Indonesia, but also with many of the 330,000 or so Dutch who left the ex-colony after its independence, taking his writings with them. This chapter explores the multiple subjectivities of Boon as he negotiated, both personally and through his writings, his experience as a colonial and post-colonial subject in different settings. In this way Boon becomes a culture-bearer for those who faced disruption, dislocation, and confusion as they were forced to switch homelands, following the ex-colonial power back to the metropole after Indonesian independence. Boon gave voice to the many who were unable themselves to bridge these very different cultural environments, providing an

1 Indisch Wetenschappelijk Instituut (IWI), accessed 1 December 2019, www.iwi-nu.nl.

2 Boon published about 219 "Piekerans" in *Nieuwsgier* under the pseudonym Tjalie Robinson. In the 1950s he published 75 of them in two collections: *Piekerans van een straatslijper*. In 1965 he consolidated them into one volume, adding 10 extra columns. This so-called 'umpteenth edition' has been reprinted each decade since 1965 by the Boon family publishing house Moesson. In the 1980s Boon's widow published another 31 columns under the title *Piekeren in Nederland* (The Hague: Moesson, 1983). A total of 116 Piekerans are therefore known in the Netherlands.

3 Multatuli is an alias of the Dutch writer Eduard Douwes Dekker (1820-1887). In 1860 he published *Max Havelaar, of de Koffij-veilingen der Nederlandsche Handel-Maatschappij* (Max Havelaar, or the Coffee Auctions of the Dutch Trading Company), a so-called 'double novel' or 'frame story' about the colonial civil servant Max Havelaar who tries to generate support in the Netherlands for his protests against colonial abuses in Indonesia. *Max Havelaar* is a classic in the Netherlands, researched, reprinted, and turned into a film in 1976. In 1987 it was refashioned as a musical presented on Dutch television, in Belgium it has been presented as a *Suske en Wiske* comic, and in 2016 it was even retold as a tale with zombies. For its place in the collective memory of the Netherlands see Pamela Pattynama, *Bitterzoet Indië: Herinnering en nostalgie in literatuur, foto's en films* (Amsterdam: Prometheus/Bert Bakker, 2014), 72-92.

outlet, a level of understanding, and ultimately a meeting point to collect and connect the memories, family histories, and objects of an otherwise culturally dispersed community.

Boon was raised in Indonesia, the son of a sergeant in the Royal Netherlands East Indies Army, and migrated to the Netherlands in 1954. In the 1960s and 1970s he garnered national fame in the Netherlands, receiving the Amsterdam Prose Prize in 1959 and publishing two short story collections under his other alias, Vincent Mahieu. He also gained notoriety by publishing the magazine *Tong Tong: Het enige Indische blad in Nederland* (*Tong Tong: The Real Indies Magazine in the Netherlands*) from 1958-1974.[4] Today, in the Netherlands, appreciation for Boon is divided: Vincent Mahieu is situated in the world of literature, Tjalie Robinson is seen as the journalist, and *Tong Tong* finds Boon as the sympathetic social worker writing to emancipate his readers. In contrast to this literary compartmentalisation, the IWI posits a 'theory of everything' for Boon, uniting his cultural output in three large projects that will eventually cover all relevant aspects of Boon's life and work. The *Kètèngan project* will reprint all of Boon's work published between 1942 – 1958, utilizing first editions of each text to ensure authenticity. The IWI website project, entitled *Aangespoeld* (Washed Up) provides the social and historical background to situate Boon within the context of Indies culture, and the *TT project* will complete Boon's bibliography with his work from *Tong Tong*.

Using the *Kètèngan project* and a close reading of Boon's text "Intro" (1954), this chapter makes use of the concept of 'cosmobilities' within transnational biography by linking literary language and literary social strategies to the colonial situation that generated them. The perspective Boon put forward in this text challenged the outlook of the IWI on the cultural identity of the Indies diaspora, triggering the *Aangespoeld* project as a result. It concludes with a proposal to approach and analyse *Tong Tong* as a history book and 'framing story' in one, a necessary preparatory step toward a potentially decolonised biographical representation of Boon.

Traditional editions of Boon's writings

Boon lived and wrote in the twilight of Dutch colonialism in Asia. After the Japanese occupation of the archipelago (1942-1945) Indonesian sovereignty was finally recognised in 1949 by the Netherlands and two new national states arose: Indonesia and the Netherlands. This was not the theme of Boon's work, though there is much in his writings that touches on this process of disengagement. In 1954 Boon was among the 330,000 Dutch people who left the former colony between 1942 and 1962. The migration experience is not central to his work, although he did point repeatedly to a sense of grief and loss of homeland, departure, and the difficulties of integration. This chapter wants to emphasize the fluidity,

4 In 1959 Boon won the Amsterdam Prose Prize for *Tjies: Vertellingen*, 2nd ed. (The Hague: H.P. Leopolds Uitg. Mij., 1958). As Vincent Mahieu, he published two story collections in the Netherlands, *Tjies: Vertellingen* and *Tjoek: Vertellingen* (The Hague: Leopold, 1960). Some stories have been translated into Bahasa Indonesia, English and German. Boon edited *Tong Tong* under the pseudonym Tjalie Robinson; the name of the magazine refers to the Indonesian wooden clock used in cases of public happiness, grief or doom. *Tong Tong* was continued by Boon's widow Lilian Ducelle and still exists under the name *Moesson*.

the multiplicity and the autonomy of his life. Boon lived alternately in rural and urban areas, moving around in Indonesia, switching between Indonesia to the Netherlands, and even spending four years in Whittier, a small city in the Los Angeles area. He was a teacher, a headmaster, a sports journalist, boxing trainer, civil servant, and customs officer, working in advertising, publishing, and business. He served as a sailor, a soldier, a captain, a prisoner of war and the head of the Dutch Information Service in the Indies. He also was a husband, a widower, a divorcee, and a father of seven born between 1936 and 1952. He moved between different social positions, in different countries all over the world, operating – and writing – in the three languages in which he was raised: Petjoh, Indies, and Dutch.

With such varied experiences, it is not easy to compose Boon's life story nor to point to genres or themes in his work. Up until now Boon's writings were conceived of as coming from three different persons, and this has led to neglect of large parts of his work and to fragmentation and modification of the rest. In 1992, for example, the editor Rob Nieuwenhuys limited the 'complete works' of Boon to the Vincent Mahieu texts.[5] Editors Wilfred Diericks and Chrétien Breukers limited their attention to Tjalie Robinson, editing an unpublished manuscript by changing the title, leaving out some chapters, changing the narrative sequence and correcting without explanation "obvious spelling mistakes."[6] Another editor, Wim Willems, also concentrated on Tjalie Robinson, claiming he had found Piekerans columns "never published before."[7] He split this 'new-found' corpus into two books under different titles, adding one text never published in *Nieuwsgier* (and certainly never published as a "Piekeran") and mutilated most of the rest, changing or omitting titles, paragraphs, sentences, words, and punctuation.[8] When interviewed, the editors explained their efforts to "portalize" Boon's work by pointing to its beauty.[9] Ever since Edward Said's *Culture and Imperialism*, we know that the colonial tradition dictates a complex process of selection, adjustment, overlooking, correcting, and neglecting of the other's opinion, using the potential 'beauty' of the work as an argument for patronizing representations of 'the East.'

5 Vincent Mahieu, *Verzameld Werk,* ed. Rob Nieuwenhuys (Amsterdam: Querido, 1992).

6 Tjalie Robinson, *Didi in Holland,* ed. Chrétien Breukers and Wilfred Dierick (Nijmegen: Nova Zembla, 1992). Boon's typescript *Didi naar Holland* (*Didi to Holland*) is in the Literatuurmuseum (Museum of Literature) in The Hague.

7 Wim Willems, *Tjalie Robinson: Een land met gesloten deuren* (The Hague: Statenhofpers, 2011), 7-11; back cover; Wim Willems, *Tjalie Robinson, Kind van Batavia: Verhalen van een straatslijper* (Amsterdam: Prometheus, 2011). After "systematically researching in the newspapers" Willems selected in total 69 Piekerans before mutilating 42 of them in these two publications. See Edy Seriese, "Tjalie ont-dekt: over de houdbaarheid van teksten of 'Niet alles kan mee (zoals de oplet-chauffeur spijtig zei),'" *Indische letteren* (March 2012): 42-55.

8 Willems, *Tjalie Robinson, Kind van Batavia*, 13-23. The non-Piekeran text is titled "Anak Betawie" (meaning Child of Batavia, the colonial name for Jakarta). It was first published in *Oriëntatie* (December 1949): 7-16, the Dutch cultural monthly in Jakarta directed by Rob Nieuwenhuys.

9 Susan Legêne introduced the term 'portalise' for one of four ways native agents in a dominant culture try to bring the work of unknown writers into their national canon. Susan Legêne, "Historiography and the Hinges of Biographical Representation." Lecture at the expert meeting Unhinging the National Framework: Platform for the Study of Transnational Life Writing, Utrecht University, 30 September 2016.

Multatuli had already experienced this with his *Max Havelaar* in 1860.[10] Boon was furious about this process, withdrawing his texts when he could, and eventually withdrawing himself entirely from the Dutch literary sphere. In order to evade this colonial practice, he established *Tong Tong* as an autonomous publishing house in the 1960s, protecting the integrity of his products.[11] The IWI's *Kètèngan project* therefore aimed to print a truly complete edition of Boon's texts, conforming to the original sources as first published by Boon himself.

Within the same colonial traditions, cultural agents in the Netherlands also defined the image of Boon. In 1957, when Boon had just started as an editor of the monthly *Onze Brug* in The Hague, Rob Nieuwenhuys wrote an introductory article titled "Who is Tjalie Robinson?" presenting Boon as the "chronicler" of "kleine boeng" (meaning "baby brother" or "the little man in the street").[12] 'Kleine boeng' was a colonial construction for talking about race and colour, superiority and dependence. Nieuwenhuys effectively condemned Boon to the 'black hole' in the galaxy of Dutch colonial narratives, all of which concentrated on the Dutch leaving their country to conquer the world (for better or worse depending on the political view of the writer). These narratives never mentioned the 'kleine boeng' at all. However, the many supplementary tales tangential to the colonial narrative, published on a large scale throughout the Dutch colonies, portrayed 'kleine boeng' repeatedly in dramas, comedies, novels, and short stories in a variety of publication formats. All of these forums considered the 'kleine boeng,' also referred to as 'Indos,' as a problem for civilisation. They presented them as paupers, poor and yet conceited because of their 'mixed' descent, unable to choose between East and West, ruled by their passions, their sons easily tempted to gambling and drugs, their girls seductive and sly, lacking the 'natural' high standards of the Dutch. This narrative gave the Dutch the moral justification they needed to rule their colonies.[13]

---

10 *Max Havelaar* was edited in 1860 by Jacob van Lennep. He changed the manuscript by adding subtitles to the chapter titles and leaving out the names of cities, villages and dates in order to weaken the anti-colonial message, and omitted critical notes on religion. The book was also sold at a high price and was not made available in the colony itself. It took several editions before it was finally published according to Dekker's liking. "Edition zero," edited in 1949 by Garmt Stuiveling, restored the original *Max Havelaar* manuscript.

11 Tjalie Robinson, "Amsterdam 18 mei 1955, Zeer geachte mevrouw Maria Dermoût," collectie Johan van der Woude, Gelders Archief, Arnhem. On Tong Tong see: Bert Paasman, ed., *Tjalie Robinson: De stem van Indisch Nederland* (The Hague: Stichting Tong Tong, 1994); Pattynama, 2014; Fridus Steijlen, *Een Indische skyline: Indische organisaties in Nederland tussen 1980 en 2010* (Amsterdam: AUP, 2018).

12 Rob Nieuwenhuys "Wie is 'Tjalie Robinson?'" *Onze Brug* (1 September 1957). Nieuwenhuys totally ignored Boon's self-presentation, and even reprinted this article in *De Gids* (1960): 147-150. In December 1954 Boon had published a Piekeran titled "Who is Tjalie Robinson?" in *de Vrije Pers* (December 1954) and, apparently, also in *Nieuwsgier* in Indonesia. It is possible Nieuwenhuys had not read this article, but he must have known about its content. He was well acquainted with Boon since working together with him on *Oriëntatie*, the Dutch literary-cultural monthly Nieuwenhuys edited in Jakarta between 1947 and 1952. He had introduced Boon to the literary world in the Netherlands, and he took part in the ongoing discussions Boon informally held in his home in Amsterdam from 1954 with the Dutch and Indonesian people he knew and who came to visit him. See Adriaan van der Staay, *Trage vertellingen* 1 (Leiden: Opmeer Drukkerij, 2008), 7-13, a collection of memoires printed privately and available in the IWI collection.

13 See the serialised novels of P.A. Daum, e.g., *Goena goena* (1889) and *Nummer elf* (1893), about the thematic use of seductive spells, and later the novels and dramas of Victor Ido such as *The Pariah of Glodok* (1900) and *The Paupers* (1911).

Nieuwenhuys' article in 1957 actualised these terms and this interpretation in the post-colonial Netherlands, ignoring Boon's own thoughts on the matter.[14] In the one biography of Boon, dating from 2008, Boon is still presented as the "Indo-writer" originating from a 'mixed' and 'kleine boeng' family, desperately running back and forth between East and West, then giving up his writing to help emancipate "his" people.[15] To overcome this colonial legacy, the IWI projects stay true to the time, location, and text of Boon's publications, starting with the "Piekerans" as originally printed in *Nieuwsgier.* This creates a 'point zero' for Boon's real bibliography, laying the groundwork for a future transnational biography of Boon that will explain his nationality and mobility from the perspective of 'cosmobilities.'[16]

Transnational and border-crossing

Boon had Dutch nationality by birth, but he only spent 15 of his 63 years in the Netherlands. Before he turned 20 Boon visited the Netherlands twice for about six months, even going to school in Amsterdam. But the Indies were his home, and he lived in Java, Borneo and Sumatra before leaving for the Netherlands at the age of 44. In the following 19 years he migrated to the USA for a period of five years, returned to the Netherlands, and from there twice visited Indonesia and the Dutch colony in the Caribbean, Suriname. For those Dutch living in the Indies, professional mobility throughout the archipelago, holidays for months in Europe, schooling for years on other continents, and family ties stretching across continents were the norm. It provided its inhabitants an outlook far beyond (Dutch) national borders.[17] These circumstances generated a matching mindset cultivated by the unique frame in which schooling, education and upbringing took place. This mindset can be seen in Boon's life, for example by the relaxed way he travelled the globe, by his equal love for Indonesia and the Netherlands, and by his interest in Latin America. It can also be seen in his work, for example in the way he utilizes the Dutch idiom and the languages he knew: Dutch, Indies and Petjoh.

Boon's language use reflects the colonial, decolonial and postcolonial situations he lived in over time. Since Dutch was the language of the coloniser, it ruled the government organisations and till decolonisation also the press. Until World War II Boon, a sports journalist, wrote in Dutch, the language used by the colonisers like Boon's father, and by people educated for a period in the Netherlands or in the Indies at Dutch-speaking schools, like Boon himself. Boon also debuted

---

14 Nieuwenhuys did something similar in response to the work of Lin Scholte, who wrote of the humiliating names children of soldiers were given in the Indies. Readers of *Tong Tong* reacted vigourously and Boon had to defuse the matter with the article "Nieuwe scheldnamen" in *Tong Tong* (30 September 1964). See Edy Seriese, "Anak Nieuwenhuys of literatuur?" *Indisch Anders* (25 May 2015), https://indisch-anders.nl/lin-scholte-anak-nieuwenhuys-of-literatuur/. Accessed 25 May 2020.

15 Wim Willems, *Tjalie Robinson: Biografie van een Indo-Schrijver* (Amsterdam: Bert Bakker, 2008).

16 Sarah Panter, Johannes Paulmann, and Margit Szöllösi-Janze, "Mobility and Biography: Methodological Challenges and Perspectives," *Jahrbuch für Europäische Geschichte/European History Yearbook* 16 (Berlin: De Gruyter Oldenbourg, 2015): 1-14.

17 See Elizabeth Buettner, *Empire Families: Britons and Late Imperial India* (Oxford: OUP, 2005).

as a cartoonist in 1946 and as an author in 1948 in Dutch.[18] From 1951 on, however, he began writing the "Piekerans" in Indies and later, when he was in the Netherlands he wrote "Ik en Bentiet" in Petjoh."[19] Indies and Petjoh were not considered languages in colonial times, just slang for the lower classes.[20] Boon did not use these languages to get an easy laugh at 'kleine boeng' as was common in Dutch colonial texts. Instead, he used them to write literature, thus proving that Indies and Petjoh were real languages, and not just contact languages, registers, let alone linguistic 'mishmash.' By introducing literature written in Petjoh and Indies, Boon was overcoming intellectual colonialism. This is present at all levels of his texts: the idiom, the grammar, the metaphors and other literary forms. An example will be provided here with "Intro," the opening pages of his first book publication, *Tjies: A Collection of Tales,* published by Boon himself (as Vincent Mahieu) in Indonesia in 1954.[21]

"Intro" appears to be a tale, but it was also a meta-text, one in which Boon, by comparing novels and tales, formulated his views on literature and life. My book, writes Boon, is not high-brow "European literature" akin to novels or short stories. It is "only a small bundle of tales . . . hunted" down by him with his "tjies" (a small gun). As a writer, he saw himself rather more like a Grimm Brother than a novelist, a humble craftsman actually recording tales. The true producers of the tales, he continued, are the storytellers, "we, from the Morgenland," a place where "everybody is a taleteller" ever since "Sindbad." By these very words at the beginning of the collection, the author withdraws all literary pretention, evading in this way having the collection judged by (colonial) literary standards of the time. *Evading* is a tried-and-true strategy for escaping a dominant system. The simple, non-literary words and concepts like "recording" and "tales" and "storytellers" were Boon's signs for this strategy. Boon used the strategy to clear the way for his "vertellingen" in *Tjies* and for the "Piekerans" published as a collection that same year, referring to

---

18 The cartoon series "Taaie en Neut" was published from June 1946 to August 1948 in the Dutch military weekly *Wapenbroeders* edited by Boon. Boon's article "Oom David" was published in the Dutch cultural monthly *Oriëntatie* (March 1948), edited by Rob Nieuwenhuys.

19 The "Piekerans" were first published in *Nieuwsgier* and other dailies and monthlies in Indonesia. "Ik en Bentiet" was first published as a series in the Dutch monthly *Onze Brug* in the Netherlands. The first editions of the books *Piekerans van een straatslijper* date from 1954 and 1956 in Indonesia. *Ik en Bentiet* was not published during Boon's lifetime, his widow published the book in December 1974 in the Netherlands.

20 Indies is comparable to Afrikaans in South Africa. De Vries considered Indies, as well as Petjoh, a "variety of Dutch," also saying that Petjoh has a grammar different from that of Indies. Here Petjoh and Indies are considered "mengtalen" (hybrid languages). See J. de Vries, "Indisch-Nederlands," in *Wereldnederlands: Oude en jonge variëteiten van het Nederlands,* ed. Nicoline van der Sijs (The Hague: SDU, 2005), 59-78. Mingaars mentions Boon as a writer in Petjoh and Indies, but only used Mahieus' *Tjies* as a source. See Peter Mingaars, ed., *Indisch Lexicon: Indische woorden in de Nederlandse literatuur 'Een vervliegende woordenschat'* ('t Goy-Houten: HES & De Graaf, 2005), xxvii-xxxix.

21 Vincent Mahieu, "Intro," in *Tjies: Een bundel vertellingen* (Bandoeng/Amsterdam: Gambir, 1954). "Almost" the whole edition was lost in "the riots due to the political changes" as Boon put it in T.R., "Tong Tong vertelt," *Tong Tong* (15 December 1968): 4-5. The next printing was published in December 1955 in Bandoeng. In 1958 a part of this collection was reprinted by H.P. Leopold in The Hague. Entitled *Tjies Stories,* it left out the "Intro" and "Five Sing-Song vertellingen" but included "Het vriendje van de rups" and "Wharrr-wharrr-wharrr." This Leopold edition formed the basis for discussion of *Tjies* up to 2009. See Edy Seriese, "Het pak van Sjaalman: Kijk op Indische Letteren," *Indische letteren* (September 2010): 185-189.

them with the word "opstellen" (simple essays), another modest word that denotes a not-literary text. Nevertheless, the fact that these words were located in a preface in a collection meant that they actually gained a literary connotation.

Combined with the modesty that the word "tales" implies, Boon used another strategy to evade the powers that be, one we can refer to as *acknowledgement*. This strategy explicitly concealed current norms by underlining them, for instance the superiority of novels over tales. It is a proven strategy to silence the enemy. But Boon went further. His "Morgenland" was not just a simple word meaning 'land of dawn,' suggesting an innocent writer fantasy like Thoreau's *Walden* or More's *Utopia*. The word was nothing less than a sign of a third underlying strategy we can refer to as *revaluation by comparison*. Combined with the name "Sindbad," it refered to the *Thousand-and-One-Nights* told by Scheherazade, a complex manuscript of ancient tales. The humble name Morgenland was a gentle attack on the basic colonial conception of inequality due to diversity. For, by connecting the two story-sets, Boon related his *Tjies* to a famous classic of literature, one highly regarded also by Europeans. And since the *Thousand-and-One-Nights* originated from Asia, India and Africa and stretched back before the Christian era, Boon not only bypassed colonial literary standards, he also claimed cultural autonomy for these 'tales.' This emphasised a concept of literature totally different from the colonial one, with different characteristics and forms, like orality, interactivity between storyteller and listener, open endings, and multiple voices.

To make this revolutionary statement of cultural autonomy, Boon used the European literary form of the preface, traditionally the place for writers to position themselves and their work. Boon's simple word "Intro" was part of this strategy of *disguise*, meant to hide what Boon was really doing: drawing a line between his tales and the tales of Scheherazade, bypassing colonial history. The strategy was hidden because it did not disclose that the tales are independent from colonial history, and even suggested the possibility of an independent future. This is only made clear when Boon claimed tales will always exist because of the human need "to escape death, temporarily or forever." Boon did not mean to replace one superior literary form or system by another, but to substitute the basic colonial false standard of race by what he saw as an actual and universal human need. In Boon's view, everybody was alike in their search for immortality, and telling tales is a way to reach the future in a way that could avoid and ignore colonial values by creating new idioms, images, literary characteristics and even history. He and all his peers "from the Morgenland" knew *by experience* that a tale was the only way "to escape oblivion and death temporarily or forever" through the endless process of telling and retelling, listening and hearing.

This process had proven its immortality by Scheherazade's everlasting fame. It is a process in which everyone can participate by telling their own life story, 'the one life of thousands,' implicating that everyone is equally valued and indispensable. "Intro" therefore ends with a call: "Who will continue to tell?" It looks like a simple call for more tales; it offered in fact an opportunity for everyone to prove their existence outside the 'black hole' of the colonial narrative. It was wrapped, of course, in a non-literary form, the postscript – a signifier again, this time for the low-key strategy of *ignoring the dominant culture* to live an autonomous life on one's own merits on its margins.

Boon was in fact declaring independence for everybody, not as individuals but as indispensable members of a self-governing community. All of Boon's work was about this type of autonomy and immortality, turning the colonial system and mindset into another galaxy, offering its inhabitants a way out 'temporarily or forever.' His proposed strategies and idiom however were deeply rooted in that colonial mindset, twisting, denying, and overcoming its inhuman prejudices. Boon's 'insurgency' was to disconnect literature from the colonial concept of writing and writers, instead connecting it to the shared human need for tales and storytellers. In order to describe this work, we need additional concepts combining insights from sociology, linguistics and literary science, connecting language data to social strategies and to colonialism. We need to interpret Boon's simple and old-fashioned Dutch words and his slightly divergent use of well-known literary tools as literary strategies rooted in colonial society. We can do this by using the technique of close reading, in particular to understand how exactly Boon's texts were disconnecting his idiom and strategies from connotations too easily recognised as 'colonial.'

Refiguring the archive: return to the collectors

Boon described tale-tellers as a group with only one collective characteristic: they, like he, came from Morgenland. But Morgenland is not a real country, though it is clearly understood to be located in 'the East.' So who were the tellers? And what exactly did they tell? To search for answers to these questions, it is necessary to look at the Boon archive with different eyes.[22] The archive, now housed at the IWI, consists of all the volumes of *Tong Tong* plus a large assortment of diverse items: books, incomplete magazine sets, photos, films, audio in diverse formats, personal documents like diaries, sets of correspondence, handwritten and typed essays, and all manner of personal belongings from before, during, and after the war. These materials were collected in one place because of Jan Boon (Tjalie Robinson)'s call for "memories" in 1958 in *Tong Tong* to make the magazine "the most beautiful story book".[23] It would be a storybook about the Indies, containing 'all' the experiential knowledge gained in the former colony, as a gift to the Netherlands to help it write its colonial history. Up to the mid-1990s, when I became the managing director of the IWI collection, the archive lay stored away in an attic. My first task was to categorise the material. A number of individuals who had worked with the magazine during Boon's lifetime helped out. During this process, these volunteers revealed, piece by piece, the history of the archive itself.

Even after Boon died, they told me, people from the Indies, like Boon having migrated to the Netherlands between 1940 and 1960, continued to bring their personal documents and files to the archive, for it was the one place in the

22 An inspiration for this 'rediscovery' was Carolyn Hamilton et al., eds., *Refiguring the Archive* (Dordrecht/Boston/London: Kluwer, 2002).

23 "If only 1/1000th of all people from Indië would record their memories in *Tong Tong* it would be the most beautiful storybook the Netherlands ever had." Tjalie Robinson, "Zwijgende rijsteters," *Tong Tong* (28 February 1958): 1.

Netherlands that would accept their collections intact. Archives such as the Netherlands Institute for War Documentation (NIOD), the Royal Institute of Southeast Asian and Caribbean Studies (KITLV), Museum Bronbeek, and The Royal Tropical Institute (KIT) as well as individual academics or journalists, would only take loose items. They would then use these items in what the tellers called the 'sandwich method.' Personal belongings, former parts of a real life, appeared in expositions, readings, radio and TV programs, and in academic articles, intermingled between diverse, unrelated items, sandwiched into an unrecognizable context, presenting an unfamiliar story. The alienation this caused – losing one's own story by misuse of one's own familiar property – is hard to quantify. Protests against this practice were countered by claiming that the context they were now in was 'academically sound' and the loose items served as 'illustrations' or provided compelling 'quotes.'

It was only in 1985 after Lou de Jong published his history of the Indies that these individual feelings could be clustered together, recognised now as a collective experience.[24] A law suit was filed against the Dutch government by the Committee for the Historical Rehabilitation of the Netherlands East Indies (Comité Geschiedkundig Eerherstel Nederlands Indië), together with hundreds of individuals and Indies organisations.[25] They asked for another kind of history, written not by one man but by a diverse group of scholars including people with experiential knowledge of the Indies.[26] The case made its way through the courts for over five years, from February 1985 till June 1989, and the judgment was ultimately negative, with all claims being rejected. One beneficial outcome, however, was a major expansion of the IWI collection. In the context of the case, Boon's call to help write history was renewed in the magazine *Moesson* (formerly known as *Tong Tong*) and answered in the form of an archive devoted exactly to that task.

This background revealed that the push for academic categorisation of the archive's contents in 1995 actually undermined the original goals that it, and *Tong Tong*, were established for. As a result, the IWI from then on gave space for the volunteers to tell their own stories and add them to the archive, wrapping the items that visitors requested with additional stories from their own experience. This way of presenting the archive's contents became known as 'Indies friendly' or 'Indies

---

24 "These ordinary people, who had never been involved in policy or administration, who lived far away from the source of colonial politics in The Hague . . . were and are, overlooked in historiography or made scapegoats of Dutch colonialism." Ralph Boekholt, *De Staat, Dr. L. de Jong en Indië: Het proces van het Comité Geschiedkundig Eerherstel Nederlands-Indië tegen de Staat der Nederlanden over deel 11A van 'Het Koninkrijk der Nederlanden in de Tweede Wereldoorlog' 29 maart 1986- 10 april 1990* (The Hague: Moesson, 1992), 9. Boekholt emphasised the impossibility for cultural minorities to go against the dominant culture: "Nobody is approachable. The Minister, the author, nor the judge. This history is untouchable, the author is untouchable. And yet in this standard work written on behalf of the government by the national historian, is also told about life and work of ordinary people in pre-war Indië . . . [in a] one-sided, negative, and most grievous way." Boekholt, *De Staat*, 26.

25 Gerard Jonker, supported by A.C. Broeshart and A. N. van Milligen de Wit, founded the Comité Geschiedkundig Eerherstel Nederlands-Indië (GENI) in The Hague. *Moesson*, the former magazine *Tong Tong*, directed by Boon's widow and Ralph Boekholt (born 1952), joined immediately. The GENI sued the Dutch Government based on "serious objections against the content, tenor, line of reasoning, structure and details of volume 11a" of de Jong's historiography. See Boekholt, *De Staat*, 105-108. Van Milligen de Wit and Boekholt are two of the founders of the IWI.

26 Boekholt, *De Staat*, 8.

hospitality.' It also was life story-telling the way Jan Boon had described in "Intro": story-telling brought about by the need to escape the colonial narrative. Once understood, this development of the archive caused a major shift in IWI policy. From that point on, new donations of documents and materials were accepted in complete form, with a renewed interest in the stories that came along with them. Telling stories became part of the archive. Throughout, we maintained rigorous academic standards concerning preservation, and have even greatly enhanced this aspect by donating the collection to reputable Dutch heritage institutions to enable us to concentrate on and develop our digital archive.[27]

Return to the source: the 'personal story'

Gradually, the collection was digitised and put on our redesigned website, with pictures, identification numbers and traditional keywords referring to the physical IWI-collection, with full-text-search also available. Keywords were generated from the questions visitors from the Indies were asking, from the texts and stories that came along with new donations, and from the life stories our volunteers were telling our visitors. Names of cultural enterprises, prison camps, schools, small villages that had been birthplaces, companies, ships, persons and families, and all kinds of everyday words like 'onderneming' (kind of plantation), 'tjebok,' (hygienic acts), 'bultzak' (mattress) and 'wadjan' (special kind of frying pan) became part of the archival narratives. The stories behind the new keywords were collected in the *Kumpulan Project*, a series of group meetings in which over 300 people in total shared their life memories.[28] One effect of this project was that many loose items in the archive became connected again, not just as common categories but also with the lives that once gave them their meaning. Another outcome was the collection of themes expressed by the storytellers themselves to tell their histories: ancestors and family relations, music and musical taste, daily life in the Indies, food and the Indies kitchen, nature and natural care, the three wars they experienced, and their adjustment in the Netherlands. The results were recorded and displayed through exhibitions, readings, articles and photo books, and made digitally available through various formats, including the IWI website, bringing to life new possibilities for combining collection items with stories. In this way the digital archive effectively returned the IWI-collection to its original owners, who now have daily access from wherever they may be.

The project *Aangespoeld*, meaning 'stranded' as well as 'washed ashore,' followed in 2007. It allowed for the underlying life stories found in the personal archives to be (re)constructed in texts and images. Beginning with a gallery of honor of Indies' migrants, it soon extended into a virtual collection of life stories told by individuals or small groups of storytellers. The texts in *Aangespoeld* were written by the director of the IWI and approved to the last comma by the participating storytellers. Corresponding images came from the personal archives of the storytellers and

27 The physical collection was donated to the National Museum of World Cultures in Amsterdam, the Bronbeek Museum in Arnhem, and the Royal Netherlands Institute of South East Asian and Caribbean Studies (KITLV) in Leiden.

28 See for *Kumpulan* Liane van der Linden and Bibi Panhuysen, eds., *Verhalen vangen: Verzamelen, ontsluiten en presenteren van immaterieel cultureel erfgoed* (Amsterdam: Imagine IC, 2003), 46.

from the IWI collection. Once on the website, the individual life stories were connected by hyperlinks, so that a digital visitor could roam throughout the IWI collection to gather additional information, and to a timeline and to Google Maps to visualize and realize the times and locations of the stories' details. *Aangespoeld* is the 21st century way of visiting the IWI collection, imitating the 'Indies-friendly hospitality' once found only with direct personal interaction with the archive's volunteers. The website now holds over 60 life stories, the oldest of a person born in 1869 and the youngest born in 1954. *Aangespoeld* does not simply repeat the physical IWI collection. With the stories now connected to each other and to the spaces in which the lives took place, the project reveals the vision of the storytellers on the whereabouts of their lives, a place held within their heads called 'Indies,' an adjective rather than a noun that points to a kind of 'Morgenland.' *Aangespoeld* turned out to be an interface that made this space accessible and visible, every single story now a part of a greater whole, and every single storyteller a coauthor in that whole. Brought together, the 60 biographies told their own story. A story with enormous historic significance.

Return to the background story

This larger story is not actually told in *Aangespoeld*, it is simply made manifest by the project. The story, paradoxically familiar and unknown, refers to the genesis of Indonesia and postcolonial Netherlands as nation states, but favouring the Indies tales over the Dutch or Indonesian colonial stories. In this story no one is 'kleine boeng,' just (many types of) 'Indies people,' a heterogeneous group with many languages, nationalities, and professions. This 'Indies' has all kinds of religions: Hinduism, Buddhism, Catholicism, Protestantism or eclectic amalgamations of indigenous-western influences. It is populated by many nationalities with native languages like Dutch, English, Javanese, Sundanese, Indies, Petjoh and more. The life stories that make up this background story have residences connected to particular periods of life, such as school or retirement, rather than permanent addresses. They tell stories of a lifetime of perpetual mobility between distant locations.

At its center is the family, obviously the object of first love and loyalty. No single story starts without an introduction to the family and to ancestors. The word 'family,' however, does not mean exactly what we think of as a nuclear family. This is a 'grootfamilie,' a combined extended and self-chosen family of at least three generations – blood relatives and other intimates – functioning across networks that span the globe.[29] Some family lines reach back 500 years to Portuguese colonial times in Asia, still recognizable in the names and the music of many storytellers.[30] The family as a self-organizing network offered individual members their basic security in matters of marriage, work, friendship, money and other forms of loyalty. Daily family life was intergenerational, intercultural, multilingual, international and not limited to kin. The family, in short, was

29 Edy Seriese, "The house the family built: The heritage of the 'Indies factor,'" in Catalogue to the exhibition *Suspended Histories* (Amsterdam: Museum Van Loon, 2013), 16-21.

30 *Krontjongan: Vertellingen uit de Indische muziek* (DVD, Amsterdam/Almere/Zeewolde: SiC/IWI/Sebastian Productions, 2008).

the one place where cosmobilities and tell-and-tale-abilities were formed and developed. This took place, for example, when children travelled for fun or family visits and learned to write letters, and also when housewives were trained to prefer having guests rather than an empty living room.[31] That this life style is not as well-known anymore does not mean it did not exist or does not continue to do so. Its traces can be found in family stories and photo albums, in newspapers, TV-programs, and literature, in archives and museums, in case-law and minutes from parliamentary debates.[32] Indies people introduced their culture, told their stories, and built their archive, and when taken all together in *Aangespoeld* it overarches the story of Dutch colonialism. By returning to the storytelling and the personal archives of our collectors, *Aangespoeld* became an alternative kind of historiography, stemming from the social and historical background of Jan Boon and his peers. For the storytellers in *Aangespoeld* are the people known by Boon as 'we from the Morgenland.' We know that because of "Intro," reprinted in *Tong Tong* in 1968.

Turn to the writer: his literature

Boon did recognise the necessity to rewrite the 'history of the Indo,' or in his words a "rectification" of the colonial story that presented Indos as "children of shame" with "faked birth certificates." He wanted a Dutchman to write it, for it concerned in his eyes the rehabilitation of "the father" and not of his offspring. To Meyer Ranefft, former chairman of the Colonial Parliament (de Volksraad), Boon pointed out the historical nonsense of the colonial narrative and proposed a revised vision on Indos as some "of the millions and millions (of) descendants of Europeans" who left the continent to give birth to "new states and peoples of mixed descent" all over the world. That would be a history Boon could feel as a part of himself, since it demolished the enforced racial hierarchies and boundaries between 'colonised' and 'coloniers.' "Though history doesn't know," he wrote, "we are a people of our own, having our own country, our own traditions, our own dignity."[33] So he turned to the people who also belonged to that history, with a call to testify, tell their life stories, and he shaped *Tong Tong* into a place where, as he put it, "everybody" could write down their memories without running up against any "European standard" on "literature" or "journalism."[34]

---

31 Noted by Beb Vuyk in a lecture in 1974, according to Bert Scova Righini, *Een leven in twee vaderlanden: Een biografie van Beb Vuyk* (Leiden: KITLV, 2005), 423.

32 On the cultural influence of Indies people in the Netherlands and elsewhere see Hans van den Akker etal., *Reisgids Indonesië: Oorlogsplekken 1942 – 1949* (The Hague: Open Kaart, 2010); Nelien Drewes, "De geboorte van een Indische vertelling:De geschiedenis van Indisch tijdschrift Tong Tong 1956 – 1977" (PhD diss., University of Amsterdam, 1999); Andrew Goss, "From Tong-Tong to Tempo Doeloe: Eurasian Memory Work and the Bracketing of Dutch Colonial History, 1957-1961," *Indonesia* 70 (October 2000): 9-36; Florine Koning, *De Pasar Malam van Tong Tong: Een Indische onderneming* (The Hague: Tong Tong, 2007); Gert Oostindie et al., *Postkoloniale monumenten in Nederland* (Leiden: KITLV, 2011); Steijlen, *Een Indische skyline.*

33 "Amsterdam, 18 juli 1955 Zeer geachte Heer Meyer Ranneft." See also "Amsterdam, 21 juli 1955 Zeer geachte heer Meyer Ranneft" and "Amsterdam, 13 augustus 1955 Zeer geachte heer Meyer Ranneft" in Tjalie Robinson, *Schrijven met je vuisten: Brieven van Tjalie Robinson,* ed. Wim Willems (Amsterdam: Prometheus, 2009), 77-84, 89-91, 89-91.

34 Boon, "Tong Tong vertelt," 5.

Boon reprinted "Intro" in 1968, explaining that this was in response to popular demand since *Tjies* had been reprinted without it. He also included his "P.S.," making it explicit that this call for storytelling was answered in *Tong Tong*: "Hundreds of Indies people started to tell (stories)," he wrote, "left- and right-wing people, of all religions, 'kandjengs' and 'kleine boengs,' from high and low places in society, Dutch and Indonesian 'and everything in between.'" The reprint in *Tong Tong* not only identified the writers in the magazine (including Boon) as 'we from the Morgenland,' it also showed that 'Morgenland' was more than just a metaphor. Though not representing a nation-state, it was a social reality with inhabitants who first began by sharing their memories in a magazine, and later contributed to *Aangespoeld*, building a complete archive to claim their existence.

Conclusion

Boon's life and work are therefore a testament to the fluidity of identity and subjectivity, as he searched for methods and means to escape the 'colonial gaze' and the colonial idiom through his own language and publications. A transnational actor *pur sang*, Boon challenged all the narratives that, as Edward Said later exposed, maintained the barriers between the colonial worthy and the colonised worthless through 'hidden' distinctions based on class, race, and gender. His simple act of reprinting "Intro" signaled the success of the low-key strategy of 'the *Tong Tong* community in Europe.' To Boon, a magazine was both the perfect disguise and frame to visualize 'Morgenland.' *Tong Tong* should therefore be analysed, described and criticised as historiography, not comparable to Lou de Jong's work from the 1980s or others after him, but with Mochtar Lubis and Jean Gelman Taylor who methodologically assimilated oral histories into their national histories of Indonesia.[35]

Rob Nieuwenhuys did something similar in *Oost Indische Spiegel*, disguising his life memories as literary historiography.[36] The IWI sees the magazine as the history book it is, to be used to expand our knowledge of the history of the 'Indies' and its inhabitants, especially concerning the social and historical background of Jan Boon, his peers, their ancestors and offspring. *Tong Tong* was the frame that represents Boon perfectly, expressing his thoughts and stories on immortality and autonomy. However, the IWI's goal to reconstitute this meaning via the *TT project* also approaches, analyses and describes *Tong Tong* as the most exciting *literary* object in Dutch since 'the bundle of Sjaalman.'[37] Starting with a close reading of all the texts, we categorise them by looking for genres, sub themes,

---

35 Mochtar Lubis, *Het land onder de regenboog* (Alphen a/d Rijn: A.W. Sijthoff, 1979); Jean Gelman Taylor, *Indonesia: Peoples and Histories* (New Haven: Yale University Press, 2003).

36 Rob Nieuwenhuys, *Oost-Indische spiegel: Wat Nederlandse schrijvers en dichters over Indonesië hebben geschreven vanaf de eerste jaren der Compagnie tot op heden* (Amsterdam: Querido, 1972). This still influential collection is an inventory of all Dutch literary texts connected with the Indies. It shows the same strategies Boon presented in "Intro" but makes use of a different literary colonial strategy. See Edy Seriese, "Indo-centrisch of egocentrisch: Rob Nieuwenhuys, *Oost-Indische Spiegel* als exponent van de 20-eeuwse Mestiezencultuur," *Sporen van een Indisch verleden (1600-1942)*, ed. Wim Willems (Leiden: C.O.M.T, 1992), 179-196.

37 Sjaalman is the nickname for Max Havelaar, the main character in Multatuli's novel. Being a 'bundle of Sjaalman' is the main characteristic of Indies literature, see Edy Seriese, "Het Pak van Sjaalman: Kijk op Indische Letteren," *Indische letteren* (*September* 2010): 185-189.

style characteristics and literary strategies, in the language provided by *Tong Tong*, uncoupled from any national framework. The key decision was *not* to produce a biography of Boon until all the preparatory work was finished. Boon as a subject and a literary figure is thus reconstituted, no longer fragmented and erased by colonial cultural amnesias, but complete and immortal.

Bibliography

Akker, Hans van den, et al. *Reisgids Indonesië: Oorlogsplekken 1942-1949.* The Hague: Open Kaart, 2010.

Boekholt, Ralph. *De Staat, Dr. L. de Jong en Indië: Het proces van het Comité Geschiedkundig Eerherstel Nederlands-Indië tegen de Staat der Nederlanden over deel 11A van 'Het Koninkrijk der Nederlanden in de Tweede Wereldoorlog' 29 maart 1986- 10 april 1990.* The Hague: Moesson, 1992.

Buettner, Elizabeth. *Empire Families: Britons and Late Imperial India* (Oxford: OUP, 2005).

Drewes, Nelien. "De geboorte van een Indische vertelling: De geschiedenis van Indisch tijdschrift Tong Tong 1956 – 1977." PhD diss., University of Amsterdam, 1999.

Goss, Andrew. "From Tong-Tong to Tempo Doeloe: Eurasian Memory Work and the Bracketing of Dutch Colonial History, 1957-1961." *Indonesia* 70 (October 2000): 9-36.

Hamilton, Carolyn et al., eds. *Refiguring the Archive.* Dordrecht/Boston/London: Kluwer, 2002.

Koning, Florine. *De Pasar Malam van Tong Tong: Een Indische onderneming.* The Hague: Tong Tong, 2007.

Krontjongan: Vertellingen uit de Indische muziek (DVD, Amsterdam/Almere/Zeewolde: SiC/IWI/Sebastian Productions, 2008).

Susan Legêne, "Historiography and the Hinges of Biographical Representation." Lecture at the expert meeting of Unhinging the National Framework: Platform for the Study of Transnational Life Writing, Utrecht University, 30 September 2016.

Van der Linden, Liane, and Bibi Panhuysen, eds. *Verhalen vangen: Verzamelen, ontsluiten en presenteren van immaterieel cultureel erfgoed.* Amsterdam: Imagine IC, 2003.

Lubis, Mochtar. *Het land onder de regenboog.* Alphen a/d Rijn: A.W. Sijthoff, 1979.

Mahieu, Vincent [Jan Boon]. *Tjies: Een bundel vertellingen.* Bandoeng/Amsterdam: Gambir, 1954.

Mahieu, Vincent [Jan Boon]. *Tjies: Vertellingen.* 2nd ed. The Hague: H.P. Leopolds Uitg. Mij., 1958.

Mahieu, Vincent [Jan Boon]. *Verzameld Werk,* edited by Rob Nieuwenhuys. Amsterdam: Querido, 1992.

Mingaars, Peter, ed. *Indisch Lexicon: Indische woorden in de Nederlandse literatuur: "Een vervliegende woordenschat."* 't Goy-Houten: HES & De Graaf, 2005.

Nieuwenhuys, Rob. *Oost-Indische spiegel: Wat Nederlandse schrijvers en dichters over Indonesië hebben geschreven vanaf de eerste jaren der Compagnie tot op heden.* Amsterdam: Querido, 1972.

Oostindie, Gert, et al. *Postkoloniale monumenten in Nederland.* Leiden: KITLV, 2011.

Paasman, Bert, ed. *Tjalie Robinson: De stem van Indisch Nederland.* The Hague: Stichting Tong Tong, 1994.

Panter, Sarah, Johannes Paulmann, and Margit Szöllösi-Janze. "Mobility and Biography: Methodological Challenges and Perspectives." In *Jahrbuch für Europäische Geschichte/ European History Yearbook*, edited by Sarah Panter, 1-14. Berlin: De Gruyter Oldenbourg, 2015.

Pattynama, Pamela. *Bitterzoet Indië: Herinnering en nostalgie in literatuur, foto's en films.* Amsterdam: Prometheus/Bert Bakker, 2014.

Righini, Bert Scova. *Een leven in twee vaderlanden: Een biografie van Beb Vuyk.* Leiden: KITLV, 2005.

Robinson, Tjalie [Jan Boon]. *Didi in Holland,* edited by Chrétien Breukers and Wilfred Dierick. Nijmegen: Nova Zembla, 1992.

Robinson, Tjalie [Jan Boon]. *Schrijven met je vuisten: Brieven van Tjalie Robinson,* edited by Wim Willems. Amsterdam: Prometheus, 2009.

Seriese, Edy. "Indo-centrisch of egocentrisch: Rob Nieuwenhuys, *Oost-Indische Spiegel* als exponent van de 20-eeuwse Mestiezencultuur." In *Sporen van een Indisch verleden (1600-1942),* edited by Wim Willems, 179-196. Leiden: C.O.M.T, 1992.

Seriese, Edy. "Het pak van Sjaalman: Kijk op Indische Letteren." *Indische letteren* (September 2010): 185-189.

Seriese, Edy. "The house the family built: The heritage of the 'Indies factor.'" Catalogue to the exhibition *Suspended Histories* (Amsterdam: Museum Van Loon, 2013): 16-21.

Seriese, Edy. "Tjalie ont-dekt: over de houdbaarheid van teksten of 'Niet alles kan mee (zoals de oplet-chauffeur spijtig zei).'" *Indische letteren* (March 2012): 42-55.

Seriese, Edy. "Anak Nieuwenhuys of literatuur?" *Indisch Anders* (25 May 2015), https://indisch-anders.nl/lin-scholte-anak-nieuwenhuys-of-literatuur/. Accessed 25 May 2020.

Steijlen, Fridus. *Een Indische skyline: Indische organisaties in Nederland tussen 1980 en 2010.* Amsterdam: Amsterdam University Press, 2018.

Taylor, Jean Gelman. *Indonesia: Peoples and Histories.* New Haven: Yale University Press, 2003.

Vries, J. de. "Indisch-Nederlands." In *Wereldnederlands: Oude en jonge variëteiten van het Nederlands,* edited by Nicoline van der Sijs, 59-78. The Hague: SDU, 2005.

SECTION 4

POSITIONINGS

"She is English, isn't she?"

Transnationality as part of Cissy van Marxveldt's self-presentation

Monica Soeting

Introduction

In another chapter in this volume Marijke Huisman questions whether we really need a mobile subject to unhinge the nation. To Huisman, it seems "perfectly possible to write almost any such a life from a post-national perspective, provided the biographer makes an active choice to highlight features of the subject's life that connect him to the world beyond his own locality."[1] Next, Huisman takes a step further and shows that transnational life writing does not even need a human subject. Taking the case of the reception of Booker T. Washington's autobiographical book *Up from Slavery* (1901) in the Netherlands during the twentieth century as an example, Huisman shows how an object – a book, in this case – can indeed unhinge a nation "and shed some light on transnational encounters."

Where Huisman took a step further by analysing the way in which a foreign book can influence, or used to change a mindset, I chose to take a step away from the transnational and mobile subject as somebody who literally moves from one country to the other. In this article I want to show how transnationality and mobility as immaterial values were used by Cissy van Marxveldt (pseudonym of Setske de Haan, 1889-1948), a famous Dutch author of books for adolescent girls and young women, in order to present herself in public as a member of the upper middle class. In this case transnationalism is to be understood as a form of cosmopolitism, *i.e.* the prerogative of the higher classes to feel at home in many cultures, classes and countries thanks to their financial means and higher education, while firmly establishing their own social and cultural background by doing so.[2] In this article the term mobility is used in the sense of social mobility, with Van Marxveldt transgressing, or wishing to transgress, social boundaries in order to be recognised as a member of the upper middle class. At the same time, Van Marxveldt's cosmopolitism and social mobility were gendered, as moving up the social ladder meant she also had to embrace the middle class ideal of women as caring wives and mothers, however active and cosmopolitan their actual

1 I would like to thank Marijke Huisman for generously permitting me to quote from her chapter.

2 As Calhoun writes: being able to live a cosmopolitan life is "often made possible by capital – social and cultural as well as economic." Calhoun, "Cosmopolitanism and Nationalism," in *Nations and Nationalism* 14, no. 3 (2008): 443.

lives would be. This led to Van Marxveldt downplaying the impact and success of her writing and publishing in order to comply with middle and upper middle class ideals of women as caring wives and mothers who did not have to work in order to make a living.

Another aspect of Van Marxveldt's cosmopolitism is that it was a cosmopolitanism by proxy. In order to counterbalance the conflicts between her daily life and her social aspirations, Van Marxveldt fulfilled her dream of being part of the cosmopolitan middle class in her novels rather than in real life, projecting her social ambitions on her many upper class protagonists.

Social ambitions

During her rather short life – she died when she was 58 – Cissy van Marxveldt produced 27 novels and collections of short stories, of which her *Joop ter Heul*-series about the coming of age of a rich girl from Amsterdam were, and are, the most popular of her books.[3] Having provided Anne Frank with a template for her early diary notes,[4] the *Joop ter Heul*-series were, and are still, being read by thousands of Dutch girls and young women, not only in the Netherlands, but also in the Dutch colonies and by numerous Dutch emigrants, as several readers' surveys and fan letters to Cissy van Marxveldt testify.[5] The same holds true for several other of Van Marxveldt's novels, like *Een zomerzotheid* (A Midsummer Folly, 1927) and the *Marijke*-series (1929-1934). Although all these stories seem to be firmly placed in a Dutch context and have never been published in any other language than Dutch, they appealed to readers living in other countries, from Denmark to the Dutch Easy-Indies. This may have been due in part to the transnational references in most of Van Marxveldt's books. Her protagonists proudly spend their summers in southern France, have been educated at British boarding schools, visit German spas for their health, marry non-Dutch husbands, or travel to England, Indonesia, or the United States for work.[6] Although most of them live in Amsterdam or in other towns in the western part of the Netherlands, they revel in using phrases in English, German and French, and often refer to international classics in literature and music. The question is to what extent these transnational references unhinge the 'Dutchness' of Van Marxveldt's famous novels. Were they used explicitly and solely to place the novels in an international context, or did they reflect the author's and/or readers' yearning for a more cosmopolitan life-style? The answer, I will argue, is more complex than this.

---

3 The series are still in print, the latest publication dating from 2018.

4 See Berteke Waaldijk, "Reading Anne Frank as a Woman." *Women's Studies International Forum* 16, no. 4 (July-August 1993): 327-335.

5 E.g. Dirk L. Daalder, "Wat lezen onze jongeren?" in *Rondom het boek*, ed. Roel Houwink (Amsterdam: Vereeniging ter bevordering van de belangen des boekhandels, 1935), 100-112; Maria A.E. van Lith-Van Schreven, "Het Europese kind in Indië en zijn lectuur," *Indisch Vrouwen Jaarboek 1936* (Jogjakarta: Kolff-Buning 1936): 161-187. In letters to Van Marxveldt, written in the thirties, the famous Dutch-Danish dancer Nini Theilade (1915-2018) declared herself to be one of Van Marxveldt's most fervent fans.

6 As in, respectively, the *Marijke*-series, *Rekel*, *Een zomerzotheid*, the *Joop ter Heul*-series, *De Kingfordschool*, *Kwikzilver*, *Puck van Holten*, and *De louteringskuur*.

Setske de Haan was born in 1889 in Oranjewoud, an affluent enclave in a very poor area of the southwestern part of the province of Friesland. Her father, like her mother, was the child of poor manual laborers, but had been able to escape poverty by becoming a school teacher. As an intelligent young man he managed to obtain a head teacher's certificate which secured him a much desired position as head teacher of a primary school in Oranjewoud. This was one year before his daughter and only child was born. In the years following her birth he secured jobs as a part-time teacher at an evening high school in a neighbouring town and as an examiner in Leeuwarden, the province's capital. Keen to secure a 'higher' social position for his daughter, he encouraged her to attend high school in Heerenveen, which she did but never finished. In 1908, a few months before her nineteenth birthday, she went to Great Britain to work as an au pair for an upper middle class family in Coventry. Finding a job abroad was not as spectacular at the time as it now may seem. Of Van Marxveldt's twenty-seven classmates in Heerenveen several students left for Germany after their final examination, to study mechanical engineering. One classmate found a job as a clerk in London, and another became a gardener in Paris which he left for Switzerland, only to settle in the United States; yet another classmate moved to South Africa.[7]

However, being an au pair did not suit Setske, or Céline as she was called in Coventry. Having been promised to read French and English novels and playing *quatre-mains* with her employer, she had to take care of the spoiled two year old daughter of the family and help the two maids with cleaning and shopping instead. In her diary, which she kept from July to December 1908, Setske bitterly complained about her plight and the many insults she had to suffer in the hands of her employer.[8] With insults she almost exclusively referred to remarks made by her employer about her assumed low social status as a teacher's daughter, her all too practical clothes, and her provincial, unrefined manners. Setske's life took a happier turn when she was offered a place at a girls boarding school in Bath in September 1908. Here she received a traditional upper-middle class education which involved not only learning to speak French and studying regular subjects such as geography, but also going to the theatre to watch the performance of different plays by canonical authors like Shakespeare, and attending classical concerts and public lectures.

When Setske returned to Friesland in the summer of 1909, she found it difficult to readapt to village life. After several attempts to become, consecutively, an English teacher and a journalist, she left for Amsterdam in 1912 where she enrolled in a so-called typing school. Having secured a job as a secretary with a German trading business in Amsterdam in 1913, she rented a room in the house of a widow in a respectable middle class area at the outskirts of Amsterdam. Here she led the life of a young middle class woman, going to concerts and plays with her landlady and her friends, organizing musical soirees and reading English novels. This is also where she met her future husband, Leon Beek, who was the son of Jewish parents and had been raised in the poor, Jewish quarter of Amsterdam. In order to be less conspicuously Jewish, he had at an earlier time discarded the 'n' at

---

7 Students' book of the Rijks Hogere Burgerschool Heerenveen, Tresoar Leeuwarden, coll. nr. 44-03, s.p.

8 Diary in the collection of Tresoar Leeuwarden, collection in process of being made accessible.

the end of his first name. He also at one point made attempts to have references to his Jewish background removed in the Amsterdam public records,[9] and lied about his place of birth when he first met Setske, as can be gleaned from the letters she wrote to her parents in 1913.[10]

Beek did not only do so out of fear or anti-Semitism, but also because of social aspirations. In this he followed a path many people born in the Jewish quarter had taken, to the dismay of some of the Jewish leaders, such as Bernard Kahn, one of the board members of the Dutch Federation of Zionists. At a public meeting following a serious anti-Semitic incident in Amsterdam around this time, Kahn addressed the issue of "Jewish anti-Semitism." This, he said, was typical of Jewish people who had managed to escape the ghetto and now despised the people who had not succeeded to leave the poor Jewish quarters. "Almost every Jew who escaped the ghetto thanks to his intellectual powers yesterday will tomorrow look down on his brothers and sisters from a great height," Kahn stated. "While his language hasn't yet lost the traces of the Jewish quarter . . . he feels a total different human being, draws a fat line between himself and the Amsterdam Jews and avoids going to cafés which are frequented by Jews on a Saturday."[11] After Setske and Leo became engaged, they took this 'escape' a step further and decided to emigrate to Canada. They were forced to change their plans when the First World War broke out in the summer of 1914, and married in Amsterdam in 1916.

With Leo being mobilised as First Lieutenant in the Dutch Army, and Setske having lost her job at the German trading company, she moved back in with her parents and started to write short stories for popular magazines under the penname Cissy van Marxveldt, in order to make money and to fulfil a life-long dream – as expressed in her diary of 1908[12]–of becoming an author. As her short stories proved to be successful, she tried her hand at a novel once she was reunited with her husband. Her first book *Game-and Set!* was published in 1917 and turned out to be the first of twenty-seven popular and best-selling books for girls and young women. Van Marxveldt published her last novel just before her death in 1948.

Being a best-selling author enabled Van Marxveldt gradually to move up the social ladder. The family often moved house until they were able to rent an apartment in the posh Vondelpark-area in Amsterdam. As a socially ambitious and successful novelist Van Marxveldt felt bound to abide by the ideals and rules of the upper social classes, including the ideal of the married woman "to produce a continually evolving domestic sphere."[13] For a long time this ideal was no more than that. Until 1928, when Beek had found a stable job at a department store in Amsterdam and Van Marxveldt was struck by illness, she was the breadwinner of the family.

9 The word 'Hebreeuws' on one of Beek's personal record cards has been crossed out.

10 Letters in the collection of Tresoar Leeuwarden, collection in process of being made accessible.

11 Joosje Lakmaker, *Voorbij de Blauwbrug: Het verhaal van mijn joodse grootvader* (Amsterdam: Wereldbibliotheek, 2008), 70-71. (My translation, MS).

12 Diary in the collection of Tresoar Leeuwarden, collection in process of being made accessible.

13 Nicola Humble, *The Feminine Middlebrow Novel 1920 to 1950s* (Oxford: Oxford University Press, 2007 [2001]), 109.

However, wanting to be recognised as a member of the upper middle class Van Marxveldt, rather than advertising her writing skills and her books, eagerly presented herself in public as a lady of leisure, dabbling in writing as other ladies might dabble in watercolors. This led to a conflict of interests of some sort. In an interview in 1928 with the journalist and publisher Aaldert J.G. Strengholt she was described as the "plucky little wife of an Amsterdam businessman, who lives in the museum quarter and loves to make a daily stroll to the Museumbookshop, where her books often embellish the shop window."[14] Asked by Strengholt if she planned to publish a 'real' novel, *i.e.* not a book for girls and young adult women, Van Marxveldt responded: "No, honestly: I just long to make a journey through the south of France in my own car, or through the Sahara for all I care."[15]

Complying with Strengholt's presentation of herself as a lady of leisure, playing down her writing skills and her success as a writer, and stressing that she'd rather travel than write, served several purposes. Van Marxveldt played down her skills and her literary ambitions in order to show her readers that in spite of her status as a bestselling author she valued the homely, middle class ideal of women as caring wives and mother. This also served to quell any suspicion that she was a female literary hack – much despised at the time by self-appointed intellectuals like the writer Menno ter Braak, who feared that popular female writers would take over the book market with their easy reading, middle-brow books, poisoning the minds of their readers and make them insensitive to Real Literature.[16] At the same time, protesting she'd rather drive her own car to France or Northern Africa made her look modern, rich and cosmopolitan: a fearless, affluent woman of the world as depicted in the novels by popular British authors like Agatha Christie and Barbara Cartland.[17]

Seven years later, in an interview published in the *Haagsche Courant*, Van Marxveldt again publicly confirmed her image of a member of the upper middle class, living up to the ideal of the caring wife and mother. This time she eagerly compared her writing to charity work. To the astonishment of the progressive female interviewer, Van Marxveldt explicitly stated that writing books was a hobby which she pursued only when she had time on her hands. "The author is of the opinion that a married woman and mother – extraordinary circumstances not withstanding – can and must find full happiness in her care for her family and her home," the interviewer noted.

> When I objected and said that it was possible that there are women who want more than this, and that it is egotism which forces a mother to devote her life to her children, she answered with a sweet, quiet smile that children

---

14 Aaldert J.G. Strengholt, "Cissy van Marxveldt vertelt . . . ," *Astra* 12 (June 1928): 1316.

15 "En op de laatste vraag, of ze ernaar verlangde 'om nog eens een heuschen "roman" te schrijven, of een drama,' antwoordde ze: 'Neen, eerlijk niet: ik verlang alleen naar een groote autotocht met een eigen auto door het Zuiden van Frankrijk, of door de Sahara voor mijn part.'" Strengholt, "Cissy van Marxveldt vertelt . . . ," 1320. (My translation, MS).

16 Erica van Boven, *Een hoofdstuk apart: 'Vrouwenroman' in de literaire kritiek*. Amsterdam: Sara/Van Gennep, 1992.

17 Compare Barbara Cartland's description of a modern heroine in *Sweet Punishment* (1931): "Diana had her own private airplane; she could pilot it herself . . . . It was an open two-seater Moth, painted silver-gray, with a line of deep blue." Cartland, *Sweet Punishment* (London: Hutchinson & Co., 1931), 31. With thanks to Margreeth Soeting for supplying this quote.

are allowed to be egoists in this respect. Women who have surplus time and energy may, according to her, spend this on reading, fancy work, education and social work, which can all be done at home, as long as it does not distract her attention or her personal presence too much. She regards it as an inconvenience when her work takes all her energy and makes it difficult to switch her attention to the children when they come home from school.[18]

In an autobiographical essay published in 1930, Van Marxveldt also carefully adjusted the conventional elements of a writer's life story to the middle class ideal of the woman as a mother and a care taker.[19] Describing how she had become a writer, she claimed, like most male authors, that her career as a writer had taken off with an epiphany. In her case, however, the epiphany had not been brought about by God or any other higher power, as in most autobiographies of male authors, but by her husband and father, who had encouraged her to write a book about a high school girl. This had resulted in the writing and publication of the bestselling series about the upper class schoolgirl Joop ter Heul and her friends. As in the interview with Strengholt, Van Marxveldt in her autobiographical essay stressed that writing was 'great fun' and a mere hobby instead of arduous labor, something that could be done without neglecting one's duties as a wife and mother.[20]

As the interviews and the autobiographical essay show, Van Marxveldt's representation and self-presentation as a writer were fraught with paradoxes. The same seems to have hold true for her daily life. On the one hand Van Marxveldt *was* a traditional Dutch homely wife and mother, caring for her husband and children according to middle class ideals. On the other hand, she was the untypical breadwinner of the family for a long time. Apart from this she yearned to be a modern, rich, cosmopolitan woman of leisure, feeling at home in the world, speaking different languages and enjoying different cultures, a life she could not actually live because her income was not high enough and because she suffered from ill health. This, however, was where her profession came at hand. Being a writer, writing for middle class readers with the same high class ideals, gave her a chance to live her cosmopolitan dreams, if not in reality then in her own books and by proxy of her characters.

18 "De schrijfster is van meening, dat de getrouwde vrouw en moeder – buitengewone omstandigheden daargelaten – haar volle geluk en bevrediging kan en moet vinden in haar zorgen voor gezin en huis. Op mijn tegenwerping, dat het toch mogelijk is, dat er vrouwen zijn, die daarbuiten nog iets wenschen, en dat het toch veelal louter egoïsme is, dat de moeder geheel voor zich doet opeischen, antwoordde zij met een lieven, rustigen glimlach, dat kinderen egoïst mogen zijn in dit opzicht. Wie tijd en energie overhouden, kunnen die haars inziens besteden aan lezen, handwerken, ontwikkeling en maatschappelijk werk, alles in huis mogelijk, althans zonder haar aandacht en persoonlijke aanwezigheid daarvan te veel of dwingend weg te leiden. Zij gevoelt het zelfs als een inconveniënt, dat haar werk haar nu eenmaal niet op gezette tijden loslaten wil, en zij zich niet altijd op het oogenblik, dat de schooldeuren opengaan, volkomen omschakelen kan." I.F. van Gelderen-de Witte, "Bij Cissy van Marxveldt," *Haagsche Courant*, 6 November 1935. (My translation, MS).

19 See Kathleen Chamberlain, "Gender, Class, and Domesticity in the Isabel Carleton Series," in *Nancy Drew and Company: Culture, Gender and Girls' Series*, ed. Sherrie A. Innes (Bowling Green: Bowling State University Popular Press, 1977), 39.

20 Cissy van Marxveldt and Emmy Belinfante-Belinfante, *Confetti* (Amersfoort: Valkhoff & Co., 1930).

Conspicuous consumption

A great many aspects concerning Van Marxveldt's journey up the social ladder may be gleaned not only from her public self-presentation as a writer but also – or especially so – from her novels. First of all, Van Marxveldt's pseudonym – in itself a signifier of female modesty[21]–referred to the upper class family Van Marxveld which owned a large estate in the east of the Netherlands and had ties with the royal family. Secondly, by numerous references to material goods, like interiors, dresses, meals and menus in her novels, Van Marxveldt showed her readers that she knew how things were done in an upper middle class milieu, which is typical of novels associated with the affluent middle and upper middle class, as shown by Nicola Humble and Kathleen Chamberlain. Status and class are, after all, not just determined by lineage, education and income, but also by material objects, such as the size and location of houses, interior decoration and, in cases of the upper middle and upper classes, clothes and food with cosmopolitan connotations. Marking status by material things was especially important in the case of newcomers or social climbers. Van Marxveldt, who had no lineage, education or wealth to speak of, took her refuge integrating these markers in her novels, showing her readers she knew what was *comme il faut.*[22]

A scene in a restaurant, included in Van Marxveldt's first novel *Game-and Set!* (1917), is a typical showcase of upper middle class taste in expensive foreign food and exclusive dresses, with words like cosy, soft, soft-pink, fairylike, white and sparkling being significant and indicative of a gendered, class-informed construction of a social-cultural ritual. In this story two young women, Lies and Henny – the two protagonists – are treated to dinner at a restaurant by Lies's mother, Mrs Van Deyl. The fact that they are not dining in any old-fashioned, inexpensive Dutch restaurant is made clear by Henny's description of the room where they dine and the discreet references to upper class manners, like the proper use of cutlery, table settings and decorations: "Around us we heard the cosy click-clack of forks and knives, a soft murmur of voices. . . . Our table was decorated with a couple of white carnations in a small, slim vase, and a small electric lamp adorned with a soft-pink glass shade casted a fairylike light across the white tablecloth, the wine glasses and sparkled playfully in Mrs Van Deyl's diamond ring."[23]

The ambiance shows Mrs Van Deyl, dressed in an seemingly simple, yet elegant and no doubt expensive black velvet dress, to her greatest advantage. She is presented as a true cosmopolitan lady who is at ease in expensive restaurants, feels at home in France as well as in England (where she has been educated) and exhibits

---

21 Erica van Boven, "Het pseudonym als strategie: Pseudoniemen van vrouwelijke auteurs 1850-1900," *Nederlandse letterkunde* 3, no. 4 (1998): 309-326.

22 "An understanding of the semiotic of class will include . . . material indicators as well: the location, size, type, and cost of housing; clothing; the type and number of such goods as household appliances, furnishings and 'luxuries'; the type of food eaten, and so on." Chamberlain, "Gender, Class, and Domesticity," 38. See also Ileen Montijn, *Leven op stand 1890-1940* (Amsterdam: Thomas Rap, 2003), 14-39.

23 "Om ons heen hoorden we het gezellig geklik-klak van vorken en messen, een zacht geroezemoes van stemmen. . . . Op ons tafeltje stonden in een klein, slank vaasje een paar anjers, en een electrisch lampje goot door een zacht-roze ballonnetje een feeëriek licht over het witte tafellaken, de wijnglazen, vonkte speelsch in den diamanten ring van mevrouw Van Deyl." Cissy van Marxveldt, *Game-and Set!* (Leiden: A.W. Sijthoff's Uitgeversmaatschappij, 1917), 85. (My translation, MS).

an easy manner with people from lower social classes (like the waiters). The food, consisting of turtle and curry soup, pineapple and mocha, as well as culinary words like hors d'oeuvre and compote, are distinctly non-Dutch:

> How wonderful it was to see once again brilliantly bedecked tables with flowers and to see wine pearling in crystal clear glasses with their green and red reflections. Mrs Van Deyl slowly and carefully selected the most wonderful delicacies.
>
> "Do you like tongue, Henny? I know Lies loves it."
>
> "Oh yes please, Madam."
>
> "Excellent – we're almost there, I think. How about this," she pointed her finger, "first a hors d'oeuvre, next, yes, what kind of soup, curry, turtle. . . ."
>
> "Oh no, mother, much too spicy."
>
> "Well, why don't you tell me."
>
> "All right then, let me see . . . chicken soup, Henny likes that too. Is that all right?"
>
> "Excellent. So, we'll start with a small croquet, next tongue, won't we, and then potatoes with veal steak and endive. . . . Next, chicken or duck, what do you prefer? I don't mind. All right – chicken, with a compote, a mixed compote, right? Lots of pineapple, Henny? All right child, I'll tell the waiter. Ice cream? Ice cream with fruit? Mocha for you, Lies? Excellent. And for desert, cream and jelly, I would think."
>
> She called a waiter, ordered the food. What easy manners she had.[24]

Detailed descriptions of expensive houses, interiors, food, dress and leisure – aspects of Veblen's conspicuous consumption[25]– which all have distinct international flavours, cannot only be found in *Game-and Set!*, but in almost all Van Marxveldt's novels. She also made sure that public representations of her own apartment would mirror these descriptions. In an interview conducted in 1934 by fellow writer and friend Emmy Belinfante-Belinfante, the latter described how she found Van

---

24 "Wat was het heerlijk weer eens glanzend-gedekte tafels te zien, met bloemen, en wijn te zien parelen in de kristal-heldere glazen met hun groenen en rooden weerschijn. Mevrouw Van Deyl zocht langzaam, met veel zorg, de grootste lekkernijen uit. 'Houd-je van tong, Henny? Lies is er dol op, dat weet ik.' 'O ja, mevrouw.' 'Mooi zoo – dan ben ik er nu bijna, geloof ik. Kijk eens,' ze wees met haar vinger bij, 'eerst een hors d'oeuvre, dan, ja wat voor soep, kerry, schildpad. . . .' 'Hè nee, moeder, veel te scherp.' 'Nu, zeg 't dan maar.' 'Goed, laat eens kijken ... Pouletsoep, daar houdt Henny ook van. Vindt u dat goed?' 'Prachtig. Dan eerst een croquetje, en dan tong nietwaar, verder aardappelen met kalfsbiefstuk en andijvie. Ja Henny, 'k heb goed onthouden, dat je daar zoo veel van houdt. Dan kip of eend, wat hebben jullie liever? 't Kan mij niet schelen. Goed – kip, met compôte, gemengde compôte maar, hè? Veel ananas, Henny? Goed kind, 'k zal het zeggen. IJs? Een plombière? Jij mocca Lies? Uitstekend. En voor toe-tje, slagroom met confituren dunkt me.'–Ze wenkte een kellner, bestelde. Wat een gemakkelijke manieren had ze." Van Marxveldt, *Game*, 86. (My translation, MS).

25 Thorsten Veblen, *The Theory* of the *Leisure Class: An Economic Study* of *Institutions* (Mieola: Dover Publications, 1994 [1899]).

Marxveldt's own "cosy" home filled with soft cushions and luxurious flowers: a sumptuous, upper class apartment – the apartment of a woman of the world.[26]

Yet not only references to objects signify the higher middle class status and matching cosmopolitism of Van Marxveldt characters. *De Louteringkuur* (1928, The Purification Cure) happily ends with Trix, the Dutch female protagonist, being offered a job as a cartoonist at an American newspaper, which she readily accepts. Being married to a successful businessman, Trix accepts the job out of interest, not out of necessity, marking her status as a cosmopolitan woman who feels at home in New York as much as in Amsterdam. The main character of *De Kingfordschool* (1922) marries her British boss at the end of the story, which marks her rise in society. In *Een zomerzotheid* (1927, A Summer's Comedy), a story about class differences, the protagonists constantly refer to canonical, international writers such as Shakespeare, de Cervantes, Goethe and Heine, which not only marks their higher education but also their cosmopolitan life style. They constantly sing songs in various languages and use lots of foreign words, though mostly English ones, and refer to international sports heroes and holidays abroad. When Joop ter Heul marries the rich and handsome Leo van Dil, a young banker with excellent taste, the couple moves into a villa which they name "Sweet and Merry." Several members of the "Jopopinoloukicoclub," the club of Joop and her six high school-friends (the name of the club refers to their names: Joop, Pop, Pien, Noor, Loutje, Kitty and Connie), have links with England through jobs and further education. Babs, the protagonist of *Kwikzilver* (1926), who is also married to a businessman, finds her 'destination' when her husband is forced to file for bankruptcy and she has to find a job to support her family. She is hired almost immediately by a trading company because of her knowledge of foreign languages, and because of her 'easy manners.' Like cosmopolitan Mrs Van Deyl, Babs feels at ease in different countries and seems to be above class boundaries – a sure sign of upper class membership. Interestingly enough, quite a few of Van Marxveldt's female protagonists find jobs outside their homes which they find psychologically rewarding, thus defying middle class gender ideals. All in all, Van Marxveldt's female protagonists distinguish themselves by moving across different borders – borders of nations, gender and class – without fear of losing their nationality, their social status and/or femininity. Their upper class membership makes them perfect cosmopolitans.

The English woman

In at least one case Van Marxveldt presented herself in a novel as an upper middle class British woman, albeit in a crypted way. It is important to note at this point that at the beginning of the 20th century a change in taste, "caused the Dutch elite," as cultural historian Ileen Montijn wrote, "to slowly but surely turn their attention from France to England."[27]

---

26 Emmy Belinfante-Belinfante. "Een interview met Cissy van Marxveldt," *Contact* (July 1934): 253-255.

27 Montijn, *Leven op stand,* 84: "Aan het begin van de twintigste eeuw deed een smaakverandering de Nederlandse elite langzaam maar zeker het gezicht van Nederland naar Engeland wenden." (My translation, MS).

In *Marijke's bestemming* (1934, Marijke's Final Destination), protagonist Marijke works as a nurse for a rich older woman who has taken Marijke to stay at an expensive hotel in the French resort Menton. The guest list of the hotel is distinctly international, with Van Marxveldt showing off her knowledge of supposed nationalistic traits. Thus Marijke becomes acquainted with a posh Dutch couple with a slang-speaking little son (which shows this family is able to cross social borders without having to fear a loss of status), a young French couple in love, an English gentleman and his two unapproachable, stiff daughters, and a group of merry, happy go lucky Americans. Indicating that Marijke may be a nurse, yet has a taste for and knowledge of British literature, Van Marxveldt has her read Katherine Mansfield's *Journal* (1927) to her employer in the original language. This simultaneously reflects Van Marxveldt's cosmopolitan taste and knowledge of modern, British literature, as Mansfield's *Journal* was not – and has never been – translated into Dutch. The story also briefly stages an English woman whom Marijke sets as an example for her employer who suffers from depression. "This young English woman," Marijke tells her employer, "who is paralysed at one side of her body, yet smiles every time she's driven onto the terrace, shows a lot of courage, don't you think?"[28] On the next page, the English woman is described in more detail:

> Her [Marijke's] eyes wandered to the young English woman who stared at the sea.
>
> Her perpetually cold feet were hidden under a big plaid. The nurse who was sitting next to her had just carefully replaced the disobedient arm, which was paralysed, on a cushion next to her. At that moment the English woman turned around. She softly spoke to the nurse, who laughed. Marijke swallowed. A mist appeared in front of her eyes . . . .[29]

There are several indications that the English woman is an idealised self-portrait of Van Marxveldt. Six years earlier, in 1928, Van Marxveldt had suffered a stroke, which paralysed her right arm. After convalescing in a nursing home in the east of the Netherlands, she travelled to Menton with her husband, her physician and his wife. Although photographs of Van Marxveldt in Menton show her standing next to her husband, in reality she had to use a wheelchair, just like the English woman in *Marijke's bestemming*. Thus, the English woman, who plays no actual part in the novel's plot, can be seen as part of Van Marxveldt's autobiografiction, a term coined by Max Saunders: the expression or realisation of an author's ambitions

28 "Dat jonge Engelsche vrouwtje, dat aan een kant verlamd is, en toch elke morgen lachend het terras wordt opgereden, die heeft moed, vindt U niet?" Cissy van Marxveldt, *Marijke's bestemming* (Amersfoort: Valkhoff & Co., 1934), 129. (My translation, MS).

29 "Haar [Marijkes] blikken dwaalden weg naar het jonge Engelsche vrouwtje, dat uitstaarde over zee. Haar voeten, die altijd koud waren, waren verborgen in een groote, geruite plaid. De verpleegster, die naast haar zat, had net de onwillige arm, die verlamd was, weer behoedzaam op het kussentje gelegd, dat naast haar lag. Dan draaide het Engelsche vrouwtje zich om. Ze zei zacht iets tegen de verpleegster. Die lachte. Marijke slikte eens. Er kwam een waas voor haar oogen. . . ." Van Marxveldt, *Marijke's bestemming*, 130. (My translation, MS).

and aspirations in her work as an alternative, fictional life narrative.[30] In this case the Englishness, gender, age, class and wealth of the invalid hotel guest, who is accompanied by a private nurse and like Mrs Van Deyl exhibits gentile and easy manners, can be perceived as a rephrased and idealised public self-portrait of Van Marxveldt as a member of the cosmopolitan upper middle class.

The question is whether Van Marxveldt's autobiografictional self-presentation as an English woman and a cosmopolitan member of the upper middle class was recognised as such by her Dutch contemporaries. So far no evidence has been found. However, some of her young readers were definitely confused about Van Marxveldt's nationality.

In December 1924, eight high school-girls in The Hague decided to found their own Jopopinoloukico-club after watching a play based on the Joop ter Heul-series. In a form of fan fiction *avant la lettre* each of the girls was appointed a name of one of the original club members, with one of them, Riek, having to be content with the name of Joop's sister Julie (who is definitely not a member of the club in the original series). One month later, they convened to compose a fan letter to the actress Julia de Gruyter, who played the part of Joop in the stage play. As they wrote this letter under their assumed names and addressed De Gruyter as 'Joop' a rather complicated correspondence between Joop from The Hague (who in real life was called Lenie Straatman) and Joop the actress (Julia de Gruyter) about the protagonist Joop ter Heul ensued. In one of her letters to the club De Gruyter wrote that she had actually met Van Marxveldt. This led to great excitement among Lenie and her friends. In a letter to De Gruyter-Joop, dated 30 January 1925, Lenie-Joop expressed her curiosity about Van Marxveldt and urged De Gruyter to tell her more about her meeting with the author: "Joop, will you write again? I think it's such fun, and do tell me about C.v.Marxveldt. Does she speak Dutch? She is English, isn't she?"[31] The next day Riek also wrote a letter to De Gruyter, complimenting her on her performance as Joop. She too was unsure about Van Marxveldt's identity: "I didn't know that Cissy van Marxveldt is still very young. Isn't she an English woman."[32]

Unfortunately none of the girls explained why they thought Van Marxveldt was English. As De Gruyter frequently corresponded with Van Marxveldt it seems likely that Van Marxveldt heard about the confusion concerning her nationality. If she did she must have been pleased: mission accomplished.

---

30 Max Saunders, *Self Impression: Life-Writing, Autobiografiction and the Forms of Modern Literature* (Oxford: Oxford University Press, 2010).

31 "Joop, schrijf je nog eens terug? Ik vind 't zoo leuk, en vertel dan eens van C.v.Marxveldt. Kan zij Hollandsch spreken? Zij is toch een Engelsche?" Letter from Lenie Straatman to Julia de Gruyter, 30 January 1925. Collection Julia de Gruyter, Special Collections, University Library, Amsterdam University. (Translation by me, MS).

32 "Ik wist niet dat Cissy van Marxveldt nog zoo jong is. Is het geen Engelsche." Brief van Riek Vrouwenvelder aan Julia de Gruyter, 31 January 1925. Collection Julia de Gruyter. (Translation by me, MS).

Bibliography

Belinfante-Belinfante, Emmy. "Een interview met Cissy van Marxveldt." *Contact* (July 1934): 253-255.

Boven, Erica van. *Een hoofdstuk apart: 'Vrouwenroman' in de literaire kritiek.* Amsterdam: Sara/Van Gennep, 1992.

Boven, Erica van. "Het pseudonym als strategie: Pseudoniemen van vrouwelijke auteurs 1850-1900." *Nederlandse Letterkunde* 3, no. 4 (1998): 309-326.

Calhoun, Craig. "Cosmopolitanism and Nationalism." *Nations and Nationalism* 14, no. 3 (2008): 427-448.

Cartland, Barbara, *Sweet Punishment.* London: Hutchinson & Co., 1931.

Chamberlain, Kathleen. "Gender, Class, and Domesticity in the Isabel Carleton Series." In *Nancy Drew and Company: Culture, Gender and Girls' Series,* edited by Sherrie A. Innes, 37-58. Bowling Green: Bowling State University Popular Press, 1977.

Humble, Nicola. *The Feminine Middlebrow Novel 1920 to 1950s.* Oxford: Oxford University Press, 2007 [2001].

Lakmaker, Joosje. *Voorbij de Blauwbrug: Het verhaal van mijn joodse grootvader* (Amsterdam: Wereldbibliotheek, 2008).

Montijn, Ileen. *Leven op stand 1890-1940.* Amsterdam: Thomas Rap, 2003.

Saunders, Max. *Self Impression: Life-Writing, Autobiografiction and the Forms of Modern Literature.* Oxford: Oxford University Press, 2010.

Strengholt, Aaldert J.G. "Cissy van Marxveldt vertelt . . . " *Astra* 12 (June 1928): 1312-1320.

Gelderen-de Witte, I.F. van. "Bij Cissy van Marxveldt." *Haagsche Courant,* 6 November 1935.

Van Marxveldt, Cissy. *Game–and Set!* Leiden: A.W. Sijthoff's Uitgeversmaatschappij, 1917.

Van Marxveldt, Cissy. *De H.B.S.-tijd van Joop ter Heul.* Amersfoort: Valkhoff & Co., 1919.

Van Marxveldt, Cissy. *De Kingfordschool.* Amersfoort: Valkhoff & Co.. 1923 [1922].

Van Marxveldt, Cissy. *Joop van Dil-ter Heul.* Amersfoort: Valkhoff & Co., 1924 [1923].

Van Marxveldt, Cissy. *Rekel.* Amersfoort: Valkhoff & Co., 1924.

Van Marxveldt, Cissy. *Kwikzilver.* Amersfoort: Valkhoff & Co., 1926.

Van Marxveldt, Cissy. *Een zomerzotheid.* Amersfoort: Valkhoff & Co., 1927.

Van Marxveldt, Cissy. *De louteringkuur.* Amersfoort: Valkhoff & Co., 1928.

Van Marxveldt, Cissy and Emmy Belinfante-Belinfante. *Confetti.* Amersfoort: Valkhoff & Co., 1930.

Van Marxveldt, Cissy. *Marijke's bestemming.* Amersfoort: Valkhoff & Co., 1934.

Veblen, Thorsten. *The Theory* of the *Leisure Class: An Economic Study* of *Institutions.* Mieola: Dover Publications, 1994 [1899].

Waaldijk, Berteke. "Reading Anne Frank as a Woman." *Women's Studies International Forum* 16, no. 4 (July-August 1993): 327-335.

"A caveman in a canal house"

The rejection of transnationalist biography in Hafid Bouazza's *A Bear in Fur Coat*

Sjoerd-Jeroen Moenandar

Introduction

Hafid Bouazza was born in 1970 in Oujda (Morocco). When he was seven, he joined his father, who had moved to the Netherlands as a so-called guest worker. Debuting in 1997 with the collection of short stories *Abdullah's Feet* (*De voeten van Abdullah*), Bouazza has managed to become one of the Netherlands' most prominent writers of the last twenty years. Alongside his literary work, Bouazza has been active as a translator of English and Arabic texts. He has also been, at times, a vocal presence in the public debate, writing op-eds in which he vented his spleen about what he saw as Islamic vices and the follies of Dutch cultural relativism. This critical stance, as well as an often expressed preference for topics such as drugs and aesthetic pleasure, have served Bouazza to position himself as a freethinker as well as a sort of latter-day Byronic artist preoccupied with death, intoxication and the autonomous world of art.

Apart from this image as a freethinker, Bouazza has also positioned himself on several occasions as what I have elsewhere described as a 'cultural mediator' who, in essays and through his translations, acquaints Dutch readers with Arab literature and culture.[1] As such, and because of his migrant background, Bouazza may at first sight seem an ideal subject to illustrate how transnational life writing may unhinge national frameworks. As the editors of this volume argue, personal experiences turned into life stories "are particularly valuable sources that offer intimate access to the complex layers of identity" and studying Bouazza and his work could therefore offer valuable insights in identity formation in a contemporary superdiverse Western European society. However, Bouazza's writings also serve as a warning against simply taking life stories as valid sources at face value: never naïve and often written in bad faith,[2] they destabilize their own authenticity and thereby the extent to which they offer a valid insight into what a transnational life may be like. Furthermore, Bouazza and his work are not only of interest for

1 Sjoerd-Jeroen Moenandar, "Transmitting Authenticity: Kader Abdolah and Hafid Bouazza as Cultural Mediators," *Journal of Dutch Literature* 5, no. 1 (December 2014): 55-73.

2 Sjoerd-Jeroen Moenandar, *Depraved Borderlands: Encounters with Muslims in Dutch Literature and the Public Debate* (Hamburg: Peter Lang, 2013), 161.

the study of transnationalism because they show how life stories may illuminate current notions of transnationalism, but also – and arguably even more – because they unhinge those very notions at least as much as they exemplify them.

In this chapter, I will offer a close reading of *A Bear in Fur Coat* (*Een beer in bontjas*, 2001; *Een beer in bontjas: Autobiografische schetsen*, 2004), an essay by Bouazza that is presented as autobiographical, but that rather seems to be a play on autobiography, paying special attention to this essay's remarkable narrative structure. I will link this close reading to what in sociological studies of literature is called an author's *posture*: the different expressions of an author that are meant to clarify what kind of author we are dealing with (Meizoz 2010). This analysis of literary text and author's posture will then be put in broader literary and societal contexts. I will first shortly discuss current notions of transnationlism and relate them to Bouazza's life and work. Then, I will talk more specifically about how Bouazza has used the dichotomy of barbarism versus civilisation in *A Bear in Fur Coat* to negotiate his own position in contemporary Dutch society. He does so in a rather unexpected way, seemingly reifying current islamophobic and orientalist rejections of the Muslim other. Whether he truly embraces these types of 'othering,' common among critics of multicultural society, or merely summons them in order to disrupt and shock his readers, remains the question – as is so often the case with this author. After all, all his work – short stories, novels, essays and even (as I have discussed in elsewhere) his work as a cultural mediator – is characterised by an ironic play with autobiography and exotic authenticity.[3] His play with highly charged ways of talking about a Muslim 'other' in his life writing is no exception to this.

Unhinging transnationalist frameworks

Most of Hafid Bouazza's work is literary fiction that falls outside the scope of life writing. In fact, the work that I will mostly focus on in this chapter, *A Bear in Fur Coat* is the only larger text by him that can be defined as such.[4] And even though it consists for a considerable part of an account of Bouazza's life up till then, it is not a conventional autobiography. The first edition was called an 'essay'[5] and the second edition had *Autobiographical Sketches* as its subtitle. Indeed, at first the reader seems to be dealing with an essay in which the author wants to present his thoughts on the interrelatedness of literature and biography, or rather, argue the lack thereof. Bouazza starts with several anecdotes meant to show how his work has been continuously linked to his Moroccan background by readers and critics. Then, he rhetorically suggests he wants to evaluate the validity of such an approach to literature, changing gears, as it were, to another genre. At this point in the text,

3 Moenandar, "Transmitting Authenticity.

4 However, the collection of short stories that was Bouazza's debut as an author definitely suggests an autobiographical streak by announcing on the back cover that the stories have their origin in the author's memories of the Moroccan village of his youth, only for Bouazza to then ridicule readers who read these stories as autobiographical accounts (cf. Moenandar, "Transmitting Authenticity," 161.

5 The text was originally published in 2001 as the so called 'Book Week Essay' (boekenweekessay), part of that year's Book Week (Boekenweek), an annual festival in the Netherlands celebrating books and reading. This festival always has a central theme and in 2001 this was the rather transnational 'writing between cultures.' Each year, a free book is published that is distributed to customers of bookshops, as well as a 'Book Week Essay' that explores the theme of that year.

A Bear in Fur Coat seems to move from essay to autobiography as the life story of Hafid Bouazza is being recounted in order to see whether his migrant descent is indeed relevant for his literary work.

All of this is embedded in a fictional narrative situation: several strange characters have assembled to hear the life story of their 'guest of honour,' Hafid Bouazza, and to discuss the relevance of this life story to his work. Throughout the text, there seem to be four narrators: at first, the reader feels the author himself is speaking, as is usually the case in essayist writings. Secondly, we encounter the typical narrator of an autobiography: an aged and experienced 'I' who looks back on 'Hafid Bouazza's' transnational youth, growing up first in Morocco and then in the Netherlands. Furthermore, in the descriptions of the fictional debate, there is an invisible narrator, a sort of camera-eye describing what goes on. Finally, a significant part of *A Bear in Fur Coat* is made up out of a speech given by one of the participants to this debate, Haaris Boelfachr. Haaris Boelfachr – whose name, as Henriëtte Louwerse notes, is Arabic for 'defender of pride', exactly the same meaning as Hafid Bouazza[6]–seems to be a stand-in for the author, with his speech more or less in tune with the essayist parts of *A Bear in Fur Coat.*

This dizzying narrative structure disrupts the uprightness that is normally expected of genres such as autobiography and essay. The autobiographical 'I' may or may not be Hafid Bouazza himself, because of its fictional embeddedness. The author speaking directly at us in the essayist part may or may not be taken at face value – not more, or less at least than the fictional character of Haaris Boelfachr, who may or may not be just a mouthpiece for Hafid Bouazza himself. Such play with autobiography and authenticity is typical of all of Bouazza's work. As the author himself has written, we never encounter the writer himself: "Whether one writes autobiographically or not . . . [t]he writer writes with a recreated writer's ego."[7] Bouazza seems to playfully stage such a creation of an ego in *A Bear in Fur Coat*, and whether the ensuing personas are egos or *alter* egos remains to be seen.

One clue as to the authenticity of the staged ego in this text is given by a similar play on the migrant author as a 'transmitter of culture.' Throughout *A Bear in Fur Coat*, the reader is teased with exotic images of flying carpets and Aladin's cave as symbols for the imagination that is the source of the author's literary work. In the fictional parts of the text, an enthusiastic reader takes these symbols as authentic expressions of otherness when she tells Haaris Boelfachr: "What an imagination! I feel such lightness on your flying carpet. This fairy-tale quality is something I miss in the Netherlands" (38).[8] In this reader – all dressed up in Middle Eastern paraphernalia, not knowing the difference between Morocco and Yemen – Bouazza seems to caricaturise the notion that the value of the migrant authors lies in the fact that they bring the culture of their origin country to enrich the culture in his destination country. Dutch – or Western – culture needs no enrichment, Bouazza seems to say, when he reveals, at the end of *A Bear in Fur Coat*, that flying carpets

---

6 Henriëtte Louwerse, *Homeless Entertainment* (Bern: Peter Lang, 2007), 34 n.

7 Hafid Bouazza, "Schrijven als roes," in *Roes: Een bloemlezing over drank en drugs in woord en beeld*, eds. Hafid Bouazza and Yves van Kempen (Amsterdam: Prometheus, 2010), 331.

8 "Wat een fantasie! Ik voel me helemaal licht worden op uw vliegend tapijt. Dat mis ik toch hier in Nederland, de sprookjesachtigheid."

and magic caves are more Western than Oriental: "The cave of the forty thieves . . . , Aladin's magic lamp and the flying carpet do not find their origin in the Arab works. They are made up by the European forgers of that work."[9]

What at first seemed the cultural mediation of an exotic otherness, the authenticity of which was ensured by the transnational background of the author, is now revealed to be merely an imagined otherness – a forgery instead of a faithful translation. Thus, the reading experience for many of *A Bear in Fur Coat*'s readers will go from being presented with what seems to be an aesthetically pleasing exoticness, to a sudden confrontation with the fact that this exoticness really belongs to the familiar. Louwerse has called this move from seduction to deception a "mockery of the reader" and sees this as a constant in Bouazza's work.[10] Bouazza continuously addresses transnationalist issues such as migration, multiculturalism and nostalgia for a country of origin, while the takeaway message from the mockery with which this is done might be that the work itself and the strangeness presented in it, are surprisingly *national*. In this chapter, I therefore want to raise the following question: how transnationalist is the writer's ego that Bouazza creates throughout this work?

As an approach to issues of migration, transnationalism came to the fore throughout the nineties in anthropology and sociology. It stressed the "attachment migrants maintain to families, communities, traditions and causes outside the boundaries of the nation-state to which they have moved."[11] In this, it was a departure from older approaches that tended to focus on the nation of origin as belonging to a migrant's past and the nation of arrival as the setting for their present. Instead, transnationalist approaches sought to recognise that "contemporary migrants live in 'transnational communities'" that are characterised by a constant flow of people, goods, ideas, symbols and information between these two nations. As carriers of "transnational identities," migrants and other "global or cosmopolitan subjects,"[12] so the argument goes, tend to simultaneously reinforce cultural boundaries and expand them and transnational studies try to understand how this happens.[13] As other contributions to the present volume show, "the mixing of cultures and the hybridity of identity are not only recent phenomena of a globalized twenty-first century; they are not the exceptions to the rule, but in a historical perspective these phenomena constitute the rule."[14] Thus, there have always been transnational subjects.

Hafid Bouazza, however, must definitely be placed in the more recent context of contemporary globalised and multicultural society. In such a context, a transnational mode such as the "[c]osmopolitan is a positively named and valued descriptive model

9 "De grot van de veertig rovers . . . , de wonderlamp van Aladdin en het vliegende tapijt hebben hun oorsprong niet in de Arabische werken. Zij zijn verzinsels van de Europese vervalsers van dat werk." Hafid Bouazza, *Een beer in bontjas* (Amsterdam: CPNB 2001), 52-53.

10 Louwerse, *Homeless Entertainment,* 130; Moenandar, *Depraved Borderlands,* 143-146.

11 Steven Vertovec, "Transnationalism and identity," *Journal of Ethnic and Migration Studies* 27, no. 4 (2010): 574.

12 Hannes Schweiger, "Global Subjects: The Transnationalisation of Biography," *Life Writing* 9, no. 3 (August 2012): 249.

13 Ellen Fleischmann, "'I only wish I had a home on this globe': Transnational Biography and Dr. Mary Eddy," *Journal of Women's History* 21, no. 3 (2009): 112; David Thelen, "The Nation and Beyond: Transnational Perspectives on United States History," *Journal of American History* 86, no. 3 (1999): 967.

14 Schweiger, "Global Subjects," 254.

for also/and relationships, identities, logistics, responsibilities."[15] However, at the same time this context is also partly shaped by a so-called 'backlash against multiculturalism'[16] and a rejection of transnational realities as threatening to a national sense of self. As I will discuss in the next section, Bouazza has often seemed to reject the former and embrace the latter, despite the transnational nature of his life. Thus, Hafid Bouazza throws the main question asked in transnational biography, namely "what it means to be transnational and to live a transnational life,"[17] into an interesting relief. The transnational approach seeks to tease out and analyse the "various ways transnational settings and dynamics affect the construction, negotiation and reproduction of identities,"[18] while Bouazza rejects the relevance of cultural settings and social dynamics for his work and life. Where transnational approaches assume intense linkages with their homelands among migrants,[19] Bouazza rejects these. Similarly, rather than accepting, as studies of transnationalism do, that "personal and collective identities . . . should be understood as closely entangled with each other,"[20] Bouazza scoffs at this notion when he complains, in an early column, that a Moroccan "so-called writer" tells him "that she likes to write about "our beautiful culture."[21] Culture, to Bouazza, is a private, and not a communal matter: "I answered that I preferred not to share my bath, which I have carefully run and heated."[22] And if he is going to allow people to call his author-ego anything, then it is not Moroccan or a transnational moniker like 'allochtonous' (the term normally used for foreign-born citizens of the Netherlands). Like his work, his authorship is to be seen in a *national* context: "A French writer is someone who writes in French, an allochtonous author is someone who writes in allochtonian and a Dutch writer writes in Dutch."[23] Thus, Bouazza seems unwilling to embrace the hybrid identity[24] that transnational subjects are supposed to have.

Rather than cultural identity and societal position, Bouazza claims he seeks his sense of self in language: "Language is the only country in which a writer feels at home. Language is his identity, style his passport. . . . A writer belongs to the dominant culture. He should be judged according to the measures of that culture and does not deserve special treatment."[25] And because the language in which he writes is Dutch, Bouazza refuses to be seen as transnational. Thus, at first glance, for Bouazza there seems no need, as in transnationalist approaches, to "investigate

15 Ulrich Beck, cited in Schweiger, 253.

16 Steven Vertovec and Susanne Wessendorf, "Introduction. Assessing the backlash against multiculturalism in Europe," in *The Multiculturalism Backlash: European Discourses, Policies and Practices*, edited by Stefan Vertovec and Susanne Wessendorf (New York: Routledge, 2010), 1-31.

17 Fleischmann, "'I only wish I had a home on this globe,'"109.

18 Vertovec, "Transnationalism and identity," 573.

19 Vertovec, 574.

20 Vertovec, 577.

21 Hafid Bouazza, "Allochtonen met een stem," *Vooys* 14, no. 1 (December 1996): 22-23.

22 "Een van die schrijvelaars, een Marokkaans meisje van negentien jaar, zei tegen mij dat ze graag schrijft over 'onze mooie cultuur' . . . en ik antwoordde dat ik mijn bad, dat ik met veel zorg heb laten vollopen en op temperatuur heb gebracht, niet graag deel." Bouazza, "Allochtonen met een stem," 22.

23 "Een Franse schrijver is iemand die in het Frans schrijft, een allochtone schrijver is iemand die in het allochtoons schrijft en een Nederlandse schrijver schrijft in het Nederlands." Cited in Bart Vanegeren, "Hafid Bouazza, schrijver zonder land: Als ik al ergens woon, is het in de taal." *Humo* (26 May 1998).

24 Fleischmann, "'I only wish I had a home on this globe,'" 119.

25 Bouazza, *Een beer in bontjas*, 31.

how well national borders are contained or explained"[26] in his work: he wants to be seen as Dutch, and as Dutch only.

In other words, if the 'transnationalisation of biography' means that 'culture and context' are put in the limelight to explain someone's life and work, it will find Hafid Bouazza to be a very unwilling subject. In fact, many scholars engaged in transnationalist studies have themselves warned against falling 'prey to culture-only explanations'[27] and at the very least, we could say that Bouazza's life and work illustrate this risk very well. I propose to study Hafid Bouazza and his work in this light. For now, I will focus on analysing how Bouazza negotiates the notion that being less civilised is endemic to being a certain type of transnational subject – such as a migrant from Morocco – in the highly charged context of a supposed 'clash of civilisations' between 'Islam' and 'the West' in which *A Bear in Fur Coat* appeared.

Cavemen, barbarians and bears

Even though *A Bear in Fur Coat* is a play with autobiography and truth, the reader is certainly meant to take seriously the essay's strong rejection of the tendency to categorise Hafid Bouazza and his work as 'Moroccan,' 'Moroccan-Dutch,' or 'migrant,'[28] As I have discussed elsewhere,[29] this can be read as strategic literary positioning through which Bouazza creates a *posture* that distinguishes him from a larger group of foreign-born authors who were debuting around the same time.[30] By strongly rejecting a biographical approach to his literature, and saying things such as "I hate authors who pride themselves on being Jewish, Black or Moroccan."[31] he ensures that he stands out from authors who do discuss such a background as relevant.[32] As I argued in the previous section, this implies a rejection of transnationalism as well. One particular interesting moment in the essay in which Bouazza argues against this notion is in a passage that he starts with recounting a request from a "well-known newspaper" to write comments on pictures of Dutch people in their kitchen. Bouazza claims that he was asked to do so because the editorial staff assumed he had a special way of looking at the Netherlands: "One could imagine (this is how it was phrased) . . . that a Dutch kitchen has a certain exotic quality for me . . . , because I look at it, after all, with an alien gaze."[33] This anecdote serves Bouazza to once again vehemently reject the notion that he is somehow shaped by his transnationalist biography: "I imagine an alien gaze to be an eye with pupils in which the magical scenes, beheld in the womb country, still continue to shine and in which the current surroundings are

26 Thelen,"The Nation and Beyond," 967.
27 Schweiger, "Global Subjects," 256.
28 Bouazza, *Een beer in bontjas*, 9-10.
29 Moenandar, *Depraved Borderlands*, 148.
30 Strategic indeed, because Bouazza has never really been approached as an author outside of the Dutch literary tradition by his critics.
31 Cited in Elisabeth Lockhorn, *Geletterde mannen: Interviews* (Amsterdam: De Bezige Bij, 2000), 101.
32 This, however, is a very limited group in the Netherlands. Cf. Moenandar 2007.
33 "Het was voorstelbaar (zo werd dat gezegd en wat een inzicht spreekt uit deze formulering) . . . dat een Nederlandse keuken voor mij iets exotisch heeft . . . , omdat ik er toch met een uitheemse blik naar kijk." Bouazza, *Een beer in bontjas*, 13.

obscured by the shades (and the heart by the twinkling) of the past."[34] Bouazza, however, objects to the assumption that he possesses such an "alien gaze," because he sees it as a "defect" that would leave him handicapped in his daily life:

> As far as I know, I have not shown . . . symptoms of this defect. My current surroundings do get through and have even become familiar for me. . . . so far, no one has noted that I walk around with my mouth open in surprise and cross-eyed by amazement, like a caveman in a canal house.[35]

Here, 'canal house' ('grachtenpand') does not merely refer to the typical kind of houses found in the canal area ('grachtengordel') in central Amsterdam, so beloved by tourists. It carries strong connotations of elitism and metropolitanism, based on the assumption that this neighbourhood is populated by a culturally refined, progressive elite. In such an urban environment, the transnational possessor of an 'alien gaze' would be reduced to a 'caveman': not only handicapped, but backwards too, unable to participate in modern, civilised society.

As Bakhtin has shown, words and the concepts they refer to are always unstable. Whenever we utter a word, we automatically enter an ongoing dialogue about what concept that word actually refers to, and whenever we refer to a concept, we enter an ongoing dialogue about which words should be used to do so. In other words, every utterance takes place in what Bakhtin calls 'a dialogically agitated and tension-filled environment' and implies taking position in this environment as well.[36] By using the words that Bouazza does when referring to the encounter between Dutch society on the one hand and the Moroccan and Arab culture from which he migrated on the other as an encounter between civilisation and backwardness, he certainly enters an environment that is "agitated and tension-filled." Almost at the same time that *A Bear in Fur Coat* first appeared, film author and public debater Theo van Gogh published an op-ed in which he wrote:

> To say that Islam is the biggest threat that the civilised world will have to face, still appears to be touching on the sour spot of the politically correct church and its "sticking plaster" approach. The facts tell a different story: every enfranchised citizen who would want to defend such a thing as reasonable is on the brink of a battle with Allah's representatives of the most pestilent backwardness.
>
> No Athens without Sparta, no Rome without barbarians.[37]

---

34 "Bij een uitheemse blik stel ik mij een oog voor met pupillen waarin de magische taferelen, aanschouwd in het baarmoederland, nog naschijnen en waarin de huidige omgeving omfloerst wordt met de tinten (en het hart met de tintelingen) van het verleden." Bouazza, *Een beer in bontjas*, 13.

35 "Voorzover ik weet vertoon ik . . . deze afwijking niet. Mijn huidige omgeving dringt wel degelijk tot mij door en is mij zelfs vertrouwd geworden. . . . dat ik met mond open van verbazing en ogen scheel van verwondering rondloop als een holenmens in een grachtenpand, is nog niemand opgevallen." Bouazza, *Een beer in bontjas*, 13-14.

36 Mikhail Bakhtin, *The Dialogic Imagination* (Austin: University of Texas Press, 1982), 276.

37 Theo van Gogh, *Allah weet het beter* (Amsterdam: Xtra, 2003 [2001]), 75. "Te zeggen dat de islam de grootste bedreiging is die de beschaafde wereld onder ogen moet zien, blijkt nog steeds een vloek in de politiek correcte kerk van pappen en nathouden. De feiten zijn anders: iedere kiesgerechtigde die zoiets als de redelijkheid wil verdedigen, staat aan de vooravond van een veldslag met Allah's vertegenwoordigers van de meest pestilente achterlijkheid.
Geen Athene zonder Sparta, geen Rome zonder barbaren."

A little over a year later, right-wing politician Pim Fortuyn, like Theo van Gogh an outspoken critic of Islam and Muslims, would cause a national uproar by calling Islam a 'backwards culture.'[38] And in a novel by Abdelkader Benali, like Bouazza an author of Moroccan descent, this dichotomy is also mentioned in a passage about an argument between two characters: Mehdi, a Moroccan boy, and Diana, his girlfriend. She strongly disapproves of his 'superstitions' and other cultural traces in his behavior. During what seems to be an encounter between Moroccan irrationality and Dutch rationality, the boy tries to ignore the fact that she is pregnant, because, as it is described, if he would allow himself to be moved by this: "he would burst into tears and then his anger would be exposed as ridiculous, like a barbarian being calmed down by a great humanist."[39] Although grammatically the metaphor refers to the boy's anger, rather than the boy himself, the resulting image is – as with Bouazza, Van Gogh and Fortuyn,–one of civilisation on the Dutch side and barbarism on the 'other' side.

What exactly this 'other' side encompasses may differ slightly in each case, but the constant factor seems to be its Muslim nature. If that is left rather vague in the original edition of *A Bear in Fur Coat*, it becomes all the more clear in the 2004 version. By then, Bouazza had written several op-eds, published in Dutch quality newspapers such as *de Volkskrant* and *NRC-Handelsblad* in which he fiercely attacked Muslim minorities in the Netherlands. The tone of these op-eds is striking. With biting satire and open indignation, Bouazza attacks Muslims for being sexist ("Demonstreer voor vrijheid moslima's"), fundamentalist ("Moslims kwetsen Nederland") and generally hostile towards Dutch culture and society ("Nederland is blind voor moslimextremisme"). And almost as vehemently, he reproaches the Dutch for tolerating all of this. In his op-eds, Bouazza pictures Muslims as – indeed – a backwards element in the enlightened West, possessing some of the original characteristics of the barbarian: they do not seem to have an intelligible language and seem to be devoid of reason. In one op-ed, for instance, in which Bouazza calls for large demonstrations against the oppression of Muslim women, he says he knows that his "vehement Muslim opponents" will only be able to answer this call with "roaring and screeching."[40] In another op-ed, he describes what he calls a "delightful picture" of a demonstration in Morocco against divorce rights for women:

38 Cited in Frank Poorthuis and Hans Wansink,"De islam is een achterlijke cultuur," *de Volkskrant*, 9 February 2002.

39 "Dan zou hij in tranen uitbarsten en zou zijn woede er belachelijk bijstaan, als een barbaar die wordt gekalmeerd door een groot humanist." Abdelkader Benali, *De langverwachte* (Amsterdam: Vassallucci, 2002), 294.

40 "het gebrul en gekrijs van felle islamitische tegenstanders." Hafid Bouazza, "Demonstreer voor vrijheid moslima's," *NRC Handelsblad*, 19 February 2003.

> In the foreground a white bearded man drew the attention, in the classic pose of Arab indignation – open mouth, uvula visible, hands against his temples, rocking head. The poor greybeard must have been cursed with nine daughters. And in Dutch mosques as well, Muslims were grunting disapprovingly.[41]

The way Bouazza phrases it, the almost grotesque character of this uncanny display of emotions derives from its Arabness and Muslimness and their stereotypical associations: unreasonable, fanatic, with a host of children. The message to the reader seems to be a call to wake up: the barbarians are among us.

Parts of these and other op-eds were weaved through the original text of *A Bear in Fur Coat*, so that when it was republished as *Autobiographical Sketches*, it could now be read as much as a comment on the position of the immigrant in the Netherlands, as on the position of the immigrant author in Dutch literature. The meaning of the anecdote about the request to write about Dutch kitchens from an alien perspective is somewhat subverted in this new edition because of an additional passage in which Bouazza writes how Muslim migrants in the Netherlands would like to turn their kitchens into "segregated bastions for their wives."[42] He now concludes that the suspicion that he might have an "alien gaze" is not so much the fault of the silly editorial staff of the "famous newspaper." Rather, his fellow migrants are to blame: "Maybe my scorn at the time was a bit too premature, because I have learned in the meantime that a kitchen certainly remains rather unexplored to the Moroccan gaze."[43] In other words, Bouazza has moved closer to the position of Theo van Gogh and Pim Fortuyn around the time that his original essay was published and now suggests that Muslims are indeed much like a barbarian in a civilised world. Thus, while the first edition of *A Bear in Fur Coat* can be read as a rejection of transnationalist 'double rootedness' in literature, the second edition does so for Dutch multicultural society in general. Especially in the latter case, such 'double rootedness' is discredited as opening the door to barbarism.

The texts by Van Gogh, Fortuyn and Benali – and there are many more examples to be found – show how Bouazza takes up a dichotomy that must have been easily recognizable to his readers in 2001 and 2004. In it, the encounter between 'the West' and 'Islam' is not only framed as a 'clash of civilisations'–to use Samuel Huntington's infamous and at the time often misquoted term – but, even more confrontationally, as an encounter between civilisation and non-civilisation: between Dutch refinedness and barbaric otherness. The way in which Bouazza positions himself as a transnational subject – or rather, choses to position himself as decidedly *not* transnational – is facilitated by this charged dichotomy and its inherent framing of his native culture as barbaric. The implication is that, as a

41 Italics added. "Op de voorgrond trok een witbebaarde man de aandacht, in de klassieke houding van Arabische verontwaardiging – mond open, huig zichtbaar, handen tegen de slapen, deinend hoofd. De arme grijsaard moet vervloekt zijn geweest met negen dochters. En ook moslims in Nederlandse moskeeën gromden afkeurend." Hafid Bouazza, "Moslims kwetsen Nederland," *NRC Handelsblad*, 2 March 2002.

42 "[A]parte bastions voor de vrouwen." Hafid Bouazza, *Een beer in bontjas: Autobiografische schetsen* (Amsterdam: Prometheus 2004), 19.

43 "Misschien was mijn hoon toentertijd wat al te voorbarig, want ondertussen weet ik dat een keuken voor een Marokkaanse blik zeker iets onontgonnens heeft." Bouazza, *Een beer in bontjas: Autobiografische schetsen*, 19.

culturally refined *Dutch* author, Bouazza has no desire to be transnational – since that would only position him as backwards.

In line with this is Boauzza's introduction of the essay's eponymous bear in fur coat. This is a character out of a children's story who one day wakes up from his hibernation to find the woods in which he grew up gone, replaced by a factory. The bear is ordered by the people in the factory to go back to work, but he refuses to do so, since he doesn't work there – he is merely a bear. In the story, the bear is told repeatedly that he is no bear, but a "silly man who wears a fur coat and needs a shave" until finally he accepts this description of himself and takes up his place at the conveyor belt.[44] It is quite easy to read this bear as a fitting metaphor for the transnational subject, having moved from the woods to the factory and attempting to negotiate this cultural shift on his own terms, not accepting to be turned into a man (and, at the end of the story, going back to his roots to hibernate again). Bouazza, however, refuses to see himself this way. That a dominant culture redefines its transnational members is "no evil plot" but merely a cultural "dynamics," according to Bouazza.[45] Reconfiguring the metaphor to illustrate his own position, he writes:

> I am not the kind of reader who identifies with the characters in a book . . . but it is tempting to compare my position as Dutch author of Moroccan descent of Dutch nationality with that of the bear . . . . But if I were the bear, I would take off my fur coat, with all the blood and pain it takes.[46]

If the 'fur coat,' *i.e.* how the humans in the story misinterpret the bear's fur, is taken as a signifier of 'otherness,' then Bouazza seems to be saying he'd rather get rid of what may function as such a signifier, than to accept such otherness. Anything that may suggest there is something split about Bouazza, that he has double roots or a translocalised self, will have to go. Thus, the 'writer's ego' that comes to the fore in this life writing is Dutch, rather than transnational, because the language in which it is conveyed is Dutch. The question remains, however, what is meant with Dutch. Bouazza has suggested that there may be a difference between speaking Dutch and being Dutch: "If I live anywhere, it is in language,"[47] he has said, when speaking of where he feels he belongs. Here, language functions as a way out, a place where multicultural follies and Muslim vices will no longer hold him back in how he wants to define himself: "Let us not accept any order except the order of the word, of grammar, of the ordering of sentences," he writes in *A Bear in Fur Coat* after rejecting cultural definitions of identity that he deems all too narrow. Interestingly and paradoxically enough, language itself seems to become transnational here, a means to transcend confining boundaries.

---

44 Frank Tashlin, *The Bear That Wasn't* (Mineola: Dover Publications, 1995).

45 "Hier wordt niet gesuggereerd dat er een kwaadaardig complot gesmeed wordt . . . maar dat dit nu eenmaal 'de dynamiek van de overheerser tegenover de ander' zou zijn." Bouazza, *Een beer in bontjas: Autobiografische schetsen*, 17.

46 "Ik ben niet een lezer die zich identificeert met de personages in een boek . . . maar toch is het verleidelijk om mijn positie als Nederlandse schrijver van Marrokkaanse afkomst met de Nederlandse nationaliteit te vergelijken met die van de beer . . . . Maar als ik de beer was, dan zou ik mijn bontjas, met alle bloed en pijn van dien, uittrekken." Bouazza, *Een beer in bontjas*, 9.

47 Quoted in Bart Vanegeren, "Hafid Bouazza."

And indeed, if we look at Bouazza's written work, a focus on language itself is one of the first things that strike us. Highly stylised, employing a remarkably broad vocabulary – remarkable not because Dutch is Bouazza's second language, but because he uses words that have long become obsolete, as well as a plethora of neologisms – Bouazza's work can sometimes make for a difficult read. If this is true of his literature it is also true of all of Bouazza's other texts. In his essays on literature and society, we recognise what Liesbeth Korthals Altes[48] calls "*pervasive aestheticizing*: the extension, to the public and private sphere, of norms prevailing in the autonomous aesthetic domain, such as ambiguity, or impunity of transgression and provocation." If Bouazza claims that his only home is language, it is important to remember that his use of language is always literary, in the sense that it maximizes ambiguity to playfully negotiate stereotypes and prejudices through style and vocabulary. His short stories, novels, essays, op-eds and translations never make for an easy read and their meaning is regularly obscured by a mannerism that borders on the neurotic. This obfuscation in his work, both literary and non-literary, is further strengthened by his continuous use of an "ironic tone of voice"[49] that creates a certain ambiguity. Bouazza's attacks are vicious, but whether he truly means them remains to be seen. At the same time, Bouazza's aim is certainly not to claim the exact opposite of what he says, as with classic irony. His tone of voice rather seems to be an example of romantic irony, in which such a positive outcome is lacking: "romantic irony undermines all positions insofar as they are positive, final, and limited."[50] Indeed, the way in which Bouazza presents himself and his rejection of transnationalism reminds one of Hegel's rebuke of romantic irony as "symptomatic for a self-congratulatory ego" and "a frivolous attitude that destroy[s] all seriousness by undermining every possibility to commit and communicate."[51] However, the author himself would arguably embrace Hegel's criticism as a positive. This lack of seriousness and refusal to commit allows him to escape into ambiguity, to replace the fur coat that signifies an 'authentic otherness' with, if we stretch this metaphor a bit, fake fur: that is to say, with a play on authenticity itself.

Concluding remarks

It shall come as no surprise that Hafid Bouazza has upset the transnationally minded. Another contemporary migrant author, Kader Abdolah (very popular with readers, arguably not in the least because of how he has vented out his transnationalism), once wrote in a column that Bouazza "just about kills [him]self with his longing to be Dutch."[52] And indeed, there is something quite shocking about the sometimes

---

48 Liesbeth Korthals Altes, *Ethos and Narrative Interpretation: The Negotiation of Values in Fiction* (Lincoln: University of Nebraska Pres, 2014).

49 Dan Sperber and Deirdre Wilson, "Irony and the Use-Mention Distinction," in *Radical Pragmatics*, ed. Peter Cole (New York: Academic Press 1981), 311.

50 Kai Hammermeister, *The German Aesthetic Tradition* (Cambridge: Cambridge University Press, 2002), 83.

51 Hammermeister, *The German Aesthetic Tradition*, 84.

52 "Hafid, je verlangt je bijna dood om een Nederlander te zijn." Kader Abdolah, *Karavaan* (Amsterdam: De Geus, 2003), 148.

violent images that Bouazza uses to reject transnationalism. The caveman in a canal house and the bear taking of his fur coat imply that one has to become 'civilised,' one has to shed one's 'skin,' to truly belong in the Netherlands – notions that are regularly found in islamophobic and xenophobic rejections of multicultural society. And, I would say, Bouazza's first and foremost aim when saying things like these is, indeed, to shock, to upset a multiculturalist ideology in which the transnationalist position is automatically assumed to be enriching.

The fundamentally ironic tone of voice in Bouazza's work is an important part of this, as it undermines the implied concept of authenticity that underlies such a presumed transnational position for the author. Whenever Bouazza positions himself through his life writing or essays, seemingly offering the reader a glimpse of how identity formation may take place within a transnational context, his texts ultimately reject the identities they put forward. Read in this way, *A Bear in Fur Coat* also already counters Abdolah's criticism. Rather than saying Bouazza longs to be Dutch, Bouazza's 'autobiographical sketches' arguably propose a stop to any discussion about how Dutch or non-Dutch the author is.

Thus, Bouazza and his work highlight a problematic dimension of transnational approaches. On the one hand, transnationalism is shown to complicate national categories: in today's globalised and multicultural societies, national frameworks are no longer the only ways in which people construct their cultural identities – if they ever did. On the other hand, when explaining transnational cultural identities, transnational approaches have sometimes led to what Schweiger called 'culture-only interpretations' in which categories such as country of origin and country of residence, this and that nation, here and there, were reified, rather than complicated. Bouazza's life writing undermines, maybe not transnationalism per se, but certainly such transnationalism-as-reification, and may be seen as proposing postnationalism rather than transnationalism. The notion that a retreat within language might facilitate this, is interesting, because here the celebration of a national language becomes a means to transcend national boundaries and an escape from attempts to pigeonhole the author into defined categories of national or transnational belonging. Thus – and this ties in remarkably well with the original meaning of the word barbarian – the difference seems to lie, first and foremost, in whether one recognises and submits oneself exclusively to the 'order' of language. The civilised do, the barbarians do not.

Bibliography

Abdolah, Kader. *Karavaan*. Amsterdam: De Geus, 2003.

Bakhtin, Mikhail. *The Dialogic Imagination*. Austin: University of Texas Press, 1982.

Benali, Abdelkader. *De langverwachte*. Amsterdam: Vassallucci, 2002.

Bouazza, Hafid . "Allochtonen met een stem." *Vooys* 14, no. 1 (December 1996): 22-23.

Bouazza, Hafid. *Een beer in bontjas*. Amsterdam: CPNB, 2001.

Bouazza, Hafid. "Nederland is blind voor moslimextremisme." *NRC Handelsblad*, 20 February 2002.

Bouazza, Hafid. "Moslims kwetsen Nederland." *NRC Handelsblad,* 2 March 2002.

Bouazza, Hafid. "Demonstreer voor vrijheid moslima's." *NRC Handelsblad*, 19 February 2003.

Bouazza, Hafid. *Een beer in bontjas: Autobiografische schetsen*. Amsterdam: Prometheus, 2004.

Bouazza, Hafid. "Schrijven als roes." In *Roes: Een bloemlezing over drank en drugs in woord en beeld*, edited by Hafid Bouazza and Yves van Kempen, 330-338. Amsterdam: Prometheus, 2010.

Fleischmann, Ellen. "'I only wish I had a home on this globe': Transnational Biography and Dr. Mary Eddy," *Journal of Women's History* 21, no. 3 (2009): 108-130.

Gogh, Theo van. *Allah weet het beter*. Amsterdam: Xtra, 2003.

Hammermeister, Kai. *The German Aesthetic Tradition*. Cambridge: Cambridge University Press, 2002.

Korthals Altes, Liesbeth. *Ethos and Narrative Interpretation: The Negotiation of Values in Fiction*. Lincoln: University of Nebraska Press, 2014.

Lockhorn, Elisabeth. *Geletterde mannen: Interviews*. Amsterdam: De Bezige Bij, 2000.

Louwerse, Henriëtte. *Homeless Entertainment*. Bern: Peter Lang, 2007.

Moenandar, Sjoerd-Jeroen. "The Evaluation and Positioning of Literary Work by Authors with a Muslim Background." In *The Autonomy of Literature at the Fins de Siecles (1900 and 2000)*, edited by Gillis J. Dorleijn, Ralf Grüttemeier, and Liesbeth Korthals Altes, 241-260. Leuven: Peeters, 2007.

Moenandar, Sjoerd-Jeroen. *Depraved Borderlands: Encounters with Muslims in Dutch Literature and the Public Debate*. Hamburg: Peter Lang, 2013.

Moenandar, Sjoerd-Jeroen. "Transmitting Authenticity: Kader Abdolah and Hafid Bouazza as Cultural Mediators," *Journal of Dutch Literature* 5, no.1 (December 2014): 55-73.

Poorthuis, Frank, and Hans Wansink. "De islam is een achterlijke cultuur," *de Volkskrant*, 9 February 2002.

Schweiger, Hannes. "Global Subjects: The Transnationalisation of Biography," *Life Writing* 9, no. 3 (August 2012): 249-258.

Sperber, Dan, and Deirdre Wilson. "Irony and the Use-Mention Distinction." In *Radical Pragmatics*, edited by Peter Cole, 295-318. New York: Academic Press Inc., 1981.

Tashlin, Frank. *The Bear That Wasn't*. Mineola: Dover Publications, 1995.

Thelen, David. "The Nation and Beyond: Transnational Perspectives on United States History." *Journal of American History* 86, no. 3 (1999): 965-975.

Vanegeren, Bart. "Hafid Bouazza, schrijver zonder land: Als ik al ergens woon, is het in de taal. *Humo* (26 May 1998).

Vertovec, Steven. "Transnationalism and identity." *Journal of Ethnic and Migration Studies* 27, no. 4 (2010): 573-582.

Vertovec, Steven, and Susanne Wessendorf, "Introduction. Assessing the backlash against multiculturalism in Europe." In The Multiculturalism Backlash: European Discourses, Policies and Practices, edited by Stefan Vertovec and Susanne Wessendorf. New York: Routledge (2010): 1-31.

Afterword: reflections from a diplomatic historian

Giles Scott-Smith

Life writing is situated at the crossroads of history and literary studies, and draws on a range of techniques and methodologies to merge the two under new coordinates. From the perspective of a historian, it is a challenge not just to history as discipline, but to history as practice. Since the 1960s the traditional focus of history on the 'movers and shakers' of the world and the passage of 'great events' has been gradually undermined by a series of assaults on this ingrained elitism. Class, race and gender have opened up new vistas of subjectivity by breaking open the walls of traditional social hierarchies. They have also contributed to stretching the dominant containers of historical interpretation, be they the family, the career, or the nation. As this volume shows, transnational history has directed attention away from the nation-state as the prime container of meaning and context for historical subjects. Social history – the collective – and subaltern history – the 'forgotten' – have greatly expanded the notion of historical experience from the privileged few to the limitless multitude. But these are still all histories on a grand scale, looking to re-cast our understanding of the passage of events from alternative, bottom-up perspectives, so that "both the people who claim history as their own and the people to whom history has been denied emerge as participants in the same historical trajectory."[1]

Life writing brings a new dimension to these trends. Broadly speaking, it questions the standard interpretive categories that individuals have been subjected to, in order to grant them new-found multiple meanings. More profoundly, it raises important questions such as: Does *everyone* have a history? This path of life writing is therefore to redirect the practice of history into the reconstruction of the everyday life of the everyday peoples of this world. From this perspective, those considered marginal or insignificant before, for instance due to race, class, or gender, are given a voice in the process. This can include those considered part of the class elite, but who have been kept 'historically silent' because of gender or age. It is not the recording of world-shaping events that is significant for 'meaning' – the events proceed, but largely off-stage – it is instead the reaction and response of individuals as they become caught up in the impossible-to-understand maelstrom, making decisions, charting paths of survival, and leaving traces behind of their struggles and celebrations in the process. Life writing as challenge, therefore, represents the taking of these traces and the crafting of narratives that overflow

1 Eric Wolf, *Europe and the People without History* (Berkeley: University of California Press, 1982), 23.

the established borders of 'what history should do'. The process (and its results) is refreshing, and brings to mind Robert Rosenstone's call to arms:

> What we need is history that surprises and startles us. That lets us see things we haven't seen. Hear things we haven't heard. Feel things we haven't felt about some particular period, person, moment or movement in the past. Learn things from the seeing, hearing and feeling we haven't learned before.[2]

Four broad themes run through the chapters in this book. Firstly, several of them aim to surprise, expose, and bring to light what has happened in the past, but from the dirt of the street level, not the serenity of the birds-eye view. Life writing is central to the 'narrative turn' across the humanities, where the historian attempts to gather the flotsam and jetsam left by 'the passage of a few persons through a rather brief moment in time.' While biography is generally about those who have 'earned' attention through their 'great acts' or remarkable achievements, life writing emphasizes that all lives are remarkable, in their own uniqueness and intricate detail. Linearity and one-dimensionality are out, and 'many layers of subjectivity,' as the Introduction indicates, are in. Nancy Mykoff reminds us in her chapter that all lives are full of "seemingly insignificant acts," yet these same acts mark out the lines of existence and experience. Bringing this across in an educational setting can trigger unexpected responses as students grapple with linking their own (often comfortable) everyday with the very different everyday of others elsewhere. Life writing can thus be the non-sanitised version, the confrontational 'awkward uncle' at the family party, the lines of text long deleted. Life is jagged, not smooth, and so should it be recorded.

A second theme emerging from these chapters concerns the inventiveness of the historian in teasing out and piecing together a narrative from a variety of personal records, sometimes no more than mere hints, or even silences. "Every source is a constructed and selective representation of experience," writes Alistair Thomson, "and part of the historian's task is to consider the factors that shape the source and their relevance for our analysis." The historian needs to step back and 'allow' the multiple texts to speak for themselves, but this does not represent an abandonment of the historian's craft. On the contrary, constructing a life story means an extra attention to craft in assembling something that is "partial, selective and purposeful."[3]

Personalities need to be reconstituted, like putting together a broken mirror which necessarily can never be like the original. Thus Diederik Oostdijk teases out the hidden meaning between the lines of Adrienne Rich's poetry in order to track her passage as poet from one life-stage to another, and Sjoerd-Jeroen Moenandar follows the flow of Hafid Bouazza as he plays with the otherness of his Moroccan identity within the white Dutch literary world. These are very subtle exercises in entering the mindset of the subject to suggest transitions in behaviour that may not be immediately apparent. As Ciraj Rassool remarks in his chapter, "people live out

2 Robert Rosenstone, "Space for the Bird to Fly," in *Manifestos for History,* eds. Keith Jenkins, Sue Morgan, and Alun Munslow (London: Routledge, 2007), 13.

3 Alistair Thomson, "Life Stories and Historical Analysis," in *Research Methods for History,* eds. Simon Gunn and Luce Faire (Edinburgh: Edinburgh University Press, 2012), 105-106.

their lives in a storied manner in ways that are deeply embedded in narrative," and the historian has to find the thread of that narrative and follow as far as they can.

A third theme running through all of the chapters are the connections and interconnections that take place, willed or otherwise, across space and time. Eveline Buchheim draws on Tony Ballantyne's evocative notion of 'webs of empire' that designate the systems of exchange, mobility, appropriation, and extraction that enforce social and political hierarchies. Several of the subjects in this book pass through and across these webs, in the course of which encountering the once distant suddenly in an up-close way, but able to accommodate it nonetheless. Barbara Henkes' study of a Dutch emigrant to South Africa negotiating racial difference demonstrates vividly how the formerly exotic becomes the mundane everyday, and a creeping 'casual colonialism' takes over. Lonneke Geerlings provides a marvelous series of snapshots (literally) to mark out the social topography of W.E.B. du Bois' visit to the Netherlands in September 1958, making use of Mary Louise Pratt's 'contact zone' to recreate the path of Du Bois, the venerable civil rights activist, through the streets of Amsterdam and The Hague, cities built on colonial exploitation. Such contacts can also be the source of 'deviant histories' that trouble the established, nation-based narratives of good and bad. Thus Eveline Buchheim enters the confused terrain of a wartime marriage that crossed battle lines and that may not have occurred at all.

Transnational encounters are not solely bound to the human experience – objects are just as important for their passage through time and space, and the responses that they trigger along the way. Marijke Huisman's chapter tracks the rippling influence exerted by Booker T. Washington's *Up from Slavery* as it crossed oceans, passing from its origins as a text in the United States to its later impact among those still dealing with the realities of Dutch colonialism. And just as the subjects of these chapters evolved in changing circumstances, so too does the historian's craft evolve, most recently with the addition of digital technologies that enable the charting of connections in ways otherwise hidden from view by an overflow of detail. By noting the specifics of the spreading network of correspondence maintained by the Belgian Emile de Laveleye, Thomas D'haeninck is able to reveal the patterns of interaction that the social reformer engaged in, and his involvement in circles over time that would not otherwise have been associated with him.

A fourth theme relates the adaptation of subjects to hostile or prejudiced environments, in the process nullifying or overcoming injustice and claiming the fruits of emancipation. Ernestine Hoegen follows Mieke Bouman's determination to see out a court case in threatening circumstances, her husband having fled. Monica Soeting brings to life the manoeuvrings of Setske de Haan as she takes on the visage of Cissy van Marxveldt in order to overcome the overbearing snobbery and enter the upper middle classes as one of their own. Finally Edy Seriese provides a captivating study of Jan Boon, who searched for a language and identity that reflected the lived experience of himself and his people, in so doing escaping the non-existence of colonialism. Seriese shows how Boon's task led him to adopt pseudonyms and styles to try and escape the overarching (re)interpretation of his work, as colonial mindsets appropriated his meanin, text, and authorship in order to neutralise its authentic, culturally-sophisticated voice. In doing so she shows how the colonial subject should not be allowed to attain a voice even long after their death, because these will still disrupt the tales of national endeavour and success.

As a project in all its forms, life writing is therefore challenging, surprising, energizing for releasing the subject from the rigidity of established classification, and undermining for the dominant paradigms, be it colonialism, patriarchy, or class controls. In its subversive mode, it is part of a longer, wider struggle to overcome the 'writing out of history' of the oppression of the everyday encounter. In his Preface to Fanon's *The Wretched of the Earth*, Sartre evocatively describes how the colonial elites "had the Word; the others had the use of it." But Sartre notes that the process of overcoming is not a simple replacement of one with the other.

> A new generation came on the scene, which changed the issue. With unbelievable patience, its writers and poets tried to explain to us that our values and the true facts of their lives did not hang together, and that they could neither reject them completely nor yet assimilate them.[4]

The outcome is therefore always a hybrid, a cosmopolitan mingling of identities by which one dominant social paradigm is supplanted by another. Yet this is not a smooth process, and neither is its recording simple either. Thus Cristobal Gnecco has stated: "History and heritage are still arenas – controlled by the state, by academic disciplines and by a deep and overarching sense of the nation – for the deployment of a collective 'us', which nevertheless becomes an increasingly blurred category in multicultural times."[5] The chapters in this book collectively and individually speak *of* the multicultural hybridity of their subjects, speak *with* these subjects as they are brought out of obscurity, speak *beyond* the paradigm of methodological nationalism, and speak *against* the limiting categorisation of 'subjects' that either dismisses their importance or rejects their very existence. The result is a collection of narratives that is very much present, unbound, and vital.

Bibliography

Gnecco, Cristobal. "Heritage in Multicultural Times." In *The Palgrave Handbook of Contemporary Heritage Research,* edited by Emma Waterton and Steve Watson, 263-280. London: Palgrave, 2015.

Rosenstone, Robert. "Space for the Bird to Fly." In *Manifestos for History,* edited by Keith Jenkins, Sue Morgan, and Alun Munslow, 11-18. London: Routledge, 2007.

Sartre, Jean-Paul. "Preface." In Frantz Fanon, *The Wretched of the Earth*. London: Penguin, 2001 [1961].

Thomson, Alistair Scott. "Life Stories and Historical Analysis." In *Research Methods for History,* edited by Simon Gunn and Luce Faire, 101-117. Edinburgh: Edinburgh University Press, 2012.

Wolf, Eric. *Europe and the People without History*. Berkeley: University of California Press, 1982.

4 Jean-Paul Sartre, "Preface," in Frantz Fanon, *The Wretched of the Earth* (London: Penguin, 2001 [1961]), 7-8.

5 Cristobal Gnecco, "Heritage in Multicultural Times," in *The Palgrave Handbook of Contemporary Heritage Research,* eds. Emma Waterton and Steve Watson (London: Palgrave, 2015), 268.